Phenomenological-Hermeneutical Approach to Borderline Personality Disorder

Studies on Phenomenological Mind

Series Editor: Pablo Fossa

The focus of this book series, Studies on Phenomenological Mind, is the publication of books related to phenomenological research on human consciousness. This series seeks to establish a dialog between psychology and phenomenology to explore the mysteries of consciousness. This series publishes theoretical and empirical contributions coming mainly from philosophy and psychology, integrating research from the philosophy of mind, phenomenology, and theoretical psychology. The purpose of this new series is the publication of contributions of frontier works between psychology and philosophy, with a theoretical and empirical orientation, that account for the contribution of phenomenology to psychological research on consciousness. This new series seeks to fill the gap in the links between phenomenological philosophy and psychology, in relation to the problems of human consciousness. In this sense, this series is positioned in the border zone between phenomenology, philosophy of mind and theoretical psychology, to deepen the understanding of the human psyche and to challenge and question the empirical methodologies to investigate it. In short, this publication space seeks to provide interdisciplinary theoretical and empirical contributions through a dialog about the human mind between phenomenologists and psychologists.

Phenomenological-Hermeneutical Approach to Borderline Personality Disorder

By

Cristóbal Pacheco

University of British Columbia, Canada

And

Pablo Fossa

Universidad del Desarrollo, Chile

emerald
PUBLISHING

United Kingdom – North America – Japan
India – Malaysia – China

Emerald Publishing Limited
Emerald Publishing, Floor 5, Northspring, 21-23 Wellington Street, Leeds LS1 4DL

First edition 2026

Cover photo: iStock and Natallia Yatskova

British Library Cataloguing in Publication Data
A catalogue record for this book is available from the British Library

ISBN: 978-1-80592-282-7 (Print hardback)
ISBN: 978-1-80592-284-1 (Print paperback)
ISBN: 978-1-80592-281-0 (Ebook)
ISBN: 978-1-80592-283-4 (EPUBbook)

Typeset by TNQ Tech
Cover design by TNQ Tech

Printed and bound by CPI Group (UK) Ltd, Croydon, CR0 4YY

CONTENTS

ABOUT THE AUTHORS

Cristóbal Pacheco is a clinical psychologist, researcher, and professor at the University of British Columbia and St. Mary's University. He holds a PhD in Psychology from the Pontifical Catholic University of Argentina, where his doctoral research focused on "Understanding the particular experience of individuals with borderline personality disorder from a phenomenological-hermeneutic perspective." He is an active member of the Phenomenology and Mental Health Network (PMH) at the University of Oxford. Alongside other researchers, his interests center on understanding the subjective experience associated with various pathologies and enhancing psychotherapeutic interventions through phenomenological approaches. His research fields include phenomenology, hermeneutics, clinical epistemology, and borderline personality disorder, with an emphasis on developing strategies for understanding and intervention at the psychotherapeutic level, drawing from philosophy and epistemology.

Pablo Fossa is a professor and researcher at the Faculty of Psychology of the Universidad del Desarrollo, Chile. He received a PhD degree in Psychology from the Pontifical Catholic University of Chile. His doctoral thesis dealt with the expressive dimension of inner speech in human experience from a microgenetic perspective. He did a postdoctoral fellowship financed by the National Commission for Scientific and Technological Research (CONICYT) of Chile, with a research project on trajectories of thought from a microgenetic orientation. His lines of research are related to Cognition, Cultural Psychology and Phenomenology. Specifically, his interest has been in exploring human consciousness by focusing theoretically and empirically on the border between psychology and phenomenology. He is an active member of the Society for Historical Cultural Activity Research (ISCAR), the International Society for Dialogical Self (ISDS), and the International Society for Theoretical Psychology (ISTP). He is the author of several academic articles published in important international journals, such as

Integrative Psychological & Behavioral Science, Culture & Psychology, Current Psychology, International Journal of Psychoanalysis, Human Arenas, Culture & Education, among others. He is the editor of the book *Latin American Advances in Subjectivity and Development: Through Vygotsky Route* (Springer, 2021), *New Perspectives on Inner Speech* (Springer, 2022), *Inner Speech, Culture & Education* (Springer, 2022), *Affectivity & Learning* (Springer, 2023) and *Collected Papers on Inner Speech* (IAP, 2024). He is currently a PhD candidate in Philosophy at the University of Navarra, Spain, context in which he is conducting phenomenological research on the inner consciousness of time.

CHAPTER 1

INTRODUCTION

Borderline Personality Disorder (BPD) is a severe psychiatric condition that profoundly affects both individuals and their close social environment (APA, 2013). With a prevalence rate fluctuating between 10% and 13% of the population, BPD can occur either as an isolated condition or comorbidly with other mental disorders (Mosquera, 2004). The complexity of its nosology and resistance to treatment poses significant challenges, with improvements in prognosis often remaining elusive (Skodol et al., 2002). This difficulty underscores the high research interest in BPD, especially in developing more effective treatment approaches.

BPD is typically characterized by a pervasive pattern of instability in interpersonal relationships, self-image, affect, and marked impulsivity (APA, 2013). Common symptoms include chronic feelings of emptiness, impulsive behaviors in at least two areas, frantic efforts to avoid real or imagined abandonment, and unstable interpersonal relationships that oscillate between extremes of idealization and devaluation (APA, 2013).

In terms of clinical treatment, a combination of pharmacological and psychotherapeutic approaches has traditionally been employed to achieve the best possible outcomes (Álvarez, 2001). Pharmacologically, antidepressants, anticonvulsants, antipsychotics, and benzodiazepines are commonly used to manage emotional and behavioral disturbances (Chávez-León et al., 2006).

On the psychotherapeutic front, four primary models have emerged: two rooted in Psychodynamic theory and two in Cognitive-Behavioral theory (Zanarini, 2009). The Psychodynamic models include Mentalization-Based Therapy by Bateman and Fonagy (2006) and Transference-Focused

Phenomenological-Hermeneutical Approach to Borderline Personality Disorder, pages 1–3

doi:10.1108/978-1-80592-281-020251001

Therapy by Otto Kernberg (Clarkin et al., 2006). On the Cognitive-Behavioral side, Dialectical Behavioral Therapy by Linehan (1993) and Schema Therapy by Jeffrey Young (Young et al., 2003) are widely applied.

While BPD has been well-documented regarding its symptoms, treatments, and prognosis, experiential aspects of the disorder—particularly from a comprehensive, phenomenological perspective—remain underexplored. This highlights the need for a deeper understanding of the lived experience of individuals with BPD, which could inform more empathetic and effective intervention strategies.

Karl Jaspers, a key figure in psychopathology, emphasized the importance of understanding mental phenomena comprehensively, advocating for an unprejudiced immersion into the facts of psychic life without rushing to conclusions (Jaspers, 1965). According to Jaspers, the clinical approach should balance explanation, akin to how a physicist studies matter, with understanding, which allows access to the inner world of meaning rather than relying solely on quantitative analysis (Jaspers, 1959).

In recent years, there has been growing interest in considering hermeneutic and phenomenological traditions as alternatives to the natural-science-driven models that dominate current psychotherapy and diagnostic approaches (Mook, 2010). These approaches emphasize understanding individuals within the context of their language, history, and culture. Philosophers such as Heidegger (2020), Gadamer (1982), Merleau-Ponty (1945), and Ricoeur (1981) have laid the groundwork for this interpretative focus, where "interpreting" the lived experience takes precedence over merely "explaining" it.

A phenomenological approach to understanding BPD could yield new insights into the subjective experiences of those diagnosed with the disorder. The field of phenomenological psychiatry, as pioneered by figures such as Stanghellini and Lysaker (2007), has already demonstrated the value of exploring first-person experiences in conditions such as schizophrenia (Irarrázaval, 2015) and bipolar disorder (Doerr-Zegers, 2011).

At an international level, institutions such as the Center for Subjectivity Studies at the University of Copenhagen have contributed significantly to understanding subjective psychiatric experiences through phenomenological lenses. Their research includes studies like "The Ontology and Epistemology of Symptoms" (Parnas & Urfer-Parnas, 2017) and "Empathy in the Phenomenological Tradition" (Jardine & Szanto, 2017). One particularly notable contribution is the Examination of Anomalous Self-Experience, developed by Parnas et al. (2013), which offers a structured approach to examining the lived experience of psychiatric disorders.

However, despite some promising research, clear methodological guidelines for applying hermeneutic phenomenology to BPD remains scarce. For example, Camille Abettan (2015) has reflected on the limitations of phenomenological psychiatry in diagnosing BPD, suggesting that the role of phenomenology is not to determine who is ill but rather to explore the existential threats revealed in an "uncovered existence."

Other studies, such as those by Paul Cammell (2016) and Houben et al. (2015), have explored emotional instability and self-destructive behaviors in individuals with BPD, while Marlene Dor's (2015) doctoral thesis offers a phenomenological analysis of the lived experience of BPD patients in New Zealand. Yet, many of these studies, while insightful, lack clear phenomenological and hermeneutic methodologies, making it difficult to replicate their findings or apply their insights more broadly.

In summary, while the theoretical groundwork for a hermeneutic phenomenological approach to BPD has been laid, there remains a critical need for methodological clarity and consistency. Such an approach would not only deepen our understanding of the subjective experiences of individuals with BPD but also challenge the stigmatizing assumptions often made by both the general public and mental health professionals.

The aim of this study is to develop a structured hermeneutic phenomenological methodology for understanding the lived experiences of people with BPD. This approach will focus on narratives related to emotional, relational, cognitive, and self-image experiences, contributing to a holistic understanding of the disorder. The anticipated outcomes will offer valuable insights for psychotherapists and mental health professionals, fostering more empathetic, individualized care.

The research objectives are as follows:

- To develop a structured methodology for exploring the lived experience of individuals with BPD from a hermeneutic phenomenological perspective.
- To identify and analyze the experiential narratives of individuals with BPD, focusing on emotional, relational, cognitive, and self-image dimensions.
- To evaluate the effectiveness of a hermeneutic phenomenological approach in capturing the depth of BPD's subjective experience.

This study aims to generate a significant scientific contribution by offering a comprehensive framework that can be applied not only to BPD but also to other mental health conditions. Through this framework, clinicians will gain a clearer understanding of which experiential elements are essential in therapeutic work and which should be carefully considered to ensure holistic patient care.

CHAPTER 2

INSTABILITY AS A PRINCIPLE—DIVING INTO BORDERLINE PERSONALITY DISORDER

Borderline Personality Disorder (BPD) is a complex mental health condition that deeply affects the lives of those who suffer from it. Its prevalence is estimated at 1–2% of the general population (Grant et al., 2008). BPD is characterized by a wide array of symptoms that impact emotional regulation, interpersonal relationships, and cognitive functioning (APA, 2013; Gunderson & Links, 2008; Paris, 2019).

The diagnosis and management of BPD present significant challenges for mental health professionals due to the variability in symptom presentation and the complexity of the disorder (Paris, 2019). Furthermore, societal stigma and misunderstandings about BPD often prevent affected individuals from receiving proper treatment and support (Sansone & Sansone, 2015).

According to the American Psychiatric Association (2013), the key symptoms associated with BPD include:

- Intense efforts to avoid real or imagined abandonment.
- Unstable and intense personal relationships, characterized by alternating between idealization and devaluation.
- Emotional instability due to heightened reactivity to mood states.
- Chronic feelings of emptiness.

Phenomenological-Hermeneutical Approach to Borderline Personality Disorder, pages 5–7

doi:10.1108/978-1-80592-281-020251002

- Intense and inappropriate anger, with difficulty controlling it.
- Transient stress-related paranoid ideation or severe dissociative symptoms.

The etiology of BPD is multifactorial, involving genetic, biological, and environmental factors (Ruocco et al., 2019). Recent research has focused on brain function abnormalities, particularly in regions related to emotional processing (Cremers et al., 2021). Childhood trauma, including emotional or physical abuse, has also been identified as a significant factor that may increase vulnerability to developing BPD (Zanarini et al., 2002).

Treatment for BPD requires a comprehensive approach that addresses the disorder's various dimensions. Dialectical Behavioral Therapy and Cognitive Behavioral Therapy are widely regarded as effective therapeutic approaches for treating BPD (Bateman & Fonagy, 2009; Cristea et al., 2017; Linehan, 2018). These therapies focus on helping individuals manage intense emotions, regulate mood, improve interpersonal relationships, and challenge dysfunctional thought patterns.

Dialectical Behavioral Therapy, developed by Marsha Linehan (1993), has proven effective in reducing self-injurious behaviors, suicidality, and other symptoms of BPD. Cognitive Behavioral Therapy, on the other hand, helps individuals identify and change dysfunctional thoughts and behaviors associated with BPD, thereby improving overall functioning and quality of life (Young et al., 2006).

In addition to therapy, medication is sometimes recommended to control symptoms. Antidepressants, particularly selective serotonin reuptake inhibitors, can be helpful for managing depression and anxiety, while mood stabilizers, such as lithium or valproic acid, can help control impulsivity and mood swings (APA, 2013; Paris, 2019; Stoffers et al., 2012).

This integrated approach, combining therapy and medication, is tailored to the unique needs of each individual, offering a solid foundation for managing BPD and improving the quality of life for those affected.

BPD can significantly impact the social, occupational, and emotional functioning of individuals. Emotional instability, impulsivity, and difficulties in emotional self-regulation often make it challenging for those with BPD to maintain stable, satisfying relationships (APA, 2013). Social stigma, discrimination, and isolation are common experiences for individuals with BPD, further exacerbating the challenges they face (Gunderson & Links, 2008; Sansone & Sansone, 2012).

Stigma surrounding BPD can hinder access to appropriate care. Negative stereotypes and a lack of understanding about the disorder often lead to discrimination, making it difficult for individuals to seek help (Sheppard et al., 2023). This isolation can worsen BPD symptoms, making everyday functioning even more difficult (Borschmann et al., 2012).

Continued research into BPD is essential for improving our understanding of its underlying causes and treatment options (Choi-Kain et al., 2017). BPD is a complex disorder involving a dynamic interaction between biological, psychological, and environmental factors (Gunderson & Links, 2008). Current research is focusing on potential biomarkers, neurobiological abnormalities, and genetic factors that contribute to the development and persistence of BPD (Ruocco et al., 2012). Additionally, new therapeutic approaches, such as Acceptance and Commitment Therapy and Mentalization-Based Therapy, are showing promise in managing BPD symptoms (Bateman & Fonagy, 2009; Stoffers et al., 2012).

Public awareness and education about BPD are crucial for reducing stigma and promoting empathy and understanding. Individuals with BPD often face discrimination due to a lack of awareness about the nature of the disorder and the stereotypes associated with it (Bonnington & Rose, 2014). Educating the public can help dismantle these harmful stereotypes and foster greater understanding and support for those affected by BPD.

This research aims to contribute to the destigmatization and deeper understanding of BPD by focusing on the subjective experience of individuals with the disorder. By exploring BPD from a first-person perspective, this study hopes to promote a more holistic understanding of the condition. In doing so, it seeks to inform psychotherapeutic strategies that address the core issues faced by individuals with BPD, ultimately improving their quality of life.

CHAPTER 3

UNPREJUDICED AS FULL CONSCIOUSNESS IN THE ENCOUNTER WITH ANOTHER: PHENOMENOLOGY AS AN APPROACH TO THE PHENOMENON ITSELF

Phenomenology, as both a method and philosophical attitude, invites us to approach lived experience with radical openness, free from prejudices and preconceived notions. This approach challenges us to engage with phenomena in their purest essence, opening a window to human subjectivity that transcends superficial or critical knowledge. Phenomenology emphasizes a genuine encounter with the other, where the observer becomes an active participant, discovering the depths of their own subjectivity without the constraints of prior judgments.

This chapter explores the concept of phenomenology and its evolution, beginning with its etymological roots in the Greek word phenomenon, meaning "that which shows itself." Through the contributions of key figures such as Franz Brentano and Edmund Husserl, the development of phenomenological thought is traced, highlighting the importance of intentionality and intentional experience as central elements. We also examine the work of Martin Heidegger and Maurice Merleau-Ponty, who expanded and

Phenomenological-Hermeneutical Approach to Borderline Personality Disorder, pages 9–19

doi:10.1108/978-1-80592-281-020251003

transformed phenomenology to offer a deeper understanding of being-in-the-world and perception as fundamental to human experience.

We will provide a comprehensive view of how phenomenology, from its beginnings with Husserl to the hermeneutic interpretations of Heidegger and the perceptual insights of Merleau-Ponty, offers powerful tools to approach phenomena in their most essential form. Through phenomenological reduction and epoché, we learn to suspend our judgments and preconceptions, allowing us to experience and describe reality from an authentically subjective and experiential perspective.

Finally, this chapter explores the application of phenomenology to the social sciences, drawing on the work of Alfred Schütz, who integrated phenomenological reduction into social research. This approach facilitates an unprejudiced and profound observation of human interactions and the subjective meanings that emerge from social experience, offering a richer and more nuanced understanding of individuals in their social contexts.

UNPREJUDICED AS FULL CONSCIOUSNESS IN THE ENCOUNTER WITH ANOTHER

The initial path of phenomenology is an invitation to transparency—a radical openness to lived experience, free from external critique and control. This approach challenges us to encounter phenomena in a pure, unmediated way, engaging with them as they are rather than as objects to be analyzed or explained. It is an exciting journey that enables an individual to encounter the deepest echoes of their own subjectivity without the interference of preconceived notions.

The Greek origin of the word "phenomenon" (fenomenon) means "to show itself," highlighting phenomenology's focus on how things appear in their own light (Barbera & Inciarte, 2012). The foundations of phenomenology are often traced to Franz Brentano and his concept of intentionality, which distinguishes between mental and physical phenomena. Brentano argued that a psychic fact cannot be reduced to a physical one; consciousness and phenomenon are mutually interdependent (Brentano, 1874).

Building on Brentano's ideas, Edmund Husserl introduced the term "phenomenology" in 1874, emphasizing that all experiences are directed toward objects, which he called "intentional objects" (Husserl, 2002). Husserl further explored the idea that phenomenological knowledge is "immanent"—not in the sense of being a real ingredient of experiences, but in the intentional sense, focusing on the subjective constitution of meaning (Husserl, 2012). Intentionality, rescued from Brentano, plays a fundamental role in understanding cognitive experiences, emotions, and actions, though not all experiences, such as emotional impressions, are intentional (Lambert, 2006).

Husserl defined phenomenology as both a method and an a priori science aimed at establishing a rigorous scientific foundation for all disciplines. As an a priori science, phenomenology is directly related to the subject's experience, specifically their "intentional experience" (Bolio, 2012). This focus on subjectivity as a constitutive element in the definition of the world positions phenomenology in direct opposition to psychologism and positivism, which dominated European thought at the time (Husserl, 2012).

The primary aim of Husserl's phenomenology is to study experience in order to reveal consciousness through phenomenological reduction (Barbera & Inciarte, 2012). This involves "bracketing" or suspending all judgments about the external world, a process known as epoché (Figueroa, 2008). Through reduction, Husserl sought to purify phenomena and examine them without the influence of preconceived beliefs.

Husserl identified two types of reduction: eidetic reduction, which focuses on the essence of objects, and transcendental reduction, which brackets the belief in the reality of the world. Eidetic reduction allows us to perceive the essential structure of an object, even as its physical characteristics change. For example, we recognize a die as a die, even if its color or shape changes. Similarly, we recognize the essence of a person, despite the physical changes they undergo over time.

Transcendental reduction, on the other hand, disconnects our belief in the empirical reality of the world and focuses instead on the structures of experience itself (Husserl, 2012). This shift reveals that science cannot be founded solely on empirical observations; phenomenology offers an alternative by focusing on the subjective experience of reality (Quepons, 2012).

The reduction process enables the subject to approach reality from the standpoint of intersubjectivity, a key aspect of Husserl's notion of intentionality. Consciousness, Husserl argues, should not be understood as a container for objects but as the interpretive act of engaging with the world. This interpretive approach allows us to explore how personal experience shapes our understanding of reality (Husserl, 1982).

BEING-IN-THE-WORLD AND THE INCARNATION OF REALITY

The development of a critique of positivist reason frames the observer in the challenge of establishing a naked observation devoid of ornaments or technicalities, as well as the development of an associative freedom, which allows an understanding over an explanation of the phenomena of the world. The approach to this being ejected into the world is an encounter with the individual intentionality referred to by Husserl in his link to the world of things, but it is also an encounter with a being predestined to the possibility of death, a being with a traced path, in which an adaptation to reality and a "taking charge" of his position in the world prevails.

The call of the active observer responds to the opening to an understanding of this being in the world and its incarnation in reality. The question of being in the development of an interpretative phenomenology, as opposed to Husserl's descriptive phenomenology, arises from the hand of Martin Heidegger, disciple of the aforementioned author, who develops a hermeneutic turn to the development of a new phenomenology, whose main task is to teach the art of thinking (Heidegger, 2008). This new proposal of thinking implies focusing on things from the beginning and from their origins. For him, phenomenology must be a method and not a science of essences, much less a philosophical doctrine (Heidegger, 2008). For Heidegger, the function of phenomenology is to put something in evidence and visible to itself. Unlike what was established by Husserl, this phenomenological turn moves away from the transcendental consciousness previously proposed, focusing on a life in its factuality, which implies a descent into the world of existence (León, 2009).

The understanding of being in the world leads to the development of the concept of "Dasein," which has several meanings, being able to define it as "the way of being of an entity in the world," opening the question to the "there" of being and its explicit understanding in its relationship with the world (Barbera & Inciarte, 2012). From this perspective we can understand that the man ejected in the world is not a man of realities but of possibilities, not of truths, but of experiences immersed in the act of existence. Heidegger preserves Husserl's radicalism regarding what is established and proposed by phenomenology, but now focuses on life from its historicity (Pöggeler, 1986). As there is a return to the world of things, to the factical elements, the call to the understanding of being in the world gives way to the image of interpretation over description, calling it hermeneutic phenomenology, which is characterized by:

1. Phenomenology must not start from "intuition" if this intuition is understood as intuition of objects, but rather it must start from "understanding."
2. Since Heidegger replaces the transcendental self by factual life, "the sphere of time" and "historicity" comes to the foreground: factual life is history and it is "historically" as it understands itself.

In this way, the history of events becomes the guiding thread of phenomenological research (Pöggeler, 1986). In the link between hermeneutics and phenomenology, the alliance of two concepts is impregnated, which engage the development of an analytical-existential vision at an ontological level, from a Heideggerian perspective. The factual life and the encounter with another in a delimited historical context entail the development of an action oriented to "understanding," as an action emitting particular meanings, not reflective but interpretative of the experience. In the words of Heidegger (2020) in his book "Being and Time," it is relevant to refer

> Philosophy is a universal phenomenological ontology, which has its starting point in the hermeneutics of "Dasein", which, as an analytic of existence, has fixed the end of the thread of all philosophical questioning at the point from which it arises and in which, in turn, it has repercussions. (Heidegger, 2020, p. 61)

For Heidegger (2020), it is the "where to" that gives meaning to "Dasein," which is not attached to or on the surface of the human, but responds to the very act of humanity in action. However, this "where to" is already predetermined or conceptualized in a certain way by the figure of the observer. It can be affirmed then that the exercise of an "unprejudiced looking," exceeds the real possibilities of the observer, in relation to the prejudice established in the human being. Nevertheless, the development of a "hermeneutic circle" proposes the possibility of not discarding the preconceptions in the act of observing, but to open a space for an opportunity to know the whole through its constituent parts, generating a true process of legitimization of the interpretation from the things themselves (León, 2009). At this point it is relevant to give importance to the reflection established by the philosopher Dan Zahavi (2003), regarding the development of the hermeneutic phenomenology developed by Heidegger.

According to his statements, he affirms that Heidegger intends to create a new phenomenological method that will not lead to "theoretical deformations of life." This is, Heidegger's search is associated with the search for an atheoretical and nonobjectifiable method of ontological understanding, this method is the hermeneutic phenomenology (Zahavi, 2003). In the words of the author, in order to validate what Heidegger proposed in the development of his phenomenological approaches, regarding his approach to individual subjectivity, it can be said that "Heidegger's real contribution consists in the development of a special type of analysis, based on a non-objective reflection, a type of reflection that can give us access to a lived subjectivity" (Zahavi, 2003, p. 169). Last but not least, it can be said that the postulates established by Heidegger are relevant in the encounter with the very nature of being, giving importance to the observation of man from his history and his factual life, thus favoring an approach to his biographical development, nourished by the world of experience itself in the context of the man-world relationship.

The inclusion of the hermeneutic variable to his phenomenological conception brings a new possibility of understanding the "being," which is based beyond the "why?," into a "how?," being necessary and interpretation for the subsequent understanding. Finally, upon reviewing the postulates established by Husserl and Heidegger, it is feasible to visualize the development of ontological postulates that allow to deepen the understanding of a being immersed in an existence that goes beyond the consciousness itself, raising the importance of the mere fact of existing as a determinant in the individual constitution.

PERCEPTION AND OPENNESS TO THE WORLD OF LIFE

The phenomena of human perception create a preoperational encounter between the individual and the world of life. This connection is shaped by biological factors at the perceptual level, yet these factors alone cannot explain the individual significance attributed to certain phenomena. A truly subjective understanding requires more than simply grasping the functionality of the human biological apparatus. As Husserl proposed, relying solely on the explanatory models of the natural sciences limits our ability to understand the full spectrum of human experience. Instead, it is through exploring ideographic possibilities—elements of personal experience, culture, and the boundaries of the world as experienced—that a deeper understanding emerges.

Maurice Merleau-Ponty (1945) advocates for a phenomenological approach that emphasizes a return to the factual world, viewing the world as something already present and ready to be described through subjective experience. Understanding environmental phenomena must arise from the study of subjectivity, including its links to history, corporeality, and time. This approach fosters a holistic vision of experiential phenomena (Merleau-Ponty, 1945).

The world is not confined solely to internalized perceptions; rather, it is through the *act of living* that we come to understand our own experiences. As Merleau-Ponty notes, "The world is not what I think, but what I live; I am open to the world, I undoubtedly communicate with it; but I do not possess it, it is inexhaustible" (Merleau-Ponty, 1945, p. 14). The concept of the "worldly man" reflects an ambiguous being, capable of generating a continuous flow of meanings and particular uses of language. This being goes beyond the prereflective, requiring us to understand the person as a living entity, constantly interacting with the vital experience of the world.

For Merleau-Ponty, the practice of phenomenological reduction does not involve eliminating all beliefs or preconceptions about a phenomenon, but rather suspending them temporarily (*putting them in suspense*) to make them explicit. This allows us to visualize the individual within the context of their immediate environment, including the observer's presence (Moreira, 2004). It is through *corporeality* that the individual grasps their relationship with the world and recognizes their "self," an interweaving of perceptions and sensations. It becomes impossible to understand the identity of a subject apart from their relationship with the world of things to which they are directly connected (Merleau-Ponty, 1945).

In discussing the man-world relationship, Merleau-Ponty highlights the need to contemplate a prereflective connection, assigning central importance to perception as a constitutive element of his phenomenological framework. He writes:

> Through sensation I grasp, apart from my personal life and my own acts, a given life of consciousness from which they emerge—the life of my eyes, of my hands, of my ears, which are so many other 'natural' selves. Every time I experience a sensation, I experience that it interests, not only my 'own' self. (Merleau-Ponty, 1945, p. 231)

The inclusion of corporeality as a fundamental aspect of human life positions the individual as engaged in prereflective interaction within the sphere of elemental life. Human actions are thus submerged in elemental intentionality, closely tied to the perceptual elements that Merleau-Ponty emphasizes. What is central in this view is the body as a temporal and intentional subject—not merely a passive entity subject to causality, but an active body, intertwined with the surrounding world. As Merleau-Ponty states, the body "is what oxygenates it, makes it visible, and transforms it into something perceptible… that which ultimately keeps the visible spectacle continuously alive, animates it, and nourishes it internally" (Merleau-Ponty, 1945, p. 235).

In summary, Merleau-Ponty's concept of the embodied self-places individuals in an active role within the act of living. This intentional linking of consciousness to lived experience through perception plays a vital role in shaping the subjective world. His solution to Cartesian dualism validates the immediacy of the existing connection between body and mind in the creation of "realities."

SOCIAL REALITY AS THE CONSTITUTION OF THE WORLD OF LIFE

The incorporation of phenomenology into social research implies an approach to the factual phenomenon from the perspective of the social sciences, considering this as an opportunity to visualize the development of the construction of subjective meanings based on social interaction and representation. For Alfred Schütz, the world of life is something that simply exists independently of the individual, which is already given, and is experienced by individuals from the common sense.

The social world is something composed of laws and experiences that people are able to experience and also identify that others experience them, through the use of common sense (Schütz, 1932). From this phenomenological understanding, the formation of a unique personality at the ontological level arises from immediate and biographical experiences, being central elements such as upbringing and individual formation, being able to refer that from the personal biography of the individual and his particular position in space and time, a "repository of available knowledge" is developed, which consists in the passive storage of the "available knowledge" of experiences (Schütz, 1932).

The subject is capable of resorting to this stored knowledge, without resorting to a specific reflexive process to order each of the experiences that occur and thus achieve an adaptation to new social phenomena (Schütz, 1932). The exercise of individual self-reflection, according to Schütz (1932), is the visualization of the subject based on past experiences, not being able to visualize his experience in the here and now, because if an exercise of reflection of the here and now is developed in this instant, a new subject is being thought of, and when objectifying it, symbols are necessarily resorted to, which already account for a subject that was (Schütz, 1932).

The distinction between acts and actions is central. In order to identify the perception of reality at the individual level, acts can be understood as something inserted in the repository of available knowledge, being visualized as an act in the past or in the future, idealized, to be performed. On the other hand, an action is a concretized act, corresponding to the very execution of a specific action and the experience of performing an act (Schütz, 1932). This experience develops in the internal temporal current of the subject, which is associated with the development of a present action that reorganizes the lived experiences in order to favor adaptation to new experiences.

However, reflection represents a break in the internal temporal current, since it brings elements from the past to the present, bringing up a previous experience to the present reality (Schütz, 1932). Regarding the perception of the individual as a social entity and in direct connection with others, it can be said that the subject is capable of perceiving certain states of the other, from the common sense, being from intersubjectivity, the possibility of contact with the other (Schütz, 1932).

In the interaction with the other, it is presumed from the common sense, certain codes that define a social structure, in which we can join a common activity, influence and allow ourselves to be influenced in the development of a common interaction (Schütz, 1932). At the social level, the development of particular actions are loaded with specific meanings, even though at certain times the actor may not have intended to specify something with a specific action, it is possible that this action is interpreted as something specific by an actor or social observer. In the development of interpretation, subjectivity is used by the social actor, who resorts to his available repository of knowledge, in order to interpret the unknown, by means of what is already known, there being a difference in the meaning that the actor gives to his specific action, with respect to the observation by others of this subjectivity (Schütz, 1932).

The establishment of an everyday explanation of intersubjectivity arises at the social level as a task in which social actors and observers can be identified, who represent different observational dimensions in terms of the phenomenon of subjectivity. In the social relationship, both actor and observer represent the role of social actor; however, in the development of the act of observing, this exercise is carried out in a differentiated manner. On the one hand, the social actor has to describe the observed phenomenon or event; on the other hand, the social observer, although he also develops a description of the phenomena, his function is also associated with the interpretation of the content of his observation, proceeding to apply the "epoché" in the development of this interpretative exercise (Bergson, 1963).

A relevant advance of Schütz (1932) is the incorporation of the phenomenological reduction, inherited by Husserl to the social sciences, associating this reduction to the exercise of a possibility of avoiding common sense, as an alternative of interpretation of meanings. The possibility of using the "epoché," supposes an investigative encounter of the "meaning of an experience in the internal temporal consciousness," making it possible to go beyond what is made possible by the use of repositories of available knowledge, which block the possibilities of knowledge of subjectivity, in the development of the interpretation of phenomena (Schütz, 1932). The development of an investigation of the meaning of individual actions implies the need to establish a holistic observation, which is associated with the possibility that the observer can perceive not only the meanings deposited in the action or message of the social actor, but also the identification of the effects left by the development of such actions in the environment, such as noises, movements of objects, gestures, among others.

These indications may have a meaning for those who observe them, but necessarily for those who perform the action, establishing the differentiation between the interpretation existing between those who observe a given action and the experiential self-interpretation (Schütz, 1932). In synthesis, when visualizing social scopes from a phenomenological observation, it is possible to establish challenges related to the development of observations proper to a "natural attitude" in the interpretative work, which not only favors the development of an unprejudiced observational exercise, but also the possibility of knowing subjective aspects of personal experience.

The challenge arises during the development of the interpretation, not to make deterministic impositions regarding phenomena perceived by the figure of the observer, which, although not captured by the social actor, the observer in his interpretative exercise tries to give them some relevance, which may involve a risk both impositive and methodologically biased in the development of interpretations.

Summary

In this chapter, various definitions and theoretical approaches associated with phenomenology have been presented, which can be defined as a method or an attitude of approach to phenomena from the unprejudiced, favoring an openness in the approach to phenomena related to human experience. Since Husserl, the insertion of a method with a scientific intentionality is visualized, centered on the definition of phenomena from the "pure experience," trying to capture the origin of the phenomenon from its particular essence.

This interest entails new purposes in terms of descriptive observation at the ontological level, developing a methodological approach from reductive tasks that would allow the development of the "epoché" or unprejudiced attitude in the approach to a particular phenomenon, an attitude that favors the return to the essential of things without embellishments. The arrival of Heidegger exposes an interest in the development of "the question of being," establishing an approach oriented to factual life, moving away from the scientific intentionality of Husserl, he establishes a phenomenology of the factual facts, seeking to explain the meanings contained in the lived experiences.

It is through the incorporation of the hermeneutic turn that the phenomena of an embodied life are subject to an interpretative possibility, in order to achieve an understanding beyond the merely relational. This significantly enables an immersion in the phenomena of subjective living, being an ideal phenomenological model to promote the development of a proposal oriented to the understanding of the particular experience. Merleau Ponty, proposes a phenomenology of perception, integrating corporeality as a central element of his representative vision, being an element that has an alliance with the world of life "lebenswelt."

This subject embodied in the world with a corporeal character has an integrative approach from a mind-body sphere to the phenomena of life, being the sensations or perceptions a dimension that graphs the experiential value of the act of living, being able to identify this aspect as a central element to consider during the development of a therapeutic proposal, which can provide a key importance to perception as a graph of the lived experiences. Finally, we have gathered the approaches of a social phenomenology, carried out by Schütz, who exposes the concrete possibilities of incorporating the phenomenological reduction to a social context, where common sense prevails in the interpretation of phenomena.

It is through the exercise of an unprejudiced observation—which does not resort to the repository of acquired knowledge—, that it is possible to achieve an approach to individual subjectivity during the development of an observation, in the role of social researcher. This approach is of utmost relevance, since it is expected to achieve an approach to a person with the pathology to be considered in this research, as a social being with personal meanings and codes, who is subject to an observing action, in which the unprejudiced and attention to his particular actions can provide an understanding of his experiences at a subjective level, especially the experiences associated with a particular disorder (Table 3.1).

TABLE 3.1 Summary of Authors and Postulates of Phenomenology

Authors	Husserl	Heidegger	Merleau-Ponty	Schütz
Concepts	"Lebenswelt" the world of life: meanings are not given by causal relations, but by human meaningfulness.	"Dasein," the being here embodied in the world. The question of being arises.	"Body" as an intentional element of the act of living, not a mere receiver of stimuli. Perception is prereflexive in the capture of the act of living.	"Repository of available knowledge" as acquired knowledge leading the common judgment in approaching the phenomenon.
Purpose	Aiming to create a philosophy as a rigorous science, capable of describing phenomena from a natural attitude.	Search for meanings in factual life. The fundamental experience is found in factual life.	Resolve Cartesian dualism, establishing man as a being of experience in which mind and body play a fundamental role.	Avoid common judgment as a method of attaining knowledge about the phenomenon.
Task	Establish a scientific method, oriented to eidetic research.	Taking charge of the phenomenon of understanding and the question of being.	Avoiding the separation between mind and matter, positioning the human body as something in between.	Incorporate the "epoché" in the social sciences, as a method to achieve an approach to subjectivity.

CHAPTER 4

HERMENEUTICS: THE BEGINNING OF THE PATH TOWARD UNDERSTANDING. UNDERSTAND THE AUTHOR BETTER THAN HE HIMSELF WOULD HAVE UNDERSTOOD

Hermeneutics, as an art of interpretation, has its roots in the work of Friedrich Schleiermacher, who laid the foundations for a deeper understanding of texts—beyond the literal—, and for understanding the authors better than he himself could have done. This approach was not only initially applied to biblical texts, but expanded to philology and text interpretation in general, thus forming an essential method in contemporary qualitative research.

Schleiermacher postulated that thought is inextricably linked to language and proposed a hermeneutic based on two main components: generalization and double comprehension. Generalization involves a general understanding of the language used by the author, while dual understanding focuses on grasping both the author's form of expression and the context in which it was generated. This duality allows for a more complete and accurate interpretation of texts, considering both the general linguistic aspects and the author's specific intentions.

Phenomenological-Hermeneutical Approach to Borderline Personality Disorder, pages 21–36

doi:10.1108/978-1-80592-281-020251004

The challenge of interpreting a text lies in maintaining objectivity and understanding the historical and cultural context in which it was written. Schleiermacher emphasizes the importance of situating oneself in the historical moment of the author in order to grasp not only the symbolic content of the text but also the environment in which it was created. This requires a "respect for the other," an ethical attitude that recognizes the need to understand the other on his or her own terms and in his or her own context.

Hermeneutics, according to Schleiermacher, is not only a technique of interpretation, but a dialectical art that addresses multiple perspectives and representations of the world. This pluralistic approach views truth and knowledge as multiple and diverse constructs, requiring a deep immersion in the author's intentions and meanings. Schleiermacher's psychologistic intention goes beyond linguistic analysis, seeking to understand the author's "germinal decision," i.e., the motivation and context that drove the creation of the text.

This chapter also explores the contributions of Wilhelm Dilthey, who extended hermeneutics into the sciences of the spirit, differentiating them from the natural sciences. Dilthey argues that the sciences of the spirit focus on the understanding of human and cultural phenomena, and not on the mere causal explanation of them. Inner experience and the expression of subjective meanings are fundamental to understanding human reality from a hermeneutic perspective.

The arrival of Edmund Husserl's phenomenology and Martin Heidegger's hermeneutic turn marked an epistemological revolution, integrating phenomenological understanding with a deeper interpretation of human experience. Heidegger, influenced by Dilthey, introduces the "hermeneutics of facticity," which seeks to understand the self in its everyday, authentic life, moving away from theoretical objectifications.

Finally, Hans-Georg Gadamer and Paul Ricoeur continue and expand this hermeneutic tradition. Gadamer emphasizes the universality of language and the importance of dialog as a means to truth. His concept of the "fusion of horizons" highlights how understanding arises from the interaction between the perspectives of the observer and the observed. Ricoeur, for his part, introduces the idea of the "hermeneutics of distance," stressing the importance of separating the author's intention from the recipient's context in order to achieve a more objective interpretation rich in symbolic meanings.

This chapter offers a comprehensive overview of the evolution of hermeneutics, from Schleiermacher to Ricoeur, showing how this approach allows us to better understand texts, and thus human experience, through a deep and respectful interpretation of subjective meanings.

THE BEGINNING OF THE ROAD TO UNDERSTANDING. UNDERSTANDING THE AUTHOR BETTER THAN HE WOULD HAVE UNDERSTOOD HIMSELF

The work of Schleiermacher (2012) begins the development of hermeneutics, as an art of interpretation of linguistic elements, which initially are linked to the interpretative exercise of biblical texts and later also incorporate the discipline of philology. The author's influence on current qualitative research is immeasurable, given the opening of a wide field of work, based on the art of understanding over the explanation of particular meanings, in the development of knowledge of multiple realities.

Schleiermacher's hermeneutic program (2012) is based on the central approach that thought is limited and dependent on language, exposing in a structured way, a hermeneutics based on two main components; "generalization" (die Verallgemeinerung) and "double understanding" (das doppelte verstehen), based on the understanding of the language and the speaker (Arndt, 2013). It can be said that the first of these components is based on the general understanding of the language of the figure of speech, capturing, as far as possible, elements of the language from which certain ideas are generated or developed.

On the other hand, the double understanding is based on capturing the form of expression of the language delivered by the author, allowing to distinguish a certain individual thought associated with what is expressed (Schleiermacher, 2012). The central function of the proposed hermeneutics is based on the close connection between these two ways of perceiving a given work, from the general linguistic dimension, which is linked to the analysis of the language used by the one who transmits, which is associated with a certain intention or particularity linked to the one who expresses (Mancilla, 2020).

At the moment of performing a certain interpretation, the difficulty arises of maintaining a distance between the intentions of a certain interpreter and the message or content expressed in a certain work, Schleiermacher (2012), exposes the need to position oneself at the moment in which certain messages are transmitted, in order not only to capture the symbolism of the work to be interpreted, but also the context in which a certain expression is developed.

This need to position oneself in the reality of another is based on ethical elements that Schleiermacher (2012) considers necessary at the moment of any interpretation, since although interpretation represents an encounter with a certain language and symbols of a culture, what Scheleiermacher calls "respect for the other" (Achtung für das fremde) also arises, the other is seen as a being that deserves to be heard and understood, in view of the fact that he/she develops from similar logics to the interpreter in question.

The author gives a great amplitude to dialectical elements, not only as transmitters of a certain discourse or symbolism, but also as representatives of multiple perspectives and representations of the world, clearly based on a pluralism in the establishment of truth and knowledge (Schleiermacher, 2012). This exposes an important challenge, at the moment of establishing any interpretative exercise, which goes hand in hand with positioning oneself in an experiential perspective as a central part of the expression that delivers particular meanings, which are not only associated to a linguistic perspective, but also of a psychological and contextual character, but above all intentional.

Schleiermacher (2012), exposes a psychologist intention in his interpretative exercise, which goes beyond a linguistic exercise based on the understanding of the use and representations that a given language delivers to the intentions of a particular author, in order to understand the meaning of a particular discourse, it is necessary to return to what Schleiermacher calls "germinal decision" (Keimentschluss), constituting the perspective in which the author has something to convey. At the moment of establishing a certain discourse, it is subject to a dialogic exercise, based on the need to be heard by members of a given community, which is why language is not only a discourse of its own, but it is established to be heard and shared by those who can share a certain language, which frames the challenge that in order to achieve a genuine understanding of the message, one must resort to information present in the historical, linguistic and situational context of a given issuer (Mancilla, 2020).

For Schleiermacher (2012), linguistic or psychological interpretation is not only based on the capture and understanding of a discourse or basic intention by an author, but also represents an exercise of deep understanding of the interpreter himself, who, at the time of establishing a certain interpretation, will internally seek an element that allows him to connect with the discourse delivered and its respective meaning. This makes the interpretative exercise not only a unilateral action, but also represents a return to the interpreter's own nature, as a subject capable of finding in his own reality, universal contents that seek to be captured not only from its linguistic value, but also from an experiential dimension.

The scope of Schleiermacher's work at a theoretical, methodological and reflective level is relevant at the moment of establishing an encounter with all discourse that conveys a dimension of particularity, in view of the ethical principle that underlies all his work, the need of each person to be heard and, failing that, to be understood in its complexity. This approach exposes a significant commitment of cultural, social, historical, linguistic, psychological and intentional characteristics from a particularity that germinates a certain idea or concept, from a need that arises as a representation of its own universe of meanings and experiences.

It is possible to find the development of a dialogic hermeneutics in the author, focused on the need to establish a detailed review not only of the message delivered, but also of the figure of the receiver, this exercise has a necessary circularity, when establishing an approach to the reality of others, from the experiential dimensions of the figure of the interpreter, who will find the particular intention of a particular message in spaces of his own inner world, making this an exercise of continuous observation, distance and approach. In later years and with the work of Dilthey, Heidegger and Gadamer, hermeneutics establishes the need to become not only an interpretative exercise at a linguistic level, but also an exercise of self-observation and intersubjective dialog.

THE SCIENCES OF THE SPIRIT: A WINDOW TO THE INTERPRETATION OF THE WORLD OF SUBJECTIVITY

The framework of hermeneutics as a method, exposes an important tradition associated with the interpretation of obscure passages of ancient religious texts, enabling an instance of understanding and approach to a human dimension, from phenomena built with a vision close to divine approaches. From this approach to the human dimension, the figure of Wilhelm Dilthey arises, who in 1883 proposes the hermeneutic scope as a possibility of approaching the historical phenomenon of the human being, being able to count on a link associated with the possibilities of individual historical phenomena, as alternatives of understanding the particularity.

In his classic work "*Introduction To The Sciences Of The Spirit*," originally written in 1883, Dilthey (1986) makes a clear distinction between what can be understood as natural sciences and sciences of the spirit, stating that the natural sciences have as their object the study of phenomena that occur as an external part of the consciousness of an individual, which can be understood from a dimension associated with cause and effect (Dilthey, 1986). On the other hand, the sciences of the spirit present an approach to properly human phenomena, associated in the first place to language as a historical determinant at the individual level, as well as culture and its historical formations, associating to hermeneutics a function related to understanding over an explanation proper to the natural sciences (Dilthey, 1986).

It is fair to say that prior to the scientific-natural knowledge of the world, there is the internal experience, as a fact of consciousness and as a connection lived from within, indicating that the internal experience is not opposed to the external experience, but rather it is associated to the fact that from the subjective experience it is possible to establish an interpretation of the objective reality (Dilthey, 2000). Access to the facts of individual consciousness does not imply an approach to an isolated world devoid of meanings or lacking in relation to the objects of the surrounding world, it is associated with the identification that individuals establish of reality, being able to access this perception from the development of expression or manifestations by the subject, which can give a possibility of interpretation in order to favor an experiential understanding (Dilthey, 2000).

According to Dilthey (1986), the sciences of the spirit unite three possible kinds of affirmations, associated to the relation of the individual with the world, these are related to historical elements of knowledge associated to real facts; others express partial contents of that reality, and finally, other affirmations are associated to value judgments. Distinguishing these three types of affirmations implies an approach to a psychologistic component from a hermeneutic point of view, which was necessary according to Dilthey's (1986) proposals, who established that although psychology is capable of distinguishing the facts of the experience from a description, being able to fully integrate itself to the sciences of the spirit, it cannot fall into the task of establishing explanations that converge in a positivist imposition regarding the understanding of the human being.

From the interpretative dimension, language is every possible representation of an individual's own construction, which can be associated with the development of a written text, a painting and obviously spoken language, and hermeneutics can be understood as a polysemic approach, capable of delivering different meanings, which implies a distinctive development associated with the identification of the author's thesis of each message (Dilthey, 1986). It is possible from the above, to distinguish two types of discourse, the discourse of the object associated with what is studied in the natural sciences, which is associated not with the search for the essence of the individual but with the development of a "cut" of essential qualities, not exploring all the richness and complexity, seeking to establish a mere explanation of the phenomenon of human experience, on the other hand, the sciences of the spirit seek to explore the complexity of the human being with a permanent uncertainty associated with the arduous task of clearly expressing the knowledge and phenomena of the human being, affirming that in understanding lies the ontic character of human life, constituting a hermeneutic exercise (Dilthey, 1986).

For Dilthey (1986), life carries in itself the understanding as consciousness of meanings, this grasping of meanings takes place in a mediated way, through expressions that the individual generates (Navarro González, 2001). Between the experience and the understanding, the expression is interposed as a necessary means, which is endowed with a "dimension of meaning," which discovers the fact of understanding. It is before this that the structure experience-expression-understanding, represents the structure through which life is lived, performing the interpretation that is inherent, being secondary that the understanding is performed by oneself or by the other, being able to understand the hermeneutic act as "the act of reencountering with the self in the you" (Navarro González, 2001).

The word "reliving" takes on main relevance in Dilthey's hermeneutics, in view of the fact that it is through the exercise of reliving that the sphere of understanding is sought, the act of reliving should not be understood as the act of repositioning oneself again at a psychological level in a previously lived experience, but rather the possibility of extracting the vital meaning of the discourse, This content may be far removed from the author's life, or it may be devoid of any meaning, which is why it represents a hermeneutic act, the possibility of understanding the content, in order to visualize the meaning given by the author to what is expressed (Navarro González, 2001).

The approach to a historical dimension of meanings makes possible an approach to a dimension associated with experience, considering the individual as a subject provided with language, culture, history and multiple elements that constitute his experience and his particular interpretation of the world of life. Dilthey (1986) proposes an approach to an esthetic condition centered on the distinction between "explaining" and "understanding," as two profoundly differentiated exercises, which undeniably belong to traditions with different but not antagonistic objectives. The identification of the sciences of the spirit (also called human sciences) presupposes a prior understanding of the universe of possibilities existing in the phenomenon of particular experiences, which are subject to the transmission of a message, a message that keeps hidden a meaning, which must be interpreted to achieve an understanding regarding subjectivity in terms of the perception of the world.

It is a challenge to consider hermeneutics as a therapeutic exercise, in view of the fact that the interpretative act represents an important risk in terms of preconceptions or biases involved on the part of the intervenor. It is necessary to refer that the interpretative exercise cannot be exempt from a phenomenological attitude, which allows an unprejudiced approach to messages and particular expressions, which is why we can refer that a hermeneutic without the presence of "epoché" can represent an imposing possibility, as well as the determination of spheres of meanings from investigative or therapeutic interests on the part of the expert.

THE LINGUISTIC TURN AS AN ACCESS TO THE HUMAN PHENOMENON

The arrival of phenomenological thought at the hands of Edmund Husserl marked the beginning of an epistemic revolution of great proportions and ambitions based on the possibility of establishing an integrated philosophical science, from a critique of the prevailing positivism, approaching phenomena from an unprejudiced point of view. Despite this initial proposal, a second great phenomenological revolution emerges, from a radicalization of Husserlian thought at the hands of Martin Heidegger, who not only continues the assumptions established by Husserl, but also destroys and restructures them from a radical perspective, distancing phenomenology as a whole as a possibility of science, also incorporating the "hermeneutic turn," as a fundamental moment in the exercise of the encounter with the phenomenon itself. This is considered the true innovation proposed by Heidegger, who establishes an epistemological enlargement from a line of the in situ capture of the own phenomena of life itself and the establishment of the exercise of interpretation and understanding. In this way Heidegger arrives at the world of hermeneutics.

Heidegger (2020) maintains an understanding based on the facts themselves and as from them opens the possibility of achieving a pure understanding of the phenomena of life, from an aprioristic perspective, in order to incorporate hermeneutics to this action, he introduces the concept of "hermeneutics of factuality," which seeks to understand the original being in factual life, which is not associated to a particular exercise or theoretical development. The procedure or thread associated to the hermeneutic action from what Heidegger established, responds to what the author calls the "formal indication" (Formale Anzeige), this formal indication does not respond to a method such as Husserl's epoché, but to an approach proper to factual life, which can be associated from the affective, posing it as an "affective disposition" that allows an approach that breaks all objectification (Heidegger, 2020).

The influence of Dilthey (1986) in Heidegger is transcendental, considering the extraction of a way to achieve a genuine understanding of the individual from his everyday life (Alltaglichkeit), which constitutes the pure form of how "Dasein" sees itself in an authentic and perceptible way in its immediacy (Heidegger, 2020). The intention of Heidegger's hermeneutic phenomenology, is to appropriate the meaning already implicit in the lived experience, through a process oriented to the destruction of discourses and construction, developing an interpretative process that represents the truth of what is observed, this is associated in the development of a profound exercise, focused on the deep interpretation that allows going beyond the everyday to a hidden meaning that represents the essence and the greatest meaning in being (Heidegger, 1989).

The way in which phenomenology and hermeneutics converge in an integrated manner, can be visualized in that the identification of phenomena from themselves, as they do not offer the possibility of establishing an understanding of their own essence—just as a medical observer who identifies a disease cannot understand at first sight what is hidden beyond the mere phenomenon—, although the perception of the factical phenomenon generates a phenomenological attitude that enables the intervener a space of identification of particular truths (Heidegger, 2020). For Heidegger (2020), the function of the hermeneutics of "Dasein," consists in making "Dasein" explicit, propitiating a process of destruction of the strata that generate a concealment of being in the world, establishing a possibility of return to the things themselves, allowing to find an original "Dasein" without conventionalisms, nor conceptions that hide its true identity.

According to Heidegger (2020), interpretation must be understood as an act of appropriation of meanings and senses, responding to the question of the "how" of things or associated actions. He defines an appropriation of meaning as follows: "Meaning is the horizon of the project, structured by the prior having-been, the prior way of seeing and the prior way of understanding, horizon from which something becomes comprehensible in terms of something" (Heidegger, 2020, p. 151). From this perspective, the act of interpreting in order to come to understand implies the establishment of questions about the destiny of being, understanding being as a subject that is directed toward a place or presents a specific horizon that constitutes it as an active essence, being able to find the essence of that being in the factual experience and in the facts of immediate existence. At the clinical level, the establishment of an exercise based on the questions "how," "where to" and "from where," provides a sense of constituted identity, based on a life project in which intentions and ways of adapting to the world are identified, from patterns established in the "Dasein."

When speaking of Heidegger's hermeneutic phenomenology, we speak of a historical-contextual being, a being in the world thrown into a dimension of possible meanings, whose experience is associated with the appropriation of a sense of the world, which is not associated with a reflective exercise, but rather with the mere fact of factual existence. The hermeneutics of "Dasein" proposes to the figure of the observer a space to consider this "Dasein" from a historical, contextual and transcendental dimension, becoming an active being that emerges and converges in a dynamic sense, of difficult access, considering that the interaction from everyday life entails the possibility of change, a phenomenon that represents a hard work for the figure of the observer.

The social observer cannot abstract from the contextual characteristics of the life of the observed subject, being the hermeneutic phenomenology an approach to the being steeped in tradition, culture and experience. It is not possible to establish a method that allows to articulate in a certain or precise way a hermeneutic phenomenology from Heidegger's point of view, but it is feasible to specify that the development of a method does not fall into the author's own pretensions, rather the call to adaptability on the part of the observer, as a walker without a path that builds his path as he walks, demarcate a hermeneutic approach of a subject immersed in the world of life, in order to favor the scope of possible interpretations, comprehensions and meanings.

THE IMPOSSIBILITY OF TRUTH IN THE DEVELOPMENT OF THE EXERCISE OF INTERPRETATION

In the path of development of hermeneutics, the arrival of Gadamer occurs as a direct continuation of the work established by Heidegger and his hermeneutic phenomenology, also managing to extract elements such as Husserl's "lebenswelt" to develop a theoretical proposal based on tradition and language, typical of a Heideggerian theoretical heritage. The development of a task focused on the search for human understanding is a work of complex magnitudes and dimensions, although the tradition that Gadamer absorbs as a constituent element of their approaches, it gives clear reference to a theoretical exposition in which "truth" will depend on the figure and language of the observer.

As a result of the turn and orientation toward language, characteristic of the 20th century, Gadamer exposes a path beyond the metaphysical vision from a factual hermeneutics, based on historical-existential elements, from the emphasis on the interpretation and understanding of the individual from a linguistic sphere (Gadamer, 1982). For Heidegger this "being in the world" is a being impregnated with meanings from the "throwing" in a world that is fused to the particular life experience, this perspective is adopted by Gadamer who manages to justify the hermeneutic turn, stating that understanding is the interpretation of the phenomena experienced in the act of living, being hermeneutics an experience even broader than the consciousness of the subject (Gadamer, 1982).

Gadamer (1982) proposes the concept of "universality of language," as a sense of man's closeness to the meaning he gives to the world through the word and how in its use deep meanings of the individual's own existence can be obtained. For Gadamer (1982), the truth of the subject takes place in the word and, in accordance with this perspective, he proposes three aspects as a means to reach understanding:

1. Dialog is the place of truth, of the happening or emergence of the thing itself.
2. In it, it is the thing itself, which sets itself up as the true subject.
3. In dialog, the interlocutors participate in the happening of truth, which unfolds in an infinite process.

By considering the individual as representing a horizon of meanings, located in language, the question is associated with the method of understanding the individual as a subject in the world. Beyond a psychological sphere in which a particular motivation or meaning can be understood (remembering understanding beyond consciousness), interpreting a subject involves a fusion of horizons (Horizontverschmelzung), the essential being the understanding of how another has acquired his or her worldview, considering aspects such as history and tradition (Gadamer, 2010). From this perspective it can be affirmed that each linguistic construction of the individual is subject to a specific historical moment of the person, a particular moment that demarcates and delivers meanings, we can understand this phenomenon as "efficacious history" (Gadamer, 2010).

The encounter between the figure of the observer and the observed, supposes a historical encounter that transcends the only corporeal perspective, it is the encounter between horizons of meanings, history and tradition, which is why Gadamer (1982), proposes the need to generate a new horizon that transcends the personal historical perspective, in which the task of understanding can be carried out, this enables a distancing from an understanding based on prejudice, from this perspective understanding for hermeneutics is given from a "comprehensive horizon." The figure of the observer must not only participate in a direct relationship with the phenomenon of history and tradition, but also with the sense of collectivity and social interaction in which this language is used from a sense of belonging, it is from this perspective that the possibility of incurring in interpretative errors can emerge, before the nonconsideration of the above mentioned dimensions, being essential the defense of the words and the relevance of their use, as part of an exercise of direct transference of the linguistic elements commonly used by the person in his daily life.

In language and dialog an infinite horizon of possibilities is housed, considering the human being as an entity in an active experiential process, subject to a maelstrom of possibilities inherent to the experience of life, where language is the gateway to a presence where present, past and history converge, in addition to sensation, perception and memory; it is a living scope that contemplates the finitude of being (Gadamer, 1982). It is in the tradition how the individual is able to transfer a particular sense of historical action, from language, this transmission or communication of the "Ipseity" involves a linguistic adaptation by the sender, given the idea that the lived experience and the self thrown in this experience cannot be completely verbalized, the dialogic interaction that seeks to deliver a meaning or personal sense is subject to a selection of linguistic elements that allow to graph which is the "feeling," "thinking" or "living" characterized by a moment, being the function of the figure of the observer to penetrate in this tradition that responds to an active and changing verbalization of one's own experience (Gadamer, 1982).

History interpreted linguistically implies an unprejudiced access stripped of value judgments, regulated methods and opinions prior to the proper development of the words that arise in the dialogic interaction, this being a space not accessible to a subject that seeks explanation as a method of ontological domination, abandoning contemplation as the making of events of possible realities (Berdzenishvili, 2016). It is in the search for truth that possibilities become finite and passages narrow, paths are filled with traps and passages that alter the observation of an ambiguous and diffuse path, a path not rooted in the specific determination of "facts or evidence," but of experience and historical experiences, of events that demarcate a delimited but dynamic sense, comprehensible but mutable. It is in the search for the truth about the human being that we must extract the truth of truths, the impossibility of truth in the understanding of the person, but not as a statistical rule.

It is from the approaches addressed in this subchapter, that the preponderant role of language embodied in the subject, as a means of expression of experiences and representation of the world, can be clearly visualized. Gadamer's work is related to the extraction of a Heideggerian tradition that rescues the Dasein, as a linguistic subject and generator of particular meanings, being the hermeneutic task to achieve a dialogic understanding and interpretation from the creation of "comprehensive horizons," and being able to affirm that these spaces cannot be limited to an encounter, but to continuous instances of historical follow-up.

THE EXTRACTION OF BEING IN THE WORLD: THE INTERPRETATIVE POSSIBILITY OF THE TEXT

In direct continuation of the work carried out in Husserl's phenomenology and the development of the question of being initiated by Heidegger, Paul Ricoeur's postulates represent a meeting point of various epistemological traditions, in addition to the development of a critical position to certain elements raised by Gadamer's hermeneutics. Since his essays on hermeneutics published in 1969, Ricoeur establishes a new paradigmatic position, a position that exposes a clear distinction between sender and receiver, modulating the phenomenon of interpretation as a task even more complex than the one previously proposed by Gadamer.

As a beginning of this critical and reflexive hermeneutics, Ricoeur (1975) establishes the need to question allegories as an object of abstraction, which pretends to express human intention and experience. This criticism is based on the fact that allegories are based on intellectualization, a situation that does not allow establishing a direct connection with particular spheres of meaning. On the other hand, Ricoeur (1975) proposes the figure of symbols as an opportunity to reach the infinitude of experiences of human existence.

A symbolic representation is not only housed in a linguistic dimension, but responds to any expression in the act of living, to representations that expose the relationship of the subject with a community and the representations proper to this communion, to the development of a text or writing, as well as to experiences and aprioristic knowledge developed in the mere act of existence (Ricoeur, 1975). In order to make a distinction between allegories and symbols, it is necessary to review the following points (Valverde, 2003):

1. Expressively, the allegory is an expression of temporality; on the other hand, the symbol is an expression of eternity.
2. Theologically, the allegory is a remote reference to a transcendental meaning, the symbol is a coincidence, it embodies in its figure the power of the sacred.
3. Aesthetically, the allegory is ruinous, catastrophic; on the other hand, the symbol is beauty and totality.
4. Constructurally, the allegory is artificial while the symbol is natural.

It is from this perspective that the allegory would have a pretension toward a metaphysical vision that distances the sense of reality of the issuing figure. On the other hand, the symbolic element extracts the sacred, infinite and true from the human experience.

The symbol as a myth and truth is eternal and representative culture of a timeless reality, which transcends the spatial dimension, but represents a possible reality, rich in meanings, housed in the contents of the symbolic. From this perspective, the interpretative exercise entails the framing of a new conception by Ricoeur (1969), who establishes the need to generate a "hermeneutics of distance," based on the need to favor a distancing between the figure of the sender and the receiver of messages, based on the action of written interpretation. This action suggests that the reader or receiver must carry out a hermeneutic exercise focused on separating the "Dasein" contained in the text, rescuing the being inserted and own of meanings, corresponding to a task of "appropriation of the text" as a meaning-generating exercise.

It is from this perspective that the exercise of a symbolic analysis entails an active interpretative action, an action of autonomous appropriation by the observer, evidencing a departure from the Husserlian "epoché." The consideration of the understanding of the text proposes the opportunity of an encounter with the being in the world, from the factual or imaginary

(Ricoeur, 1975). In relation to the question of being and the development of one's own identity, several lessons can be drawn from Ricoeur, especially from his studies focused on "narrative identity" and the construction of it from the story, being fundamental for the present research to allocate a section to address this issue.

Before developing the concept of narrative identity in greater depth, it is necessary to define the concept of "selfhood," which is associated in the words of Ricoeur (1996) to "the uninterrupted continuity between the first and the last stage of development of what we consider to be the same individual" (Ricoeur, 1996, p. 111). In simpler words, selfhood is associated with the imperturbable sense of identity despite the events or situations that every individual must live, there being a basic structure that sustains a permanent sense of identity. On the other hand, the concept of "ipseity" can be defined from Ricoeur as the "maintenance of the word," centered on the identification of the self from a historical recognition of "I am and I continue to be who I said I was," recognizing a self as the one from before, the one from now and the one that can be. It is associated to an appropriation of one's own body and identity, to a definition not only in first but also in third person, being the act of distinction and personal differentiation, a contact based on the otherness and recognition of my own characteristics in differentiation to the characteristics of another (Ricoeur, 1996).

Thus, narrative identity can be defined as the development of a story about one's own life, with an approach to an autobiographical type of story, being the individual creator and narrator of a story with personal meaning, which tells the past, present of a self in a projective orientation toward the promise of a possible future, as the protagonist of a story whose end is in development (Ricoeur, 1996).

Ipseity is involved in the position of establishing "imaginative variations," which are associated with experiential variations and self-discourses that can generate identity confusion, given the emergence of stories far from the historical dimension of individual experiences, in which the protagonist of the story is subject to a reality biased by the imaginative possibilities of the one who establishes a story (Ricoeur, 1996).

From the aforementioned vision, the need arises to visualize the emerging challenge in the interpretation of narratives that represent a possible "attack" on one's own identity, which can be sustained by the permanence of "character." However, from a consideration oriented to self-discourse, visualized from a therapeutic dimension, the discourses regarding one's own identity and personal history can define an action based on the overcoming or permanence at a psychopathological level, insofar as the spheres of self-definition allow a modulation of the senses of experience and possibilities of personal visualization as an entity oriented to alternatives of change.

In Paul Ricoeur's hermeneutic vision, elements arise that encourage a reflective analysis regarding the need to establish an active role as observing figures, in order to develop the mission of "rescuing" the personal meanings housed or lost in the discourses or narratives transmitted from the symbolic. It is appropriate to point out that the usefulness of the present vision at a therapeutic level is striking especially from the establishment of intervention processes that promote the deconstruction and reorganization of identity narratives by the individual, generating real possibilities that allow the consultant an appropriation of his history and identity, thus favoring the increase of an autonomous action and in direct harmony with the processes of change, characteristic in every life narrative.

SUMMARY

In this chapter we have extensively reviewed the origins and development of the hermeneutic tradition, distinguishing it as a discipline oriented from its beginnings to the interpretation of biblical texts and its disciplinary evolution associated to the interpretation of narratives at a personal level. From Schleiermacher's approaches, it is possible to distinguish the need to develop a model that allows an approach to the understanding of the human phenomenon, considering the linguistic element as a transcription and representation of the individual subjective experience.

Regarding Dilthey's contributions, it is worth highlighting the author's rescue of elements of Schleiermacher's hermeneutics, which is based on the need to recover the value of the multiplicity of reality and, above all, to position hermeneutics as a discipline different from the objectifiable natural sciences, initiating the so-called sciences of the spirit.

Heidegger manages to establish a revolution on the grounds of what was previously established by Husserlian phenomenology, establishing a hermeneutic turn, which raises the need for phenomenology not to emerge as a possibility of approach isolated from a narrative and linguistic component, concepts that from the factual represent a greater approach to the figure of being. Gadamer inherits the concepts of tradition and history from Heidegger and gives a central role to the linguistic element, as a central element in the exercise of understanding and interpretation, also establishing a relevant role to the dialogic, as a necessary task in the development of comprehensive processes.

Finally, in Paul Ricoeur's approaches it is possible to highlight the role of symbols and how, from the narratives developed, the need to rescue the individual immersed in them arises, extracting Heidegger's concept of "Dasein" as a central element to be visualized by the author from his own elements at the discursive level, developing a hermeneutic of identity rescue (Table 4.1).

TABLE 4.1 Summary of Authors and Postulates of Hermeneutics

Authors	Schleiermacher	Dilthey	Heidegger	Gadamer	Ricoeur
Conceptos	"Generalization" "Dual understanding" "Respect for others" "Germinal decision."	"Sciences of the spirit"; "Interpretation of language"; "Reliving experiences."	"Dasein", being-in-the-world. "Hermeneutic turn in phenomenology."	"Linguisticity," understanding of the individual from the inherent character of his language.	"Narrative identity"; "Ipseity and Myssimity," "Hermeneutics of distance."
Purpose	To develop a dialectical hermeneutics, based on the need to understand particular realities, from the interpretation of linguistic, cultural and intentional elements.	To develop an understanding of the individual from a method not based on causal explanation.	Explain the meanings contained in the lived experiences.	It seeks to understand the existence of being in the world, through language.	To develop a hermeneutic that allows maintaining a distance between sender and receiver in order to develop new dimensions of understanding.
Task	From the development of hermeneutics, an understanding of the subject must be achieved, better than the subject is able to understand itself.	Through hermeneutics it seeks to develop an understanding of the experience.	To develop the phenomenon of understanding, rather than as a knowledge task.	Linguistic process that employs different ways of understanding the self.	To rescue the being in the world contained in the text or narrative.

CHAPTER 5

UNPREJUDICE AS AN APPROACH TO SUBJECTIVE REALITY. THE HERMENEUTIC PHENOMENOLOGICAL METHODOLOGY

This chapter explores the development and application of phenomenological and hermeneutic methodology in qualitative research, highlighting its capacity to capture and understand human experience in its complexity and depth. This approach is based on the detailed and reflexive interpretation of the particular meanings that individuals attach to their experiences, following a philosophical tradition that goes back to the work of Edmund Husserl, Martin Heidegger, Hans-Georg Gadamer and other influential thinkers.

Phenomenology, initiated by Husserl, focuses on the structure of experience and how phenomena present themselves to consciousness. Concepts such as "noema" and "noesis" are fundamental to this methodology, which seeks a deep understanding of subjective experience through the suspension of previous judgments, known as "epoché." Heidegger, extending these ideas, introduces the concept of "hermeneutics of facticity," which implies an interpretation based on the everyday existence and historical context of the individual.

In parallel, hermeneutics, with roots in Schleiermacher and Dilthey, focuses on the interpretation of texts and discourses. Schleiermacher

Phenomenological-Hermeneutical Approach to Borderline Personality Disorder, pages 37–56

doi:10.1108/978-1-80592-281-020251005

emphasizes dual understanding, embracing both language and authorial intent, while Dilthey differentiates between the natural sciences and the sciences of the spirit, stressing the need to interpret human phenomena within their historical and cultural contexts.

Gadamer takes these concepts further with his idea of the "fusion of horizons," proposing that understanding arises from the interaction between the horizons of the interpreter and the interpreted. Gadamer's hermeneutics stresses the importance of dialog and the co-construction of meanings, essential elements for a deep and dynamic understanding of human experiences.

This chapter also examines contemporary developments such as Claire Petitmengin's microphenomenology and Jonathan Smith and Mike Osborn's Interpretative Phenomenological Analysis (IPA). These methodologies combine phenomenological precision with the interpretive richness of hermeneutics, providing effective tools for the analysis of subjective experiences in varied contexts, from clinical and therapeutic to educational and social.

Throughout the chapter, we detail how these methodologies allow for a deep and nuanced exploration of human experiences, offering a theoretical and practical framework for researchers interested in understanding subjectivity and meaning in human experience. Examples of application in various fields are discussed, illustrating the relevance and usefulness of phenomenology and hermeneutics in qualitative research.

In summary, this chapter provides a comprehensive guide to the application of phenomenological and hermeneutic methodology, highlighting its potential to reveal the deep and complex meanings of human experiences, and its ability to enrich understanding in diverse areas of qualitative research.

Holroyd (2007) refers that this methodology is linked to a constructivist approach, which responds to the perception of the existence of multiple realities, which are constructed from particular perceptions and according to Hatch (2002), the object of study should be associated to the individual meanings that each individual gives to his own experience. According to Van Manen (2002) and Slattery (2006), this responds to the art of hermeneutics as a discipline linked to the interpretation and visualization of particular meanings of the social world, which makes this methodology an exercise based on the capture and interpretation of experience, from a subjective and linguistic perspective.

According to Husserl (2012), the elements of "noema" and "noesis" are fundamental in the development of a hermeneutic phenomenological exercise, in the first place the noema is linked to what is experience; on the other hand the noesis is associated to the way in which it is experienced by the subject, being central elements to understand in this methodology, which according to the author, must always be accompanied by an unprejudiced approach, in which personal ideas or thoughts must be suspended, regarding the phenomenon to be investigated. On the other hand, Heidegger (2008), incorporates the concept of "exegesis," which is associated with the form in which the experience is expressed, which can be linked to a verbal, paralinguistic and written content, this represents an extension of the interpretative dimension at the investigative level, being necessary to perform not only an exercise of experiential capture, but also a complex exercise of linguistic interpretation.

Gadamer (1982), incorporates elements based on conversation, as a means of interpretation and understanding of particular experiences, the author proposes the development of a conversation based on questioning and inquiry, in order to achieve an approach to the particular truth of the interviewee. According to Slattery (2006), the development of a linguistic interaction as part of the present methodology is associated with what Gadamer (1982) called "fusion of horizons," linking this concept to the fact that each perspective (interviewer and interviewee) responds to a certain horizon of meanings and experiences, and at the moment of having a conversation, the interaction of these horizons can generate new spheres of meaning in relation to the experience to be understood.

In relation to the hermeneutic approach, Gadamer (1982), exposes the need for the interviewer to maintain a continuous distance from his own meanings and the meanings of the interviewee, also indicating the need to maintain a permanent openness of the subject to be approached, in view of the possibility of the emergence of new meanings, beyond the interpretations made by the researcher. In view of this, the consideration of a hermeneutic perspective is linked to an exercise of continuous interpretation and linguistic interaction, in search of meanings of the experience under investigation.

Gadamer (1982), bases the need for a co-construction of knowledge between the figure of the researcher and the participant, from the so-called "hermeneutic circle," each verbal interaction occurs from a circularity of interpretations, reflections and new interactions from all types of linguistic relationships. In this same aspect, Holroyd (2007), argues that verbal interaction must also consider knowledge regarding contextual elements of a cultural nature, which allow a holistic understanding of the participant's perspective and the subject matter experienced.

In order to establish a structure regarding the characteristic and constitutive elements of a research that considers a hermeneutic phenomenological methodology, a general organization of the same will be developed below, which will be divided into the following subtopics: research design, participants, data collection, informed consent and the central theme of this article associated with types of interviews.

TYPE OF RESEARCH DESIGN IN PHENOMENOLOGICAL AND HERMENEUTIC RESEARCH

Phenomenological-hermeneutic research uses an intentional selection of a specific sample. According to Creswell (2012), any sample should consider subjects who present an experiential and contextual relationship with the phenomenon to be studied, which favors a closer approach to the particular experience. Creswell (2012) also indicates that the sources for obtaining a given sample must have sufficient information regarding the distinctive characteristics of a given group of participants; this qualitative information must account for the existing link between a given subject and the phenomenon to be studied, and there must be clear evidence of the existing relationship.

SELECTION OF PARTICIPANTS IN PHENOMENOLOGICAL AND HERMENEUTICAL RESEARCH

Based on the approaches of Denzin and Lincoln (2013), the selection of participants and the sample size in phenomenological-hermeneutic research should be determined by elements such as: the nature of the phenomenon to be studied and the number of subjects who have experience associated with the study phenomenon. From a perspective based on the particular experience, Rubin and Rubin (2012), have referred that each research participant must have a particular relationship with the study phenomenon, which favors obtaining a unique and unrepeatable experience, whereby a particular participant has an irreplaceable role in the development of the research.

FORM OF DATA COLLECTION IN PHENOMENOLOGICAL AND HERMENEUTIC RESEARCH

In the development of a hermeneutic phenomenological methodology, Slavin (2007) indicates the need to use a variety of multiple instruments that allow a broad understanding of the various elements that constitute the particular experience. From this aspect, Merriam (2009) refers that the development of this type of research should ideally be generated in a space that is familiar to the participant, a space that allows an uninhibited expression, without any kind of pressure based on the need to obtain a certain discourse or result.

Ramsook (2018), indicates that the development of individual in-depth interviews is of utmost relevance in the present research methodology, considering at all times semistructured instruments that allow greater flexibility and spontaneity in verbal interaction. It is also relevant to keep video and audio records that allow a detailed review of the information obtained, as well as notebooks or diaries for the collection of additional information that may arise during the research process, being this type of annotations fundamental during the process of analysis and reflection of the information obtained.

Finally, Merriam (2009) states that the present research methodology is not specifically based on a step-by-step organization, which allows establishing preestablished or rigid processes, which is largely related to the fluctuating nature of the particular experience. Ramsook (2018), refers that it must be established at all times, the consideration that participants can at all times, construct different meanings for the same situation, which makes the capture of subjective experience, a continuous process and not based on a single historical moment.

INFORMED CONSENT IN PHENOMENOLOGICAL AND HERMENEUTIC RESEARCH

In phenomenological-hermeneutic research, as in any other type of research, the development of an informed consent document is a central element to give to each participant, in order to safeguard ethical aspects such as privacy, rights, duties of each interviewee and aspects that refer to the treatment of sensitive information that will be considered during the research (Ramsook, 2018). Regarding the identification of participants, Patton (2002), expresses the need to establish pseudonyms that allow the maintenance of privacy, in addition, in the case of keeping an audio or video record of the interview process, the express consent of each participant should always be requested (Lichtman, 2011).

TYPES OF INTERVIEWS IN PHENOMENOLOGICAL AND HERMENEUTIC RESEARCH

The phenomenological-hermeneutic methodology considers the use of various instruments to capture the particular experience of each participant, this implies the development of instruments such as in-depth interviews, questionnaires and structured analysis methodologies, which allow the organization of experiences based on a coherent logic, based on the development of a sequential process that allows the identification of the particular experience. According to Bevan (2014), the development of a phenomenological interview should consider elements proper to the tradition exposed by Husserl, as well as hermeneutic considerations exposed in the approaches of Heidegger and Gadamer, for this purpose the author has developed a structure in which he clearly exposes the elements proper to a phenomenological interview. See Table 5.1.

This figure clearly describes the initial intention of all phenomenological research, which must be linked to an attitude of unprejudiced suspension of a priori knowledge on the part of the researcher. This attitude, which functions as a type of phenomenological reduction, is called "epoché." From this attitude, different types of approach to the experience will be developed, which will seek to deepen in relation to different nuances or elements of the particular experience. From this dimension, the development of three types of interview structure, involve the development of a definition as to the way of establishing certain questions in the construction of interviews.

Finally, the type of questions to be developed is described, in terms of a specific theme, which seeks to clarify the type of experience lived during a chronic illness, as well as the possibility of distinguishing experiences associated with the permanence in a care unit in the company of a physician. The present structure clarifies how to establish an encounter that arises from an intention of approach, based on the lack of prejudice, as a way of encountering the particular experience of the subject. By developing an exercise of suspension of aprioristic knowledge, it favors the consideration of the pure experience and mainly linked to the experience from a natural attitude and alien to any scientific predetermination.

In the development of a hermeneutic phenomenological methodology, it is possible to distinguish different types of interviews or modes of approach, which commit an established structure and methodology, which is associated with its application, analysis and particular delivery of results, which seek an understanding and description of the lived experience, from a dimension based on the first person of the person who experiences a particular phenomenon.

The following are some of the types of interviews considered in this methodology:

Human Sciences Paradigm for the Phenomenological Study of Max Van Manen

Max Van Manen is a Canadian researcher who has considered as a fundamental part of his methodological approaches from a phenomenological dimension, the theoretical assumptions of authors such as Heidegger, who provides a hermeneutic dimension to the experiential approach. For Van Manen (1990), the approach must be based on the interpretation of the text that represents the particular experience, this text exposes a certain

TABLE 5.1 Phenomenological Interview Structure (Bevan, 2014)

Phenomenological Attitude	Researcher's Approach	Interview Structure	Method	Sample Questions
	Acceptance of the natural attitude of the participants	Contextualization (exposure to the world of life based on natural attitude)	Contextual descriptive/ narrative questions	"Tell me about how it is being sick" or "Tell me how you got to this care unit."
Phenomenological reduction (EPOCHÉ)	Critical-reflective dialog at a personal level	Learning the phenomenon (How does it appear in the natural context?)	Descriptive questions regarding the mode of occurrence of the experience	"Tell me about a typical day in this care unit" or "Tell me about what you do to prepare for the dialysis process."
	Active listening	Clarifying the phenomenon (Meaning from imaginative variation)	Imaginative variation (establishing a variation in type of questions)	"Tell me how your experience in the present care unit would change if a doctor was present at all times."

language that evidences a certain experience. The method proposed by Van Manen (1990), exposes the following points, based on the consideration of what phenomenological research should be:

1. A study of lived experience
2. An explanation of how the phenomenon presents itself in consciousness.
3. Study of essences
4. Description of experiential meanings
5. A human scientific study of the phenomenon
6. A poetic activity
7. A thoughtful practice of consideration
8. A search for what it means to be human

For Van Manen (1990), the way to achieve an approach to the lived experience is to achieve a linguistic interpretation that allows clarifying a certain experience of a phenomenon, in order to achieve an understanding from an external observation. In the present methodology, the author considers indispensable the need for the researcher to maintain a continuous development of writing, reading and reflection, as elements of continuous observation of the experience developed by a given participant.

Van Manen's (1990) research proposal is based on six moments, which graph in detail, stages linked to the process of experiential capture. The present graph shows the author's approaches (Table 5.2).

TABLE 5.2 Research Structure Proposed by Van Manen (1990)

Stages	Meaning
Returning to the nature of the lived experience.	Formulation of a research question.
Investigate the lived experience as it is.	The experience is captured through research methods (interviews, focus groups, writing, etc.).
Reflection on the essential themes of the phenomenon experienced.	The meaning of a participant's experience is sought through reflection on his or her experiences.
Describe the phenomenon from writing.	Through writing, the aim is for the participant to be able to express his/her emotions, feelings and attitudes toward a given phenomenon.
Maintain a strong orientation toward the phenomenon.	During the research process, the focus should always be kept on the research question formulated.
To achieve a balance in the research context, based on the consideration of the parts and the whole.	The researcher must continually visualize how the information obtained from the participant's experience is linked to the central focus of the research.

The present stages methodically expose the process committed by the author, which is based on the need not only to capture the experience per se, but also on the continuous revision of the observations made by the figure of the researcher, who must continuously establish a reflective process regarding the information captured. Van Manen's assumptions (1990), harbor the need to convert the experience into a medium attainable from written contents, which allow a reach to a linguistic dimension of analysis, as well as the construction of artistic expressions of written type that represent a manifestation of the experiences associated to a certain phenomenon.

Some research that has considered the present methodology is associated with the study of aspects related to education and nursing. It is possible to point to the study of Jhagroo (2012) named *A hermeneutic phenomenological study of the lived experiences of immigrant students in their mathematics classrooms at a secondary school in Auckland, New Zealand.*

The present research has obtained information regarding the set of experiences of a group of students, linked to discrimination and the relationship with peers in a daily academic context, considering a phenomenological and hermeneutic perspective of approaching the particular experience.

Another approach from the present methodology is associated with the study developed by Kim and Park (2021), entitled *A Phenomenological Study on the Experience of Physical Education Classes of Peer Relations Alienation Students: Max van Manen's Hermeneutic Phenomenology.* This study establishes a hermeneutic phenomenological approach to the experience of alienation in an academic context, from the perspective of people who have been excluded by their peers during the development of physical education classes, obtaining from the process of analysis a wide variety of issues associated with the object of study, as well as the identification of alternatives for the resolution of this problem.

The research by Plagenz (2015), called *The Lived Experience of Nurses Working in a Modified Therapeutic Community,* explores the experience of nurses working in therapeutic prison contexts, working directly with prison population with multiple psychopathological manifestations. The study considers the analysis proposed by Van Manen and the seven steps proposed by Colaizzi (1978), obtaining significant information associated with various complexities present in this context, achieving an organized structuring of the evoked experiences.

This methodology represents an interesting approach to the experience, however, the development of this methodology requires an important understanding of its theoretical and methodological assumptions, which is not an easy task, since the description made by the author at times is not clarifying, however, his approaches adhere to an approach that respects epistemological traditions from phenomenology and hermeneutics.

Phenomenological Descriptive Method in Psychology by Amedeo Giorgi

The development of the present methodology of approaching the lived experience exposes, according to Giorgi's (1986, 2009), the need to explain the link with the phenomenon by the participant, in a detailed and careful way, hand in hand with a description based on the raw data obtained at the research level, which should follow a phenomenological psychological reduction perspective. In relation to the articulation of the present method, Giorgi and Giorgi (2003), expose four moments that will lead to the structured development of their methodological proposal (Table 5.3)

In this table, it is possible to distinguish the development of a process based on the maintenance of a phenomenological attitude, which allows at the beginning to develop a capture of the lived experience from the dimensions defined by each participant, not incurring in presuppositions of the figure of the researcher. Giorgi and Giorgi (2003) refer to two elements linked to what it means to maintain a phenomenological attitude:

1. The researcher must put in brackets any prior knowledge he/she has about the phenomenon, in order to guarantee the capture of the subject's experience.
2. The researcher does not consider the phenomenon described as real (even if it is), since it is only associated with the experience of a particular participant and is part of that individual experience.

TABLE 5.3 Phenomenological Method Steps Proposed by Giorgi and Giorgi (2003)

Obtaining a concrete description of a phenomenon from the interviewee. Faced with this information, the researcher assumes a complex attitude, based on the reading of the statements in order to establish a sense of familiarity with them.	Once an understanding and meaning of all the information obtained has been achieved, the researcher returns to the beginning of the description, establishing a slow reading of the statements. Once this reading has been completed, the researcher makes a delimitation of the "units of meaning," based on statements that can present a partial sense of the experience.
Once the second stage is completed, the researcher returns to the beginning of the information obtained and begins to transform each unit of meaning into expressions that convey more directly the psychological sense of what the participant said, information that until now has only been approached from an explicit and natural sense.	Finally, once the units of meaning considered have been transformed, a general structure of the experience of the phenomenon is articulated.

It is on the basis of these approaches, from an epistemological and investigative perspective, that the author states that the assumptions of an experiential nature will not have a dimension of reality, considering that they arise from a particular experience, which covers an understanding of the interviewee as a subject capable of building his own world of life, which is not necessarily related to the elements that can be perceived in a supposed objective world. The approaches of Giorgi (1986, 2009) and Giorgi and Giorgi (2003), are positioned from a perspective of pretranscendental phenomenology, which states that every phenomenon that is perceived as "real" is nothing more than a mere representation of the subject and his or her determined subjectivity, but not a reflection of a collectively shared reality.

The research by Isabirye and Makoe (2018), *Phenomenological Analysis of the Lived Experiences of Academics who Participated in the Professional Development Programme at an Open Distance Learning (ODL) University in South Africa*, exposes the set of experiences of academics who have had to adapt to the development of distance education, exploring the experiences associated with the training and set of relationships that they have managed to establish from the use of this educational methodology. The research has obtained information related to aspects of temporal, spatial and bodily nature, achieving very detailed descriptions associated with how these dimensions are deployed in virtual education contexts.

The application of this methodology has also been observed in the research of Anosike et al. (2012), entitled *Phenomenology as a method for exploring management practice*, the present study was linked to the analysis of the experiences of people involved in human management tasks and how their particular experiences can influence the development of such practices. The authors identify that this methodology can be very useful in the identification of particular experiences in the present context, since these elements can directly influence practices associated with management.

Finally, the research of Martínez Ávila and Alvarez Aguirre (2021), *Aplicación de la metodología de Amedeo Giorgi como sustento metodológico*, is linked to the study of the experience of adolescents who are children of parents with problematic alcohol consumption. This essay highlights how this methodology has been able to identify elements of the daily experience of the sample considered, based on the theoretical assumptions of Giorgi's approaches, which are useful for this type of approach.

It is possible to distinguish the great usefulness and context of application of the methodology proposed by Giorgi, which is linked to theoretical assumptions that respect a philosophical and ideographic tradition in the constitution and development of experience. It is possible to appreciate clarity in the present proposal, as well as the possibility that the different moments of analysis proposed may be considered in future research, resulting in a proposal that considers a broad theoretical and practical tradition in the approach to the particular experience.

Microphenomenological Interview by Claire Petitmengin

This type of interview arises from the contributions linked to Neurophenomenology initially made by Francisco Varela (1996) and based on the development of the "entretien d'explicitation" proposed by Pierre Vermersch (1994, 2009, 2012), orientations focused on achieving an approximation by the person to implicit elements of their actions both physically and mentally. Its adaptation to cognitive sciences is based on the adaptation made by Petitmengin (2006), linked to the description of the lived experience from a second-person perspective, presenting a wide application to clinical contexts, as well as therapeutic or exploration contexts at an individual level.

Based on the approaches of Petitmengin et al. (2019), the microphenomenological interview has had applications in various contexts, among which are:

1. Clinical and therapeutic context (Balzani et al., 2013; Depraz et al., 2017; Pacheco, 2021; Valenzuela-Moguillansky, 2013).
2. Cognitive and educational research (Bitbol & Petitmengin, 2016; Van-Quynh, 2017)
3. In research related to artistic expression (Petreca, 2016; Vásquez-Rosati, 2017)
4. Associated with the capacity for contemplation (Petitmengin et al., 2017; Przyrembel & Singer, 2018).

The development of this type of interview arises from an approach, based mainly on ideas of Edmund Husserl (2012) referred to the fact that most of the experience remains regularly unnoticed or at a prereflective level. Based on the approaches of Petitmengin et al. (2019), a large part of our daily activity, linked to feeling, observing, listening or deciding, is not immediately accessible from our reflective capacity nor from the possibility of delivering verbal descriptions, which is why an exploratory model that favors an approach to the prereflective elements of experience is required.

In order to access this set of experiences, a certain capacity or skills are required on the part of the interviewer, which are clearly identified and described, mainly linked to theoretical assumptions from phenomenology, in addition to the approach to the experience from the development of certain types of questions and indications, in order to achieve a description regarding aspects of the experience that remain regularly unnoticed (Bitbol & Petitmengin, 2013; Petitmengin, 2006, 2007, 2011; Petitmengin et al., 2013). Based on these approaches, a figure describing the main moments of approach proposed by the microphenomenological interview will be developed below (Figure 5.1).

Initially, this figure exposes an approach based on the lack of prejudice, from the "epoché" proposed by Husserl (2012), linked to the suspension of previous knowledge that is present in relation to the phenomenon of study, a characteristic attitude of the phenomenological encounter. Secondly, an approach to the particular experience is promoted, beyond an explanatory dimension, which means that the exploration is oriented to the evocation of an experience lived from the particular, for which an experience focused on the "here and now" is used, otherwise the development of a memory that allows establishing a connection with the most representative elements of the experience to be evoked must be motivated.

The aspects to be considered during the interview development are associated with synchronic and diachronic elements of the experience. Petitmengin et al. (2019), indicate that the synchronic points to the landscape or space defined by the subject, from which a certain experience develops, which allows an understanding at a spatial level of the experience. On the other hand, the diachronic is linked to the understanding of how the experience develops over time, the evolution of the experience in the previously proposed landscape, thus distinguishing spatial-temporal elements in the description of the particular experience.

During the development of the microphenomenological interview, Petitmengin et al. (2019), propose the development of questions that guide the evocations by the interviewee. In the exploration of the diachronic elements of the experience, questions such as *"How do I start this?"; "What happens next?"; "How does this end?"* are recommended. By way of conducting an exploration of the synchronic elements of the evoked experience, the development of questions such as, *"When you see this, how do you see it?"; "How do you realize it feels this way?"; "What does that look like that you are seeing?"* are suggested. The questions developed do not seek to direct the interviewee in the development of his or her evocation, but rather to provide guidance and structure to the evocation developed, as an exploratory exercise that has flexibility and adaptation to the characteristics of the evoked experiences.

Once the transcription of the interview has been developed, an analysis based on 5 moments will be developed, which involve the structuring of the experience in an organized manner based on temporo-spatial elements, as well as on aspects associated with its particular description.

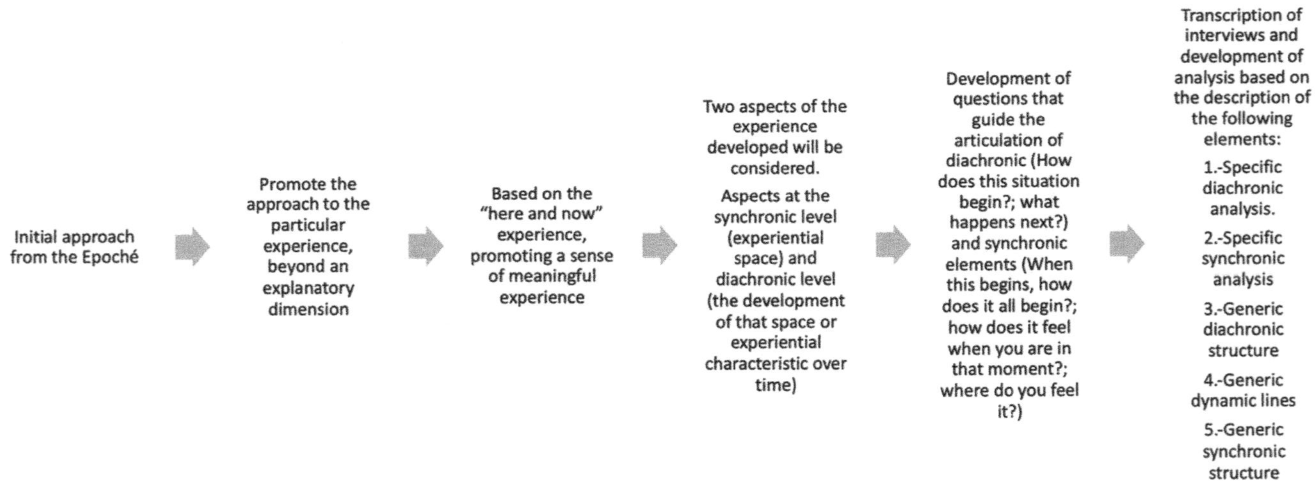

Figure 5.1 Microphenomenological interview moments, based on approaches of Petitmengin et al. (2019).

The objective of each of the analyses to be developed is described below, based on the approaches proposed by Valenzuela-Moguillansky and Vásquez-Rosati (2019):

1. *Specific diachronic analysis:* It is associated with the analysis of the temporal elements in which the experience occurs and the micro-phenomena observable in the development of that timeline.
2. *Specific synchronic analysis:* It is linked to the analysis and observation of characteristic aspects of the evoked experience, which allow a detailed visualization of the micro-characteristics that make up a given experience.
3. *Generic diachronic structure:* An order of the experience(s) is established based on the emergence of specific moments of evocation, establishing a sequential ordering that allows a clear distinction of the development of a given experience and its distinctive moments in a given period of time.
4. *Generic dynamic lines:* This stage is associated with the identification of a specific characteristic to be explored, which is part of the evocation obtained. It is intended to establish an ordering of the moments in which the characteristic of the selected experience emerges, allowing to distinguish micro-moments in which a specific phenomenon of the experience is clearly visualized.
5. *Generic synchronic structure:* In the present point the experiential comparison is considered, based on what was obtained in the specific synchronic analyses carried out. It is very useful at the moment of visualizing common elements that different evoked experiences may present, based on their constitutive characteristics.

It is possible to distinguish the development of several investigations that have considered at a methodological level, the use of the micro-phenomenological interview, which have managed to structure elements of evoked experiences, considering aspects at a temporal level, as well as characteristics present in micro-moments of the experience. Pacheco (2021), in his research *Stress in borderline personality disorder: a review of the particular experience from a micro-phenomenological perspective,* from a sample of three people with borderline personality disorder, has explored the set of experiences that they present in relation to stressful situations, achieving a structuring of the different experiences, as well as a comparison of the results obtained, managing to distinguish associated elements, among which are physical, emotional and sensory effects of exposure to stressful situations in the sample considered.

In the research by Duarte et al. (2020), *Episodes of meeting in psychotherapy: An empirical exploration of patients' experiences of subjective change during their psychotherapy process*, a sample of nine persons who participated in a psychotherapeutic intervention process was considered. From the development of micro-phenomenological interviews, moments of connection and intimacy during the development of psychotherapy were explored, identifying emotional aspects and differentiated phases that arise during the development of a therapeutic interaction, which demarcate spaces of intimacy and connection.

Finally, in the research of Rietdijk (2018), *A micro-phenomenological study of processes and mechanisms of insight meditation*, a micro-phenomenological interview was conducted with three people who have an intermediate experience in Vipassana meditation practices. The research manages to identify different moments and characteristics present during the development of the meditative processes, as well as to distinguish sensations experienced by interviewees during the development of the meditation practices performed, achieving a deep structuring of the experiences, distinguishing micro-moments that occur in short periods of time.

We have been able to distinguish the main approaches of the microphenomenological interview, which is an interesting approach and exploration of the characteristics of evoked experiences, considering a phenomenological dimension in its approaches. It is possible to distinguish the high interest of structuring and ordering of results that the present methodology proposes, which favors the development of an orderly distinction of experiential elements. These can be ordered from a temporal-spatial dimension, being able to identify micro-moments that occur during the course of the experience, which may be highly relevant and which in various methodological approaches are not considered, which positions the micro-phenomenological interview as a relevant source of exploration of the particular experience.

INTERPRETATIVE PHENOMENOLOGICAL ANALYSIS (IPA) OF JONATHAN SMITH & MIKE OSBORN

IPA is a type of interview and analysis proposed by Smith and Osborn (2003), which bases its epistemological foundations on the approaches of Husserl (2012), Heidegger (2020) and Merleau-Ponty (1945), proposing a phenomenological approach to the experience itself, beyond any theorization and a respective hermeneutic analysis of the discourses obtained during the development of lived experiences. IPA proposes an in-depth approach to the particular experience from a phenomenological and hermeneutic perspective; in the words of Smith and Osborn (2003), "The interview seeks to understand what the experience is like from the point of view of the participants" (Smith & Osborn, 2003, p. 51).

This methodology considers 4 key elements at a theoretical level, which will lead its development and subsequent analysis, these are:

1. Consideration of a phenomenological, hermeneutic and ideographic approach (Smith, 2004).
2. Incorporation of hermeneutic elements to the phenomenological dimension (Larkin et al., 2006).
3. IPA is part of an interpretive circle between participants and the interviewer (Smith, 2004).
4. Reflection is a fundamental element during the development of the analytical process of IPA (Finlay, 2008).

It is feasible to refer that the initial intention of IPA was to develop or apply philosophical principles of phenomenology and hermeneutics to research in psychology, continuously seeking to expand its limits as a methodology for approaching experience. Based on Smith et al. (2009) "IPA is concerned with the detailed examination of the lived human experience, its goal is to carry out this examination to the extent that the person can express the experience in his or her own terms" (p. 32). Its commitment to the deep exploration of human experience makes the present method a flexible approach with possibilities of going beyond the approach of psychological or psychopathological aspects, being able to cover a wide range of experiences considering the deep interpretative possibilities of the linguistic contents.

The 7 steps related to interview analysis proposed by IPA are developed below (Figure 5.2).

This graph shows the development of the analytical process linked to IPA, which is characterized by an initial approach in the development of the interview, from a theoretical suspension considering the Husserlian "epoché" as a transcendental and necessary phenomenological reduction in the approach to natural experience. A hermeneutic analysis is considered based initially on a consideration of the narrative contents of the text (interview transcript), through a natural attitude and a literal reading based on the definitions of each participant with also on their content and linguistic uses.

Subsequently, an initial analysis is considered, which is linked to the development of initial annotations linked to representative elements of the evoked experience, making a selection of emerging themes in the developed interview. Once representative information has been extracted, the existence of possible connections at the thematic level will be sought on the basis of the experience captured, in order to establish semantic networks based on representative elements at the experiential level.

The next step is associated to consider again a suspension based on the "epoché," in order to achieve an unprejudiced approach to the analysis of

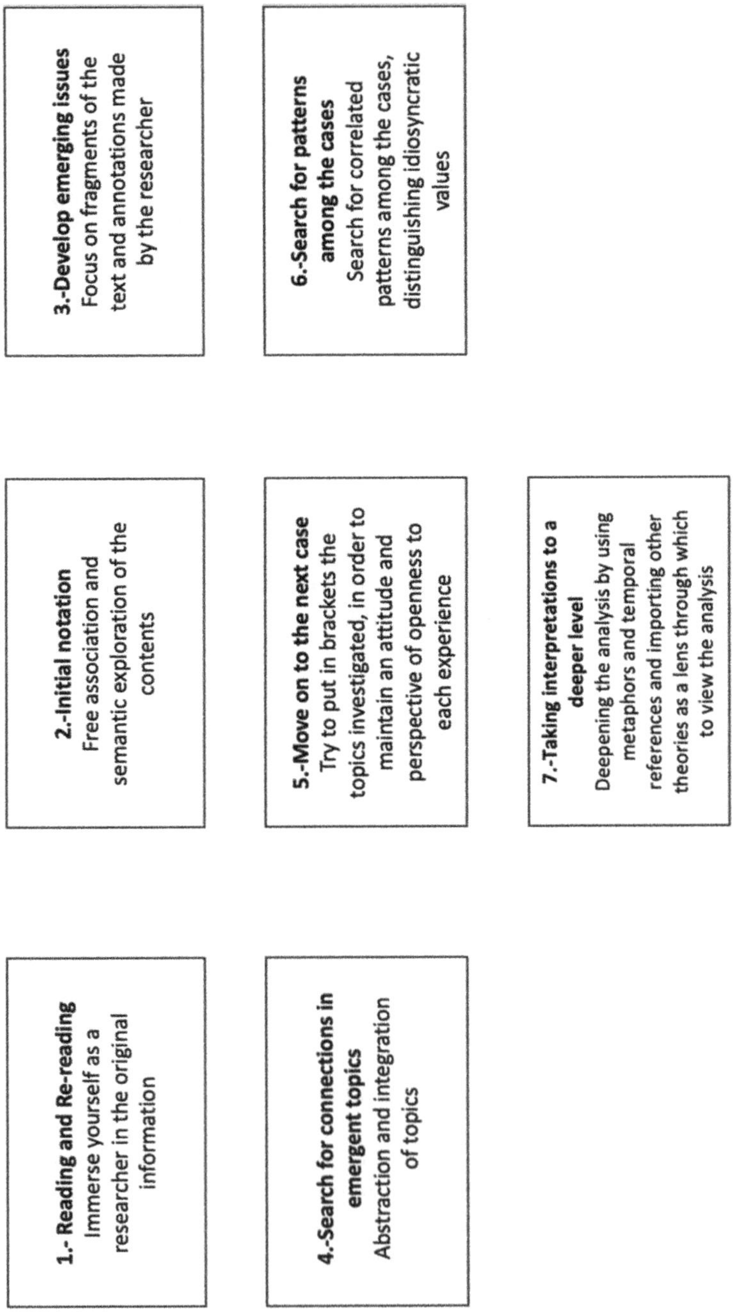

Figure 5.2 The 7 steps of IPA analysis. Charlick et al. (2016).

new cases, with the objective of distinguishing their own particularity, as well as to initiate later the search for patterns of meaning or representations among the experiences obtained. This process represents a central scope in the present analysis, given the possibility of establishing semantic networks of content, based on representative elements of the captured experiences, being able to develop subsequent analyses based on the linking of the experiential elements with theoretical aspects associated with the object of study, achieving a new dimension of meanings.

Regarding its use at the research level, it is possible to refer to the article entitled *Using interpretative phenomenological analysis in autism research,* based on the research conducted by Howard et al. (2017). The present one considered a sample of 10 interviewees who present autism, exploring their particular experiences, managing to obtain results that point to elements related to their experiences at a personal level. It is important to highlight that the present research develops a critical analysis regarding the application of this type of interview, given the high linguistic consideration it presents, which makes its application with this type of population complex.

The research of Iqbal et al. (2017), *An Interpretative Phenomenological Analysis of a Religious Conversion,* exposes an in-depth analysis of the experience of 1 interviewee and her experience associated with religious conversion over a period of 40 years. The present study obtained results related to the impact that religious conversion had on her life, distinguishing aspects associated with conflicts with Judaism, spiritual search, and life changes after her conversion. The researchers explain the usefulness of this type of methodology, in the exploration of particular experiences associated with the object of study, being able to evoke deep experiences at an experiential level, which can be structured from a thematic dimension.

Finally, the research developed by Said et al. (2020), entitled *An Interpretative Phenomenological Analysis of Challenges Faced by the University Teachers in Pakistan Amid Covid-19,* explores the experiences presented by a group of professors belonging to 21 universities in Pakistan, in relation to the development of online teaching in Covid-19 periods. The present research exposes in detail the set of experiences related to online teaching in the present period, referring to a set of challenges and adversities associated with the experiences of the interviewed participants, identifying thematic units and subthemes associated with the present object of study.

It is possible to distinguish that the present methodology, from its hermeneutic phenomenological consideration, commits a deep exploration of the particular experience, being able to be of great utility in the approach to diverse subjects of study, linking diverse possibilities of development as far as the obtained information is concerned. The different stages of analysis proposed represent a sum of very useful elements in consideration of the orientation in their respective interpretation, which in many moments can represent a challenge in this type of methodology.

CONCLUSION

The development of a research that considers a hermeneutic phenomenological perspective will always present the challenge of establishing a methodology that allows a structured articulation at the research level, which allows the adaptation of philosophical approaches at the methodological level. The present task is simplified by resorting to interviews that have incorporated the dimensions described above, carrying out an approach and analysis that respects phenomenological and hermeneutic traditions, managing to develop a work of approach to experience from a natural perspective, provided in many instances with a necessary linguistic dimension of interpretation.

Research in phenomenology and hermeneutics has been characterized by its methodological complexity; however, its depth and theoretical approach to capture the human experience in first person has been valued. The systematization of this type of methodologies allows the researcher to have greater methodological clarity of the steps to follow when using a research approach based on phenomenology-hermeneutics.

Future lines of research will have the mission of integrating these methodologies in order to take the best of each one of them and thus be able to capture the deepest aspects of human subjectivity. Future researchers should be trained in phenomenology and hermeneutics, as well as in some of their methodologies in order to be able to conduct research in philosophy, psychology and social sciences in general. This type of methodologies presents a wide spectrum of application, being possible to use in philosophical research, clinical, education, social and cultural processes, among others.

CHAPTER 6

MY LIFE IS A ROLLER COASTER: THE SUBJECTIVE EXPERIENCE OF BORDERLINE PERSONALITY DISORDER

The present chapter focuses on exploring the subjective experience of borderline personality disorder (BPD) using Interpretative Phenomenological Analysis (IPA) methodology. BPD, characterized by intense emotional instability and impulsive behavioral patterns, poses a significant challenge for both individuals with BPD and mental health professionals. In order to capture the complexity of these experiences, it is essential to resort to a methodology that allows for a deep and detailed understanding of the individual experience.

IPA, developed by Jonathan Smith and Mike Osborn, is based on phenomenological and hermeneutic principles, combining a detailed focus on lived experience with an interpretative analysis of personal meanings. This methodology is particularly suited to investigating BPD, as it allows access to individuals' personal narratives, capturing how they perceive and make sense of their everyday and emotional experiences.

This chapter presents a detailed analysis of interviews conducted with a sample of 10 people diagnosed with BPD, both men and women. Through these interviews, we seek to understand how individuals

Phenomenological-Hermeneutical Approach to Borderline Personality Disorder, pages 57–82

doi:10.1108/978-1-80592-281-020251006

describe and experience their daily lives, their interpersonal relationships, and their emotional management. IPA not only facilitates the capture of these experiences in their particular context, but also allows an interpretation of how these personal meanings are constructed and evolve over time.

The chapter title, "My Life is a Roller Coaster: The Subjective Experience of Borderline Personality Disorder," reflects the fluctuating and often turbulent nature of life with BPD. The narratives collected illustrate the breadth and depth of emotional experiences, providing a rich and nuanced view of life with this disorder. Through IPA, the nuances of these experiences are highlighted, revealing not only suffering and hardship, but also coping strategies and moments of resilience.

In summary, this chapter employs IPA to unravel the complexities of the subjective experience of BPD, providing a window into the lives of those who suffer from it and offering a deeper understanding that can inform both clinical practice and future research in the field.

IPA focuses on the in-depth understanding of how individuals interpret and make sense of their personal experiences. This methodology is characterized by the identification and analysis of superordinate themes and subthemes that emerge from in-depth interviews with participants.

The results are structured into superordinate themes and their respective subthemes, which reflect the different dimensions of the lived experience of individuals with BPD. This organization allows for a clear and comprehensible presentation of the complex experiences and perceptions of the participants, providing a detailed and nuanced view of their experiences. IPA, by incorporating a hermeneutic analysis and a phenomenological approach, facilitates the capture of the particularities and richness of subjective experiences, thus allowing for a better understanding of the phenomena under investigation.

The following is a list of superordinate themes and associated subthemes, which demarcate the set of experiences observed, based on in-depth interviews, which established a consideration based on the aprioristic suspension, characteristic of phenomenology and a discursive analysis characteristic of hermeneutic approaches (Table 6.1).

All the superordinate themes and subthemes will be developed in a differentiated manner, making a clear definition of the meaning of each experience obtained and their respective implications at a personal level, in order to distinguish the present results as significant experiences for the interviewees. All the topics to be developed will have a specific reference, linked to quotes from the participants, as a basis for the results to be delivered.

TABLE 6.1 Superordinate Themes and Subthemes Obtained in IPA

Superordinate Themes	Subthemes
Particular types of thinking	• Catastrophic thoughts • Differentiated perception of reality • Limited perception of reality
Unstable personal relationships and experiences of vulneration	• Feeling strange and different from others • Instability in relationships • Dependence in relationships • Early experiences of vulneration
Unstable emotions at the individual and relational level	• Rage • Feelings of guilt and frustration • Feelings of emptiness • Emotional instability
Intense emotion-seeking and self-punishment	• Self-harm • Self-sabotage • Risk behaviors • Need for self-punishment • Continuous need for stimulation • Impulsive decisions
Know the diagnosis and receive mental health treatment	• Experience of being diagnosed • Experience in mental health care

TYPES OF PARTICULAR THOUGHT

The present superordinate theme is linked to the types of thinking observed in the interviewees who present BPD. These types of thoughts are characterized by constituting certain ways of relating to experiences or situations on a daily level, giving rise to various difficulties or discomforts in terms of the interpretation of various scenarios on a personal, interpersonal and social level. This table shows the prevalence between the associated subthemes and the experience of the participants of this research (Table 6.2).

Catastrophic Thoughts

Catastrophic thoughts, characterized by the perception of potentially harmful events that may occur at a personal level, generating fear and

TABLE 6.2 Presence of Subthemes Associated With Superordinate Theme N°1 Among Participants

Subtopics	Participant 1	Participant 2	Participant 3	Participant 4	Participant 5	Participant 6	Participant 7	Participant 8	Participant 9	Participant 10
Catastrophic thoughts	X			X	X	X				
Differentiated perception of reality			X	X		X		X		
Perception of reality in limits			X		X	X	X	X	X	X

discomfort, are detected in the interviewees. These thoughts arise spontaneously during everyday activities, without the presence of obvious particular stressors. For example, one of them describes how, while walking down the street, he begins to imagine catastrophic scenarios when an unknown person approaches him, thinking that he might have a weapon or cause harm.

These thoughts are not limited to the perception of immediate physical threats, but also include concerns about possible accidents or misfortunes that could affect loved ones. This generates considerable anxiety and can lead to paralysis in decision making or in the execution of daily activities. The intrusive and persistent nature of these catastrophic thoughts can significantly affect the quality of life of individuals, leading them to avoid certain situations or places for fear of something bad happening.

In addition, these thoughts are associated with feelings of anxiety and anger. The interviewees experience an internal struggle as they recognize that these thoughts are not rational, but they cannot help but feel frustration and anger at having them. One of them mentions how he feels stupid for having these thoughts and gets angry with himself, showing the verbal self-aggression that accompanies these thoughts:

> it makes me angry for thinking those things, you know? Because I know they are not like that po. It's like a moment of… of… I call it 'stupidity', you know? I get stupid for a while and think those things, it makes me angry, but nothing.

In summary, the results show that recurrent catastrophic thoughts are related to the occurrence of harmful situations, both at the individual and family level. These thoughts generate a significant emotional burden, and can lead to avoidance behaviors and a reduction in individuals' ability to handle everyday situations. The constant struggle with these thoughts can lead to a sense of hopelessness and a negative self-perception.

Differentiated Perception of Reality

The interviewees show a perception of events in reality that differs from objective reality, which favors particular interpretations and generates difficulties at the individual, family, social and work levels. This differentiated perception is manifested in the tendency to interpret actions of others in a negative or malicious way. One interviewee relates how the same situation can be interpreted in different ways, affecting his interpersonal relationships: "A same thing someone says to me I can interpret… as good, I can interpret it as bad, as ill-intentioned, as destructive."

This differential perception can lead to misunderstanding and conflict, as evidenced in cases where an interviewee's emails were misinterpreted, leading to questioning the legitimacy of their own feelings and emotions.

This type of perception can cause people to feel constantly attacked or misunderstood, which negatively affects their ability to form and maintain healthy relationships.

The tendency to interpret actions of others from a negative perspective generates a cycle of self-doubt and self-questioning. Respondents experience impulsive objections and interpretations, with their own perception of events predominating. Lack of objectivity in interpreting others' actions and their own emotional reactions complicates social and personal interaction. This can lead to increased emotional vulnerability and a reduced ability to resolve conflicts effectively. One interviewee mentioned that constant questioning about the legitimacy of their emotions and reactions can also generate greater emotional instability:

> It makes me lose, also sometimes, the objectivity that, I don't know, that, although I may have been angrier than I should have been, maybe it was a valid anger. Then suddenly I question myself and say 'did I really have to get angry or didn't I have to get angry, or did I misinterpret it?

Constantly questioning the legitimacy of their emotions and reactions can also lead to increased emotional instability. Individuals may feel trapped in a cycle of doubt and guilt, which affects their psychological well-being and their ability to make clear and consistent decisions.

Perception of Reality in Limits

A perception of reality based on polarized classifications of events, situations or people as negative or positive is also observed in the interviewees. This perception influences personal decision making and the functioning of interpersonal and couple relationships. One interviewee describes how he ends relationships and friendships over minor details, without giving time for an explanation, reflecting a blunt and extreme stance:

> I have ended friendships over.... simple details, I have ended relationships, uh, as in... not as a couple, but as a simpler relationship, right, simply because of some attitude that I didn't like and I didn't take the time to explain it, but I simply close myself and I close myself, so..., I tend to be very blunt.

Perception in limits leads to an extreme evaluation of situations, where events and people are classified in a binary way as completely good or bad. This generates impulsive behaviors and radical decisions, such as ending relationships over minor details or idealizing a person without knowing him or her well. These extreme personal assessments profoundly affect interpersonal interactions and relationships, leading to conflicts and breakups due to unrealistic expectations and excessive demands.

This type of perception also has a significant influence on the expectations attached to a relationship or situation, leading to demands or demands in relationships at the family or interpersonal level. This can result in disappointments and sadness when expectations are not met. For example, one interviewee mentions how his high expectations of others result in disappointments and sadness: "That I tend to expect more from others. So, when I get disappointed, uh, it makes me very sad. Sometimes I say things I don't mean…and things like that."

In conclusion, differentiated and extreme perceptions of reality, combined with catastrophic thoughts, create a complex and challenging picture for the interviewees, affecting their emotional well-being and interpersonal relationships significantly.

PERSONAL RELATIONSHIPS AND EXPERIENCES OF VULNERABILITY

This superordinate theme is associated with the set of bonding experiences at the interpersonal level, characterized by their continuous instability, in addition to experiences associated with the perception of social rejection and stigmatization. It is also possible to distinguish the presence of early experiences associated with physical and emotional violations, which have generated significant suffering in the participants (Table 6.3).

Feeling Strange and Different From Others

The interviewees' personal perception is based on a sense of social distancing, mainly based on a self-perception of strangeness and difference before society due to the presence of BPD. This self-definition is configured on the basis of the social bonding experiences that have developed throughout their lives.

One interviewee expresses his feelings clearly by mentioning: "Emptiness, anguish, loneliness. I feel like an outsider." This feeling of not fitting in and of being different extends throughout adolescence and adulthood, as another interviewee comments: "I just thought I was a freak… I always said that I was born at the wrong time, I don't belong here."

Difficulties in incorporation and belonging to specific social groups are also common. Interviewees often fail to find spaces or relationships in which they can feel understood on a personal level, resulting in distancing and continuous variation in social relationships. One of them mentions:

> I couldn't belong to any group… I fit in with everyone, I was friends with everyone… and, at the same time, I wasn't friends with anyone, because I

TABLE 6.3 Presence of Subthemes Associated With Superordinate Theme N°2 Among Participants

Subtopics	Participant 1	Participant 2	Participant 3	Participant 4	Participant 5	Participant 6	Participant 7	Participants 8	Participant 9	Participant 10
Feeling strange and different from others	X	X	X	X	X	X	X	X	X	X
Instability in relationships	X		X	X	X	X		X	X	X
Dependency in relationships	X	X	X	X	X			X		X
Early vulnerations	X			X	X			X	X	X

> swarmed, just swarmed here and there and everything. And sometimes I was far away from everyone.

In addition, there is a clear sense of stigmatization and social judgment in the face of the disease, which produces significant emotional distress and affects social bonding in various spaces of interaction. One interviewee relates how he was discriminated against when trying to enter university due to his history of suicide attempts: "It makes me feel discriminated against. It even happened to me once when I wanted to enter the university and they wouldn't let me in, because I had a history of having, of having attempted suicide."

In summary, the results show that the interviewees experience a differentiated self-perception, based on distancing from social groups and the perception of stigmatization. This contributes to the maintenance of social isolation behaviors and continuous variation in interpersonal relationships.

Instability in Romantic Relationships

Interviewees also describe experiences of instability in romantic relationships, characterized by frequent episodes of arguments due to emotional or behavioral misalignments, as well as experiences of infidelity and emotional aggression. One interviewee mentions:

> It's like a seesaw of emotions. So, with my partner we were always fighting about the same thing, because we were planning to go out and, when it was time to go out, I would throw a tantrum... and I would take off my clothes and not go out.

In some cases, boredom arises in the couple's relationship, leading to ideas of abandonment or continued exploration at the experiential level, associated with maintaining relationships outside the couple. One interviewee describes: "I want to leave. And I tell him, I always tell him 'no, I'm going to leave. I just don't want to be with you. I'm bored'."

In addition, there are experiences of joint aggression in the couple and possessive characteristics on the part of the interviewees, which leads to the maintenance of relational instability, mainly translated into psychological aggression. Another interviewee relates: "He used to say that he didn't care about me, that he was like nothing and he always tried to victimize himself.... So, it became like a very toxic circle and I literally could not get out of it."

In general terms, the observed experiences reveal multiple elements in the particular experience of people with BPD that may favor the development of unstable relationships, including psychological aggression, infidelity and a constant feeling of boredom.

Dependence in Romantic Relationships

The interviewees also show a dependency in romantic relationships, translated into the need to count on a figure that provides care and protection, representing a fundamental pillar linked to emotional stability. This situation exposes a significant demand at the couple level, in view of the fact that the interviewees' expectations translate into an important need for emotional support and, in some cases, in the need to control the actions of these referents.

One of the interviewees says:

> Eh, that person, I don't know, well, for me he meant everything, absolutely everything. So, if he went out, if he got together with someone, that made me uneasy, because I wanted to be only with him. It was an absolute and total possession.

Dependence on their partners represents a significant demand, linked to a physical and emotional effort on the part of these figures, which can sometimes deprive the referent of autonomy. Another interviewee mentions: "I feel that... that he has an additional burden, as if he always has to support me."

In summary, experiences related to dependency in romantic relationships are characterized by a significant need for containment and emotional support, which has repercussions on the maintenance of a relationship that can deprive their love referents of autonomy. These dynamics expose that the participants are highly oriented to the satisfaction of their own needs, which implies a high demand toward their partners.

Early Experiences of Vulneration

In the participants it is possible to observe experiences related to physical, emotional and sexual vulneration during early ages. These transgressions have had a negative impact on their personal development, and the participants were able to identify a relationship between these events and the onset of this personality disorder.

As one participant says:

> Uh, also when the kids, well, you know, the kids, sometimes, the bullying, the teasing. I was a very skinny girl, extremely skinny, so the kids made fun of me. So, that fact of... feeling that I was the object of criticism or ridicule from others, made me feel very, very anxious, very.... very anxious.

It is possible to distinguish in the participants, episodes of early sexual vulneration, which have had a significant impact on their development at the individual level, demarcating part of their self-perception, as well as their relationships at the interpersonal level. One of the interviewees reports the following:

> On one occasion he went to bed to make love to me on my back and... I remember feeling his penis. I have memories of feeling his erect penis, um, so, ah.... The truth, or smaller things too, suddenly he would.... As a game, he would suck my ear. I remember that at some point I didn't like him sucking my ear because it was a more sexualized behavior for me, and I told him to stop, and he didn't stop, for example.

Some of the experiences observed are associated with significant physical and sexual violations, which have occurred at an early age, a situation that has generated significant anguish and discomfort in interviewees, lacking spaces of containment and parental support, which significantly demarcates the way in which they establish relationships at the primary level. Two of the interviewees report the following:

> Obviously I kept quiet until I grew up, then she broke up with him and then I don't remember until I was 10, my mother beat me very badly, in fact, I had an eye stroke and she hit me in the stomach and threatened me with a knife. The issue of abuse, because my parents are pastors, it was very hard for them to understand, in fact they don't understand it, they tell me "we love you as a son, but the sin you do is like no.

Early experiences of physical, emotional and sexual vulneration have been observed in the interviewees, events characterized by difficulties in the articulation of effective parental protection exercises, resulting in significant episodes at a personal level, which are related by participants as key events in the understanding of the origin of their respective personality disorder.

UNSTABLE EMOTIONS AT THE INDIVIDUAL AND RELATIONAL LEVEL

The present superordinate theme is associated with the set of emotions that develop at the individual and relational level in the participants, which experientially are mostly representative and frequent in their particular experiential developments. The set of manifestations to be exposed has a significant impact on the development of self-verbalizations, emotional self-regulation practices and interactions at the social level, representing this superordinate theme, a category of great significance in the set of experiential results obtained (Table 6.4).

TABLE 6.4 Presence of Subthemes Associated With Superordinate Theme N°3 Among Participants

Subtopics	Participant 1	Participant 2	Participant 3	Participant 4	Participant 5	Participant 6	Participant 7	Participant 8	Participant 9	Participant 10
Anger	X	X	X	X	X	X	X	X	X	X
Feelings of guilt and frustration	X	X	X	X	X	X	X	X	X	X
Feelings of emptiness		X		X		X	X			
Emotional instability	X	X	X	X	X	X	X	X	X	X

Anger

In the interviewees it is possible to observe experiences associated with anger, which does not always evidence a specific motivation or cause and can be directed toward their own person or toward external referents as a means of expression and regulation of such sensation. These manifestations represent an important risk factor in terms of the absence of self-care and the maintenance of interpersonal relationships.

One interviewee describes this sensation as follows:

> It's like a choking sensation… a terrible choking sensation that, if you don't scream, if you don't yell, if you don't throw something, if you don't react, I've already learned to handle it, right? I take a pillow and scream, because if I don't, I'll burst, but if you don't do something to calm it down, it doesn't calm down.

This description illustrates how anger can build up into an emotional explosion that needs to be released somehow.

Another interviewee mentions how, despite the tears, he insults himself at the same time: "Despite the tears and everything, I insult myself…. I insult myself at the same time. I smile, I insult myself. 'You're stupid, you're an idiot, you deserve it.'" This verbal self-aggression reflects the internalization of anger and severe self-criticism.

The feeling of anger influences the development of maladjusted emotional and behavioral behaviors or expressions in various social contexts, which can have a negative impact on work performance, family, social and couple relationships. One interviewee describes how anger can lead to hating the people you love at certain times:

> It leads you to feel because…. Sometimes even that you can come to hate the people you love at certain times, because you feel like they plan everything or do everything to hurt you or say it to hurt you. And…. of being in a nice moment where everything is love and peace, you can get to feel in…. Even hatred for that person in the same day.

Finally, it is possible to observe in a group of experiences that self-directed anger is regularly associated with feelings of frustration regarding one's own behavior or personal decisions, which can manifest itself in verbal self-punishment and feelings of anguish regarding personal characteristics associated with BPD. For example, one interviewee mentions: "Ah, it makes me angry [laughs], it makes me angry to think those things, you know? Because I know they are not like that."

The development of anger as an emotion that has an important influence on their behaviors, decisions and thoughts can be seen in all the interviewees. This emotion shows a significant influence not only at the behavioral and relational level, but also in aspects related to self-punishment and verbal or physical aggression, associated with situations of error or frustration. A double directioning of anger can be identified, which is regulated by means of aggressions at the interpersonal level and verbal and physical self-aggressions.

Feelings of Guilt and Frustration

The emergence of feelings of guilt and frustration can be observed in all the cases interviewed, clearly showing the development of these feelings in situations interpreted by those evaluated as the result of their own responsibility, sometimes perceiving the impossibility of achieving effective self-control of their thoughts, emotions or behaviors.

One interviewee describes his feeling of guilt as follows: "I feel guilt... because it's as if I am generating the thoughts myself, it's clear, I am generating them, but I say 'but why are these thoughts coming? I don't want to think about this."

Frustration also manifests itself in the feeling of loss of control over impulses and life in general. One interviewee mentions,

> It feels...there we go with the frustration again. Of feeling like you're not able to control your.... your impulses, you feel like a little bit, uh.... I don't know, I don't know how to describe the feeling of feeling like you're not able to control yourself, you kind of feel like you lose control of your.... of... of your life, of your emotions.

In other experiences, there is a tendency to self-punish and question actions, mistakes or thoughts, which represents a striking way of dealing with situations that generate frustration and guilt. One interviewee recount how he physically punishes himself: "And in the end it was like it didn't matter and it was like: 'damn, for being naïve it happened to me, it's my fault' and then I started to cut myself."

In all cases, feelings of guilt and frustration arise, which are associated with behaviors, decisions, thoughts or difficulties in achieving effective emotional and behavioral self-control. These emotions can lead on several occasions to the development of physical and psychological self-harm behaviors as a means of self-regulation of guilt and frustration.

Feelings of Emptiness

In the interviewees it is possible to observe the presence of feelings of emptiness, characterized by a physical sensation in the chest, accompanied by pain and pressure in that area. In addition, these feelings are characterized by a significant difficulty in enjoying experiences, as well as by dissatisfaction and personal demotivation in the absence of a vital purpose.

One interviewee describes this feeling of emptiness:

> You feel a hole, you feel... that something is missing, that breathing becomes difficult, that suddenly it starts to burn, that emptiness is like... it's like... it's not like heartburn, because it's not like that, but it's like a burning in the chest, uh... you start to shiver, sometimes you start to get a little more..., especially in the back, it happens to me... and you start to lose a little sense.

In summary, feelings of emptiness in the interviewees are characterized by physical sensations, dissatisfaction and demotivation in various daily activities, as well as by a loss of vital meaning and individual purpose.

SEARCH FOR INTENSE EMOTIONS AND SELF-PUNISHMENT

The present superordinate theme is associated with the set of manifestations at the behavioral, psychological and emotional level, which have repercussions on the development of risk behaviors that may imply a possible damage to the integrity of the participants. The emergence of these manifestations involves the articulation of various behaviors, which represent a set of representative characteristics at the experiential level in the course of BPD (Table 6.5).

Self-Harm

The development of self-harm behaviors is a relevant part in several participants, who use this practice as a form of emotional and physical self-regulation, as well as a punishment mechanism for actions or behaviors perceived as incorrect. Self-harm allows participants to reconnect with their reality and experience a sense of relief, albeit temporary. One participant describes this process: "It's emotional, it's physical, it's mental... self-injury.... it makes me reconnect... that I am here, that I am alive, that... I am in reality, and then it gives me a feeling of tiredness."

In addition, some participants mention playing with risk when consuming medications, seeking a sense of relief through self-injury. This is reflected in the testimony of one participant: "Because sometimes there were situations that overwhelmed me... then I started to play with risk, like what if I take 15? what if I take 20?"

TABLE 6.5 Presence of Subthemes Associated With Superordinate Theme N°4 Among Participants

Subtopics	Participant 1	Participant 2	Participant 3	Participant 4	Participant 5	Participant 6	Participant 7	Participant 8	Participant 9	Participant 10
Self-harm		X		X		X	X	X	X	
Autosa botages	X	X			X	X	X	X	X	X
Risk behaviors			X	X	X	X		X	X	
Need for self-punishment		X				X	X	X	X	
Continuous need for stimulation			X	X		X		X	X	
Impulsive decisions			X	X	X			X	X	

These practices are often seen as a personal ritual that has been incorporated into daily life, intended not only for self-regulation but also as a punishment for bad behavior. One participant describes it as follows: "It's that it's quite complicated, because it was, it even became part of a ritual. I mean, I don't think I'm a satanist [laughs], but it's like part of a weird ritual that I had."

The ritualism of self-harm is also observed in the way some participants resort to cutting different parts of the body or taking medication. These practices are developed as an accepted and necessary daily exercise, both for self-regulation and punishment for actions considered inappropriate. For example, one participant relates: "I... what I felt was like... that this would make me feel better, I wanted to... I wanted to erase myself, I wanted to... disappear. That was the only thing I wanted."

The depth and severity of self-injury varies, and some participants have experienced deep cuts on different parts of the body, which can result in hospitalization and urgent medical attention. This situation underscores the seriousness of these behaviors and their impact on participants' physical and emotional health. One participant shares her experience: "I started cutting my arms and then I started cutting my legs. I had never cut my legs before. And I cut my legs super deep, too."

In summary, self-harm in participants is not only a method of emotional and physical self-regulation, but also a ritualized mechanism that is integrated into their daily lives. These practices reflect a complex and painful attempt to manage emotional distress, and underscore the need for appropriate psychological intervention and support to address these self-destructive behaviors.

Self-Sabotage

Self-sabotage is present in most participants, developing behaviors or thoughts that undermine the achievement of objectives or goals. This tendency ranges from breaking off relationships before they can fully develop to convincing oneself that one is not capable of achieving something. Self-sabotage manifests itself as a form of protection against fear of failure or rejection.

"It is a way that has been repeating itself and I have never understood why, now I think it has to do with borderline. It is an insecurity and it is a way of.... self-sabotage."

These self-sabotage practices lead to self-disqualifying self-verbalizations and, on occasion, self-harm. "Damn, it's my fault, for being naive it happened... and that's when I would start to cut myself."

Self-sabotage can also be a response to insecurity and fear of failure, leading participants to avoid situations in which they might fail, even before they try. This behavior is self-defeating and perpetuates a cycle of failure and self-recrimination.

Risk Behaviors

Risky behaviors are common, arising from a need to achieve intense experiences immediately. These practices, which include substance use and sexual promiscuity, seek immediate gratification and can threaten physical and emotional integrity. One of the participants said: "This very thing of looking for new things often leads you to border a little on illegality… it's more exciting."

Some participants mention that these behaviors are a way to overcome emotional distress. "Going out, drinking, having this sexual promiscuity and made me feel like this joy like for moments and then the more depressive state would come."

The search for intense experiences and immediate gratification can become an addictive cycle, leading individuals to constantly seek new ways to experience strong emotions. These behaviors can have significant negative consequences, such as health problems, financial difficulties and damage to interpersonal relationships.

Need for Self-Punishment

There is a perception of the need for physical self-punishment, seen as an obligatory practice in the face of mistakes made. This self-punishment is carried out both at the level of thought and physically, with a logic that validates the action as necessary.

"It's like Machiavellian. It's like a satisfaction, on the one hand, it's like… like two people are generated… like a personality that punishes the most vulnerable one… and enjoys seeing the suffering."

Some experiences show that self-punishment follows a ritualistic practice, with regulations and guidelines established by each participant. "And there were like self-injuries. For example, like every time I wrote something, I would cut myself and, afterward, I would put the blood, just like… there."

Self-punishment can be a way of dealing with guilt and the feeling of having failed at something. This type of ritualized behavior reinforces self-criticism and perpetuates a cycle of self-aggression and emotional pain.

Continuous Need for Stimulation

The search for pleasurable stimuli is a constant in several participants, responding to a hedonistic practice that seeks novel experiences that provide adrenaline and personal satisfaction. This need for new experiences can lead to risky and addictive behaviors, one of the participants says: "Basically, I think it is more than anything else a search for pleasure, but it is also mixed with a bit of feeling good in that... in those situations."

This search can have an addictive effect due to the short duration of the pleasurable experience, leading to a continuous search for sensations of well-being and pleasure. "Damn, it was like all wonderful, so it kind of came out of my pores [laughs] and after a while it would pass."

Participants constantly seek new stimuli to escape routine and emotional discomfort. This search for immediate pleasure can lead to emotional and physical dependence on activities that provide temporary relief but do not resolve the underlying problems.

Impulsive Decisions

Impulsive decisions are common, guided by a particular emotion that requires immediate action in response. These decisions usually arise in the presence of discomfort or displeasure, seeking a quick solution to the particular emotion.

> There's always something, there's always something... at the beginning it's not so much, but as the days go by it becomes more and more unbearable until it gets to a point where you... you know what? I don't want to work anymore, I'm leaving.

These impulsive actions can have consequences that directly affect the quality of life of participants, impacting their emotional, interpersonal and financial well-being. "Ah, I feel like leaving the place where I am, I feel like throwing everything away, just like that, from one second to the next, without thinking about it."

Impulsive decisions reflect an inability to manage emotions effectively, leading to actions that can have long-term negative repercussions. This type of behavior can result in abrupt and frequent changes in participants' lives, affecting their stability and overall well-being.

KNOWING THE DIAGNOSIS AND RECEIVING CARE

The present superordinate theme responds to the set of experiences associated with having had a diagnosis associated with BPD, as well as having received mental health care, observing in general terms the presence of hopelessness, tranquility and the need for specialized care in order to achieve a better understanding and approach to the problems associated with BPD (Table 6.6).

Experience of Being Diagnosed

In the cases interviewed, it is observed how significant the experience of being diagnosed is, which provides greater clarity about the course of BPD, as well as diverse emotions such as hopelessness, tranquility and confusion. One participant describes:

> But I had not given it any importance, I did not know anything... and that is when I began to understand, when I began to read and investigate, I began to understand why my behaviors were like that and why I felt I was a strange person, not little capable, not incapable, as many treat us, not crazy, no. I feel different and I feel I am a person with many capabilities, with many... possibilities. I feel different and I feel I am a person with many capabilities, with many... possibilities, but the weak part I feel I have is my emotions.

Another participant recounts a negative experience:

> It was the worst experience of my life, I was going because I was already thinking that I wanted to kill myself, imagine. I mean, I had everything ready for my suicide and they go and tell me.... 'this is for the rest of my life, eh... there is no cure, therapy is expensive, very expensive, eh...' [laughs] 'eh, they are addicted to several things, you are going to have, I don't know, problems with this, with that, but don't worry, with time, at 40, 50 years old, the symptoms start to subside' and I would take the account and say 'I am 30' [laughs] and all that 'and the medicines are expensive, so buy them in the epilepsy league, eh, hope everything goes well, good luck'.

In most of the experiences, a mixture of tranquility, anger and despair is observed in the face of the diagnosis. For example, one participant mentions:

> When the psychiatrist finally told me what it was, and that this diagnosis included all these things that were happening to me, at the time it was like... reassuring for me, like saying 'wow, finally I know what this is called, it didn't have a name, it didn't have a face'. And having a name gave me hope of being able to treat it.

Another participant expresses:

> It was like, I don't know, it was like a condemnation, like I had no way out. It was like my life was always going to be like that, um, I never thought I was

TABLE 6.6 Presence of Subthemes Associated With Superordinate Theme N°5 in Participants.

Subtopics	Participant 1	Participant 2	Participant 3	Participant 4	Participant 5	Participant 6	Participant 7	Participant 8	Participant 9	Participant 10
Experience of being diagnosed	X	X	X	X	X	X	X	X	X	
Experience in mental health care	X	X		X		X		X	X	

> going to reach a point where I was going to stop going to therapy or stop taking medication. I thought my whole life was going to be about taking medication. My whole life was going to be that, that I wasn't going to be able to be in control or.... of me. Um, it made me sad, it made me angry, very angry.

In some cases, the diagnosis offers a starting point for better emotional management. One participant indicates:

> It made me feel calm, because they gave me my medication and I started to regulate myself a little more, so I felt good, because I said: 'finally I will be able to control the things that are happening to me' and in fact I noticed a big change since I started with the medical treatment and all those things.

However, one of the experiences shows that the diagnosis did not generate any significant change due to an already consolidated perception of self-identity. "Um... no... as I say, like I said, like no, there wasn't much, it didn't have much significance for me... it's like it didn't change anything. Whether I have BPD or not, I am still a failure in life."

In summary, the experiences of being diagnosed with BPD vary widely, from providing clarity and hope to provoking feelings of hopelessness and confusion. These experiences significantly influence the therapeutic course and the perception of one's own abilities and limitations.

Experiences in Mental Health Care

In several cases, experiences in mental health care have been mixed. Some participants have had negative experiences with professionals who were not adequately trained to treat BPD. One participant describes her experience: "Eh, horrible... horrible, because there are few specialists in Chile dedicated to borderline. So, the normal thing is that you...get a psychologist or a psychiatrist...who doesn't know what it is to be borderline."

Another participant shares:

> But my experience at the beginning was terrible. It was horrible, I mean, I would have stayed with those first experiences, I would have killed myself. I would kill myself or end up with a suicide attempt, I was at my worst. I was at my worst moment and they tell you [the diagnosis] in the worst way.

However, some participants found support and hope in their therapists. One participant report:

> So, he's like this. So, look, he gives me strength, he gives me energy, he gives me encouragement, he laughs, he grabs his head when I tell him about the shit I do. It's a joke, I mean, he... I feel very comfortable and he is always, always looking up, always hopeful, like this, like this... the good side of things.

The psychotherapeutic process is validated as a necessary intervention, which favors the development of tools at a personal level to effectively address certain aspects of BPD. A participant indicates:

> Yes, quite a lot, you know? [sic] Because I don't know, I've always been a movie buff, you know? [sic] So I would tell her: 'you know what, this and that happened to me and I think it's such and such', you know? [sic] And then she would tell me: 'well, what if you see it in another way'. She makes me see different scenarios regarding a subject and I, like this: 'you were [sic] right'. So, in the end I saw that I was just reading, you know what I mean.

In conclusion, experiences in mental health care vary, highlighting the importance of having professionals trained in the treatment of BPD to provide effective and hopeful support.

SUMMARY OF IPA INTERVIEWS RESULTS

Regarding the *Superordinate theme N°1: Particular types of thinking*, it is possible to refer that the types of thinking observed in part of the present population have a direct influence on their individual, social and relational disposition, having an observable impact on the articulation of relationships, behaviors and decisions that can motivate the emergence of various difficulties in the adaptation to a variety of situations and social interactions. It is possible to clearly distinguish emotions such as anxiety, frustration and anger, which are directly linked to this type of thoughts, emotions that have led those evaluated to the development of certain types of impulsive actions.

Regarding *Superordinate theme N°2: Unstable personal relationships and experiences of vulnerability*, the present one is largely linked to experiences of social bonding, in which those evaluated have not achieved a successful adjustment or bonding, either by personal or external action. These experiences highlight a permanent feeling of isolation and differentiation at the social level, in addition to continuously perceiving episodes of stigmatization when presenting BPD. It is also important to highlight that early experiences of vulnerability are identified as a set of key experiences in the understanding of the evolution of this disorder by the participants, being mainly experienced with anguish and helplessness.

Superordinate theme N°3: Unstable emotions at the individual and relational level, exposes an important experiential element in the participants, considering that the presence of this type of experience has had a relevant influence on their personal development, constituting emotional instability, a personal characteristic that generates significant discomfort in the participants. It should be noted that the emotional characteristics observed may influence the development of socially maladjusted behaviors, which may considerably affect the quality of life of the interviewees.

In relation to the *Superordinate theme N°4: Search for intense emotions and self-punishment,* it is relevant to highlight the present manifestations as characteristic elements of the present pathology, being evident in the set of visualized experiences, the significant effects that they can present in the vital development of the evaluated persons, from an emotional, behavioral and psychological dimension. The validation of practices aimed at self-aggression and exposure to certain risk behaviors implies the need to understand the present experiences as a testimony that living with BPD can regularly involve the development of actions that voluntarily attempt against one's own life, in addition to being continuously subject to the development of addictive behaviors that can greatly affect the well-being of the persons involved.

Finally, with respect to the *Superordinate theme N°5: Knowing the diagnosis and receiving mental health care,* it is possible to refer that the experiences associated with knowing their respective BPD diagnoses, present diverse effects at the emotional level, among which are the sensation of tranquility, anger, hope/despair, being evident in all cases, a better understanding of the present pathology and sense regarding the personal characteristics associated with BPD. Regarding the experiences of mental health care, it is possible to indicate that these are associated with the participation in care with professionals who do not have sufficient preparation to address the present pathology, this situation has had a negative impact on the quality of care provided, on the other hand, the participation in processes led by professionals who have experience in the care of BPD, have been very relevant in terms of the evolution in general terms of the participants.

SUBTHEMES ASSOCIATED WITH SUPERORDINATE TOPICS

Below is a chart that summarizes the subthemes developed in the results obtained from the in-depth interview, which considers the IPA protocol for its interpretation (Figure 6.1).

Selection of Subtopic to Be Explored in Microphenomenological Analysis

Based on the superordinate themes and subthemes developed, it is relevant to consider three criteria that have served as a guide for the selection of the subtheme explored in the development of the Microphenomenological interview. The criteria are the following:

Figure 6.1 Summary of IPA results.

1. Increased occurrence in terms of interviewed cases
2. Relevance provided by interviewees, based on collected speeches
3. Discussion with experts in Microphenomenological interviewing.

Responding to **Criterion N°1**, it can be indicated that the occurrence of subthemes has been similar in four specific themes. The following subthemes have been observed in all participants, as a constitutive part of their respective experiences with BPD.

- Feeling strange and different from the others.—Belonging to Superordinate theme N°2: Unstable personal relationships and early vulnerations.
- Anger—Belonging to Superordinate theme N°3: Unstable emotions at the individual and relational level.
- Emotional instability—Belonging to Superordinate theme N°3: Unstable emotions at the individual and relational level.

In relation to **Criterion N°2**, it can be seen that interviewees have given great relevance to issues associated with emotional instability, which significantly influences their daily development, which is seen as a characteristic element in all the stories, marking a significant experience that is directly related to BPD. Emotional instability is associated with a representative element of the BPD experience, which in turn groups various elements in its development, being able to distinguish elements at the level of thought and behavior, which involves a broad and multifactorial analysis.

Finally, based on criterion 3, contact has been established with three experts in Microphenomenological interview, PhD Alejandra Vásquez (Biologist); PhD Camila Valenzuela (Biologist) and PhD Valeria Motta (Philosopher). Based on the development of three individual interviews with researchers, it has been possible to identify the importance of emotional instability as an element to explore in the development of Microphenomenological interviews, the foundations provided by the researchers are the following:

- The transversality of the emotional instability dimension allows us to visualize not only emotional elements, but also other aspects of the participants' experience.
- The possibilities of capturing the prereflexive sensory experience of the Microphenomenological interview would allow the exploration of emotional instability from its original constitution, its development and its respective termination, establishing a structured sequence of the experience of emotional instability.
- The importance of emotional instability and how it is present in an underlying way in the experiences collected has been appreciated in the stories reviewed.

Based on the criteria reviewed above, we proceeded to conduct a microphenomenological exploration of the experiences of emotional instability in participants of the present research.

CHAPTER 7

MOMENTS OF CHAOS. A TEMPORO-SPATIAL OBSERVATION OF EMOTIONAL INSTABILITY FROM A MICROPHENOMENOLOGICAL ANALYSIS

The present chapter focuses on the analysis of the emotional instability present in people with borderline personality disorder (BPD), using a microphenomenological methodology. This approach is distinguished by its detailed focus on capturing subjective experiences, paying special attention to the temporal and spatial aspects of these experiences.

Microphenomenology, developed from the approaches of Edmund Husserl and adapted by authors such as Claire Petitmengin, is dedicated to exploring the subtleties of lived experiences, beyond what can be grasped through immediate reflection. This methodological approach allows for a close observation of the micro-moments that constitute emotional instability, offering a deep and detailed insight into how individuals experience and manage these moments of chaos in their daily lives.

Phenomenological-Hermeneutical Approach to Borderline Personality Disorder, pages 83–149

doi:10.1108/978-1-80592-281-020251007

This chapter presents a detailed structure of the results obtained from microphenomenological interviews, organized into the following levels of analysis:

1. **Specific diachronic analysis:** It focuses on the temporal development of emotional experiences, observing how they unfold over time.
2. **Specific synchronic analysis**: Examines the simultaneous aspects of the experiences, considering how different elements are interrelated at a given time.
3. **Generic diachronic structure:** Proposes a general framework for understanding the development of emotional experiences over time.
4. **Generic dynamic lines:** Identifies dynamic patterns in emotional experiences, highlighting recurrent features and changes.
5. **Generic synchronic structure:** Offers a comprehensive view of emotional experiences at a specific moment, integrating several simultaneous aspects.

This organization facilitates the understanding of the temporo-spatial dynamics underlying emotional instability, providing a holistic perspective that considers phenomenological analysis.

SPECIFIC DIACHRONIC ANALYSES

The description of this line of analysis seeks to graph the different phases from which the experiences of emotional instability evoked take place, phases that present distinctive characteristics, which compose micro-dimensions of active exploration during the present research process. The results found and their respective development are presented below (Figure 7.1).

The present evocation is composed of **four distinct phases**, which show an evolution in terms of the development of an experience of emotional instability.

The **first phase** is associated with the first physical, emotional and thought level sensations that arise before the triggering experience, which marks the beginning of emotional instability. Some of the verbalizations exposed in this stage are the following:

"The mere fact that he told me that he had to raise my rent caused me to burst into tears, and it was an emotional thing and I asked myself 'why, why? Why? If it is something that I have to face, it is a normal thing, it is a simple thing, it is an everyday thing'."

Participant 1

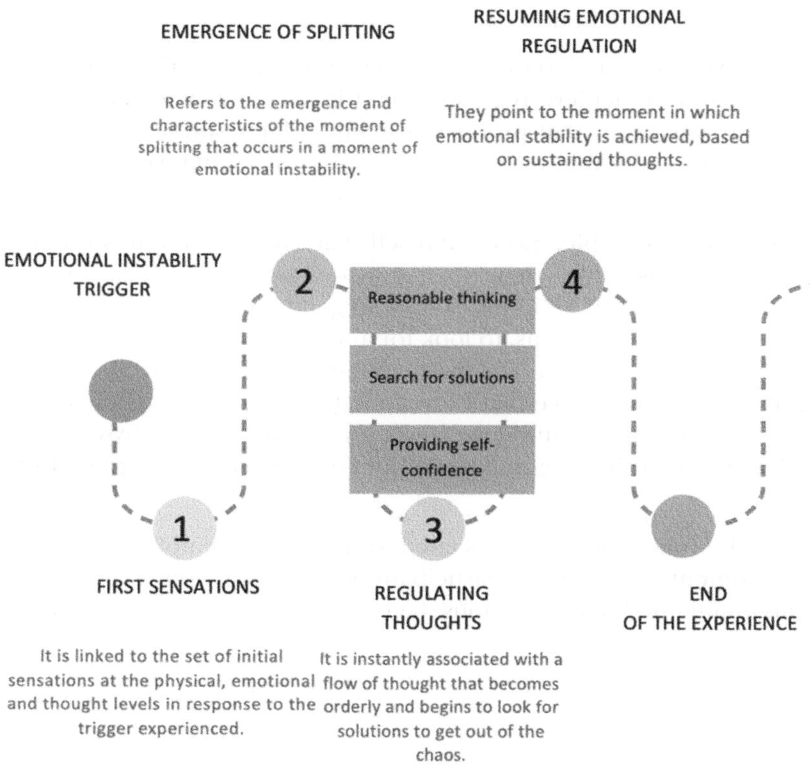

Figure 7.1 Specific diachronic analysis—participant N°1.

"I feel a kind of desperation in my chest, as if it is something that I am not going to be able to solve, and that's when anguish and fear set in."

"It's like an oppression, it's like a desperation, a hopelessness, it's a super strange feeling and very, very strong, it's something uncontrollable."

In a **second phase**, a sensory change arises, characterized by the emergence of splitting, a sensation that is described with a certain level of strangeness by the interviewee, showing a change at the perceptive level of her physical and sensory capacities. These are some of the most representative accounts of this pase:

"I don't know how to explain it, but know that lately I am experiencing very difficult situations, I call it a splitting of my person."

"Let's see, I still feel in the chaotic body or in the chaotic mind, but it is a strange unfolding, because at the same time I observe myself from the outside, but very, very calmly, as if I were not myself, that's what scares me."

"The splitting is like a 'whoa, that happens very fast, but it's something that leaves you a little bit'. Well, it leaves me a little bit worried because I'm like, how does it happen, how do I do it?"

A **third phase** is related to the emergence of thoughts by the participant, which are useful to achieve regulation and interrupt physical, emotional and thought sensations that produce instability. These thoughts favor the return to emotional stability. Some of the most representative accounts of this phase are:

"That more reasonable, more adult self that says 'we have to solve this, we can't leave it like this', then it's like a [defense] mechanism surely, I don't know, my own self looks for to solve to get out of the chaos."

"I start to think of solutions, to look for alternatives, I don't know, I start to make plans for the future, for the medium and short term, then I start giving myself the confidence that I can do it, that I am going to make it."

"I start to give myself confidence, and I myself start to trust myself again, to think that everything is going to be fine, that everything is going to be wonderful."

Finally, the **fourth phase** is associated with regaining emotional stability, being a moment in which the participant is able to recover stability from thoughts maintained in the previous stage (Figure 7.2). These facilitate the

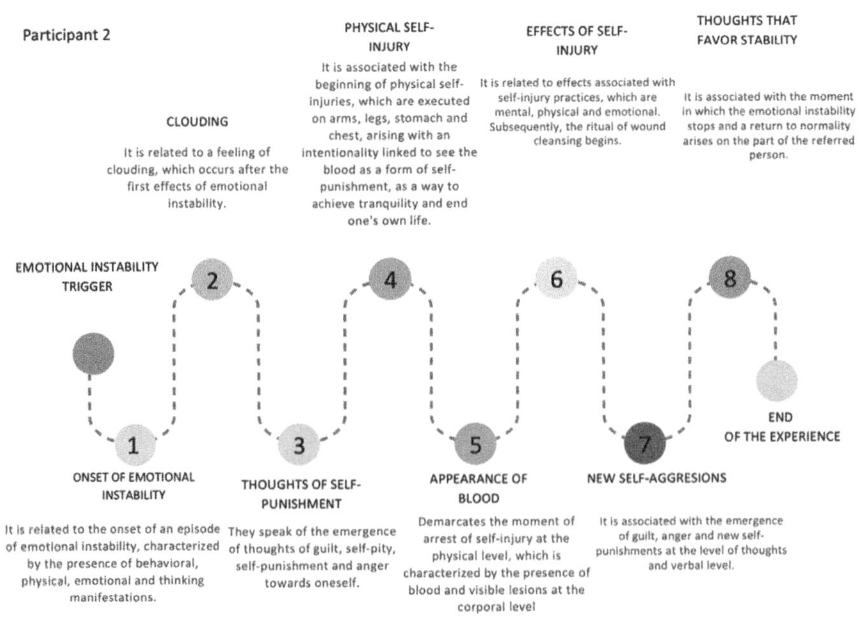

Figure 7.2 Specific diachronic analysis—participant N°2.

regulation of their discomfort at the physical, emotional and thought levels. Some of the most representative accounts of this phase are:

"Solutions arrive, life goes on and everything flows normally, as it should flow, until another event happens again, which interrupts my tranquility, that is my life."

"I return to an emotional routine in which I impose myself to be well, and until another small event or big event happens again and interrupts my peace of mind."

In the present case, it is possible to distinguish the presence of **eight distinct phases**, which demarcate the experience of an episode of emotional instability. The **first phase** is associated with the beginning of emotional instability, a moment marked by the presence of discomfort at the emotional level, sensations at the physical level, as well as a set of thoughts and actions that direct these first moments of instability. Some of the most representative narratives of this phase are the following:

"I was alone in the house, and the only thing I could think of, in a crying fit, was 'sorry mom', that was the only thing that went through my head, 'sorry mom, sorry mom', because I didn't want to go on, I started to cut all over my body."

"Physically... faster heartbeats, start shivering, start crying... you're not even [sic] crying like 'ah...', no, but crying like this that falls, that just falls."

Regarding the **second phase**, an episode distinguished by the participant as "clouding over" is observed, this episode is marked by the presence of a sensation that arises after the first effects of emotional instability, characterized by the permanence in a state of reverie and changes at the level of bodily sensations. Some of the most representative verbalizations are the following:

"It was like being in a dream, like a feeling of unreality, that what was happening was not happening, in fact, the view was different, the whole world seemed alien to me, everything seemed alien to me."

"It feels like the body feels lighter, like, to feel my corporeality, as well as to feel like the arm, to feel everything, in fact, I feel in my face like everything is like a.... I feel it a lot here, for example, in the face as if, as if it were a maximum relaxation."

The **third phase** observed is associated with the emergence of self-punishment thoughts, which are mainly associated with thoughts of guilt, self-pity, self-punishment and anger toward herself and her actions. The present narratives are significant of this experiential moment:

"Self-pity, more than anything else, I think it's like self-pity, because to me, well, 'I'm a failure, I'm a mistake, I'll never be able to live in this world'."

"Self-hatred, anger, anger at the world, grief, self-pity, 'I'm alone', it's like poof... and on top of that guilt, too, a lot of guilt, but that's all in the.... it's all together, all at once."

A **fourth phase** that emerges after thoughts of self-harm is related to the development of physical self-harm, which arises as part of the feeling of rage toward herself, achieving emotional self-regulation from cuts, which are associated with seeing the blood flowing from her body and carrying out self-punishment toward herself, which ends with her own life. The most representative verbalizations of the present moment are the following:

"Then the self-harm occurs, at that moment I'm still in a trance, I'm still thinking, I'm still having the same thoughts that motivate me to continue self-harming."

"Rage and sorrow, a mixture of rage and sorrow that.... And nothing, maximum concentration, for a few seconds it's maximum concentration just in making the cuts, in making the cuts and seeing the blood, focusing a lot on that, I focus a lot on that."

"Anger, anger, rage, it's just a mixture, of course, anger at me, 'why is this happening to me again? Why do I believe again? Why do I trust again? Why can't I be normal? Why am I a failure?'"

"The grief, feeling the betrayal, feeling that in the end it's all my responsibility because I allowed that."

The **fifth phase** associated with the moment of emotional instability is associated with the emergence of blood, a moment that marks the stop of physical self-harm presented in the previous phase. Once the participant has been able to distinguish the appearance of blood at body level and the presence of distinguishable self-harm in their extremities, they identify the need to stop their self-punishment actions, also observing effects at a physical level and a feeling of well-being when they stop. Some of the most representative narratives of this moment are the following:

"Later when I saw all the blood I needed, so to speak, because it's like.... I really feel that sometimes it's almost like it's necessary to see the blood for me, when I've seen a lot of blood and everything was like just being left with empty arms, it's like... peace, it's like you're left in nothing, like when you're stuck staring at something."

"I stopped when a few minutes passed, where all that maelstrom calms down and I already have all the self-injuries and when I see the blood, but it has to be a lot of blood, then it starts to fall like exhaustion."

Once the stop of self-harm has elapsed, a **sixth phase** emerges, which is associated with the effects of self-harm, mainly at the physical, emotional and bodily level. Once these effects are experienced, a ritual of cleaning the wounds begin, which responds to a practice identified as habitual, which represents the end of a specific moment characterized by self-harm. Some of the most representative verbalizations of this moment are presented below:

"Mainly… I don't know how… No, I know if…, in the whole body, it's like I'm not aware that my hand is here, my arm is here, my leg is here, that I'm sitting like this, that it hurts here or that I'm uncomfortable, no, but it's like, it's like really the mind is completely blank, you don't feel anything and you're like stuck staring into nothing."

"After that, very automatically is like… I get up, I start cleaning the wounds with soap, with water, the whole thing, it's almost a ritual, almost like a ritual, to clean, to see how the blood drains with the water, when it turns red, to clean the wounds well."

"There's no excitement that I'm going to get caught or… what did I do? No, it's not enough, no, nothing, it's just like a ritual, almost like solemn or something, it's like… it's the right thing to do, like it's already built in, just like already, it's the right thing to do."

The **seventh phase** linked to the present moment of emotional instability is associated with the emergence of new self-injuries, which are characterized by the emergence of thoughts of guilt, anger and new self-punishments at the verbal and thinking spheres, which are associated with the self-injuries performed and their associated responsibility. Some of the most representative narratives of the present phase are presented below:

"I left marks, how am I going to hide them, what am I going to say, what will happen to me? And sometimes anger also comes, and when anger comes, I look for alcohol and pour it on my wounds, I say to myself 'Stupid, did you want it to hurt? [hope] that it hurts, [hope] that it hurts'."

"Then comes like… the desire, as well as anger toward oneself, to say 'damn', okay, it goes up a little and then it goes down again and I'm back to… okay, it's over."

Finally, it is possible to distinguish an **eighth phase** with an emergence of thoughts that favor emotional stability, which are associated with the articulation of a set of thoughts linked to self-affirmation and the delivery of support to herself, making self-verbalizations that allow her to cope with the present moment of emotional instability (Figure 7.3). Representative narratives of this moment are presented below:

"All of a sudden, it just stops, it's like a moment where it's like, again I start to feel better, 'I can, I can handle this, I didn't die before from something similar, it's not going to be the first or the last time…', I mean, 'it's

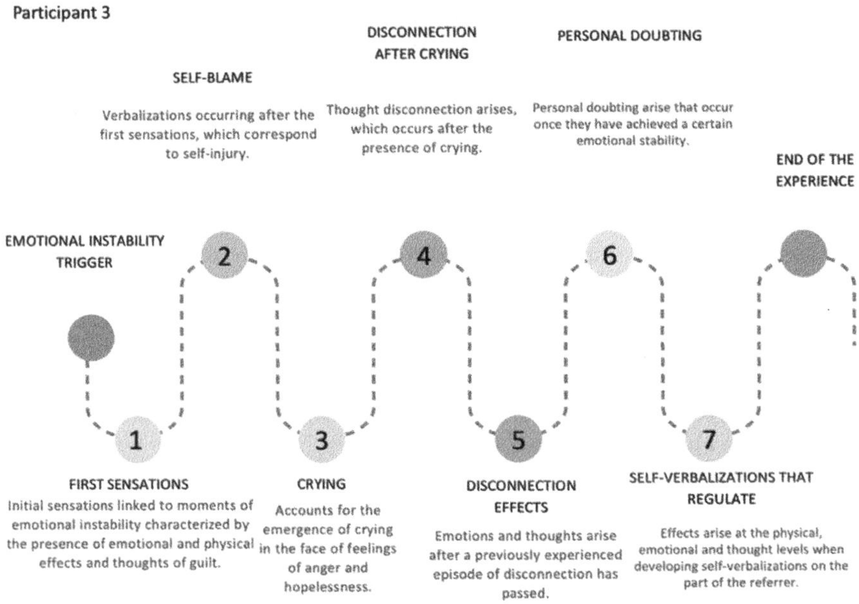

Figure 7.3 Specific diachronic analysis—participant N°3.

not the first and it's not going to be the last time it's going to happen to me'."

"It's also like a state of resignation, 'this is always going to happen to me.' If I'm going to be okay at some point… If I'm so bad, but I'm still going to be okay at some point, and then I'm going to be bad again, and I'm always going to be in this up and down state of emotions."

In the present participant, it is possible to distinguish the presence of seven **differentiated phases**, which demarcate the experience of emotional instability, being able to make a detailed description of the present micro-moments at a diachronic level. The **first phase** observed is associated with the emergence of the first sensations of instability at the emotional level, which are characterized by the presence of effects at the emotional and physical level and thoughts of guilt associated with actions performed. Some of the most representative verbalizations of this phase are presented below:

Frustration, anger, like:

> Oh, no, I'm not even good for that, I mean, for something as simple as remembering the keys, I'm a fool, how can I forget those things, things always go wrong for me, everything goes wrong, I shouldn't have existed, I'd better die, if in the end everything is already wrong.

"I felt, to begin with, a lot of heat, like you feel heat all over your body, like a pressure in your chest, like your pulse quickens, like your heart starts pumping faster, it's like the feeling more or less when you are very, like scared or in front of a situation with a lot of adrenaline, that's more or less the feeling."

"It's not just the frustration, the anger of not having brought the keys, but it's a: I do everything wrong, it's like remembering another time I wanted to do something [and] it went wrong."

In a **second phase**, a moment associated with self-reproach emerges, a space in which it is possible to distinguish the emergence of verbalizations of self-harm, which are associated with blaming oneself for a set of actions performed, being these attributed to one's own absolute responsibility. Representative statements of this phase are the following:

"I always say, if there was anyone listening, they would think I was arguing or talking to a person, because it's the same as I'm talking with you now, sometimes I'm talking to myself, sometimes I just blurt it out in the air."

"The thoughts I was having I was also verbalizing them, and like, it's like I was reproaching myself for those things, like I was blaming myself that I'm to blame for all that's going on, that it's my problem."

The **third phase** associated with the present moment of emotional instability is associated with the emergence of crying, a product of the presence of feelings of anger and hopelessness associated with the impossibility of improving their current unstable situation. The most representative verbalizations of this phase are the following:

"I started crying in a way, of, sometimes resigned, but this time it was a way like helplessness, like anger, like, I don't have, I can't do anything."

A **fourth phase** in the moment of emotional instability is associated with the emergence of a feeling of disconnection following the presence of crying, this phase being described as an instance in which a disconnection arises at the level of thought, presenting a trance-like state in which reality is not perceived from a state of unreality and self-absorption, presenting an isolation from all types of external stimuli. The most representative statements of this phase are the following:

"When I'm done crying, it's like a release, it's like I relax, let's say, a little bit, and I'm in a trance, like assimilating whether it's true or not."

"It's like you get stuck, or at least that's what happens to me, like you get stuck, like suddenly when there are people talking to you at that moment and you don't react, you get engrossed."

"It's like it's not me, but a third party that's happening to him, so it's like I start to analyze it from the outside, that's like, it would be like what happens to me a little bit, that gives the feeling that it's not me that's in that moment there."

After the phase described above, a **fifth phase** emerges, linked to the disconnection effects presented, which are associated with the emergence of greater regulation at the emotional level, as well as thoughts linked to the search for solutions to the problem that led to the emotional instability. The most representative statements of this phase are the following:

"There can still be anger and helplessness from seeing yourself in that state, but it's more manageable now, I would say it's like the normal reaction anyone would have to get angry, but within normal."

"And it's more like what am I going to do, how do I fix this, I mean, see what solution do I give it, [should] I go to someone's house, try to open a window, see if they're around to reach them somehow, it's like, there comes that: what do I do now?"

Once a certain emotional stability has been achieved, a **sixth phase** appears, characterized by the emergence of personal questioning, mainly associated with judging her own behavior and reactions at the emotional level during the episode of emotional instability, questioning the decisions she has made and critically emphasizing the type of approach she should have considered during this episode. Representative statements of this phase are the following:

"And then after that it's like 'what happened to me?', that is, 'how did I lose so much control over something, why didn't I do it right away, why...?'"

"Even after it's over, I say it out loud, 'Why didn't I do it right away, I could have done it right away?'"

"And this conversation starts with me, with another person, I don't know, because I feel that if I don't verbalize it, if I don't explain it, there will be an incognito and it won't be understood. Who will understand it: I don't know, but I explain it."

Finally, the emergence of a **seventh phase** can be appreciated, which is related to the articulation of verbalizations that favor self-regulation at the emotional, physical and thought levels. These verbalizations arise as an analytical process of the experience, facilitating its understanding from a new perspective, generating a feeling of greater well-being (Figure 7.4). The most representative verbalizations of this phase are the following:

"It is also good for me to talk about these things, as if I were another person, and to explain, and as if the feelings that I have I approach them as if

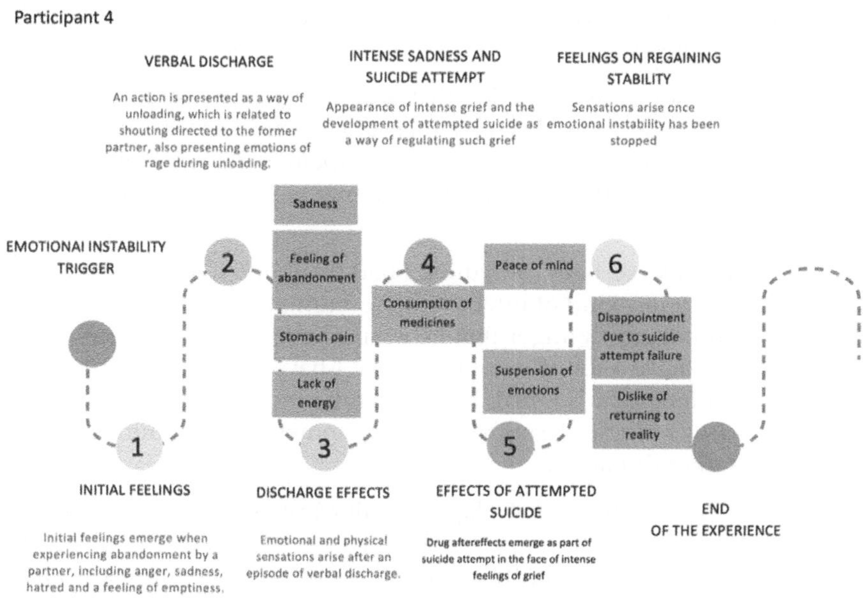

Figure 7.4 Specific diachronic analysis—participant N°4.

they were questionings or judgments that this other person makes towards me, and when I explain them, it makes me feel calmer, because it makes me also understand a different way of seeing the situation."

"This talking, these saying things, this seeing from another perspective in the background disconnects me from these thoughts of what's going to happen tomorrow or what happened yesterday, but keeps me there, in the now."

The present moment of emotional instability is marked by **six differentiated phases**, which synthesize the set of experiences presented by each participant. The **first phase** observed is associated with the emergence of initial feelings of emotional instability, which are characterized by the presence of anger, sadness, hatred and feelings of emptiness, in addition to reliving experiences of abandonment presented at other times in their lives. The main narratives belonging to this phase are described below:

"I felt betrayed, I felt rejected and I felt like I was cheated, like I thought we were on the same page and we really weren't."

"At that moment I think of thousands of things in a second, hypotheses like why, like I start to relive abandonment as a girl, so it's like that feeling, like that again, it's like it's super difficult to describe the emotions, like how to make them concrete."

"I don't know what to call it, like crisis or very unregulated it's always like that mix of feelings, as well as grief, anger, hate, a lot of hate."

A **second phase** is associated with the emergence of verbal discharge actions, which emerge as shouting directed toward the ex-partner. This action linked to verbal aggression is accompanied by emotions of rage and energy at the corporal level. The statements linked to this phase are described below:

"I unloaded, like verbally everything I had to say, but it didn't relieve me, it wasn't relief, it just kind of intensified everything."

"Anger, I think mostly anger that he wasn't being honest with me."

"I feel like I have a lot of energy, it's like I have a lot of strength, like I don't know, a feeling, it's weird, because at the moment, I feel like I have the power to say whatever I want and at that moment I have nothing to lose, so it's like it doesn't matter."

Once the present phase has elapsed, a **third phase** emerges, associated with the effects of the developed verbal discharge. These effects are presented at an emotional and physical level, being associated with the emergence of feelings of sadness, sense of abandonment, stomach pain and lack of energy. The most representative verbalizations of this phase are described below:

"There was that feeling, like the world is coming to an end, like what do I do now, what's going to give meaning to my days?"

"Pain in the stomach, but it's like gastric pain, as if there were, like, it makes me want to go to the bathroom."

"With that feeling of weight in the body, like a feeling of listlessness, like not wanting to continue."

As a result of these feelings, a **fourth phase** emerges, which is characterized by the emergence of a feeling of intense grief and a subsequent suicide attempt, in order to regulate this feeling of grief. The suicide attempt arises from the participant's consumption of medication. The most representative verbalizations of this phase are the following:

"I got home and I had more grief and like it was a grief like I couldn't stand it anymore, that's how it was like that day and, well, in other similar situations like that it's like how am I going to live with this level of grief, I can't live like that with so much grief."

"The grief I had was so great that it was like I'm not going to be able to live with so much grief, so if I can't live with so much grief and this grief is never going to go away, better not to continue, it was like for me the logical thing to do, it was like there was no other solution."

"I took some pills that I had saved, because at that point they hid the pills from me, I mean, I had to take them in front of my mother every day and I pretended to take them and save them, and when I'm like… I even remember the amount, there were 25 pills and I took them all."

Once the suicide attempt has been made, a **fifth phase** arises, which focuses on the effects of the attempt described above. The effects observed arise at the emotional and thought level, characterized by the presence of a greater mental tranquility, as well as emotional suspension, a sensation that allows a state of stillness and interruption of grief. The most representative statements of this phase are described below:

"It was liberating, because it was like after this there is no more and it's over, the pain is over, the suffering is over, it's over…"

"I felt like light, relaxed, like the problem was no longer a problem, because I didn't have to worry anymore because I had already taken the pills, so I wasn't supposed to wake up."

"The only thing I remembered is that when I took the pills I didn't feel anything, I didn't feel anything, it was like relief, like there was nothing, like my mind didn't work much anymore, I didn't think."

Finally, a **sixth phase** is presented, which is characterized by feelings that emerge when emotional stability is regained. These sensations respond to the failure of the suicide attempt presented, which in a certain way generates a state of disappointment at not having succeeded in the attempt, as well as a feeling of displeasure at having to return to reality and everyday life (Figure 7.5). The most representative statements are the following:

"I woke up and it was super disappointing, like what a drag."

"It was like dislike, like, okay, it's like coming back to reality."

In the present participant, the development of **five different phases** is observed, which are representative of the moment of emotional instability experienced. The **first phase** is associated with the first sensations evidenced, which are associated with effects at the emotional level such as feelings of anguish, physical discomfort and feelings of guilt. The most representative statements of this phase are the following:

"I felt guilty, I thought I had done something wrong, I started to get anxious comes hand in hand with thinking. My chest tightened a lot and I wanted to cry a lot."

"I feel like I'm kind of desperate in my body and I move like this (gestures with hands), then I stand up."

"I feel like my chest is squeezing and I feel a lot of anguish like in this whole area (points to chest)."

The **second phase** experienced is associated with the search for solutions to the emotional discomfort presented. These efforts arise at the level

Participant 5

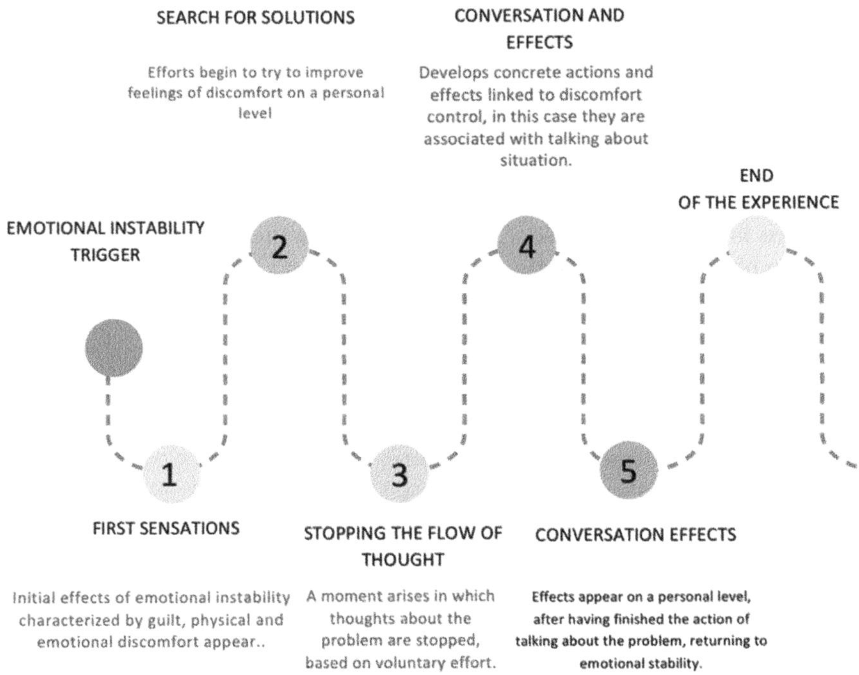

Figure 7.5 Specific diachronic analysis—participant N°5.

of thought, being representative the need to seek solutions regarding the steps or actions to be taken to improve the situation. Some of the most representative verbalizations of this phase are the following:

"Then I start smoking a lot of cigars (6 cigars) and my head keeps thinking about what to do about this."

"Anguish continues, I need to fix that situation."

Once the search for solutions to the emotional instability presented has been completed, a **third phase** associated with stopping the flow of thought emerges, at which point the participant manages to stop her thoughts and make a decision, which mobilizes her actions aimed at resolving her problem. The main statements related to this phase are the following:

"After smoking, you suddenly say enough is enough and the thoughts stop, the emotions are paused and you say I have to have a conversation

with him." "Primero en mi mente y luego digo en voz alta lo que debo hacer."
"I still feel uneasy, so I have to do something."

Once the actions determined in the previous phase have been executed, a **fourth phase** arises, which is associated with the development of conversation and the effects associated with this action. The development of this action presents effects at a physical and emotional level, mainly focused on the development of a feeling of tranquility and absence of physical suitcase. The representative statements of this phase are the following:

"I write to him and we start talking about the situation, I tell him it's wrong that we shouldn't keep doing that, that my way of being with him is not going to change."
"I feel calm, more confident to be able to talk to him, in my body I feel that my chest is not tight, I don't feel like crying."

Finally, a **fifth phase** emerges in which it is possible to clearly distinguish the totality of effects that the development of the conversation action has had. These effects can be distinguished at the physical, emotional and thought levels, being characterized by the presence of a sensation of physical well-being, a feeling of happiness, tranquility at the emotional and thought levels (Figure 7.6). The most representative statements of this phase are the following:

"I feel more relieved, I can breathe better, my chest doesn't feel so tight anymore and I feel calmer, my thoughts are calmer, my body is less tense, I'm happy, I feel like I got something off my chest, realize you're doing the right thing."
"My thoughts are calmer, before I was thinking and thinking about how guilty I felt, now that is calm, those thoughts are no longer there, doing this, talking to him I think it calms everything down."

The participant shows the presence of five distinct phases in which an episode of emotional instability occurs, these phases involve the development of various effects at the emotional, physical and thought levels. The first phase is associated with initial effects of emotional instability, which are associated with the emergence of feelings of anguish, discomfort in the chest, grief and crying at the experienced event. The most representative statements of this phase are the following:

"An instability like that, a crisis, I felt like pity, I felt very sorry because of what I was going through at that moment with the girl, where I was like with the trial issue, where I couldn't see her as much."
"It's like I couldn't keep my grief any longer, I affirm it, with grief, you know, like I couldn't stay normal, I had to cry, you know, I couldn't get

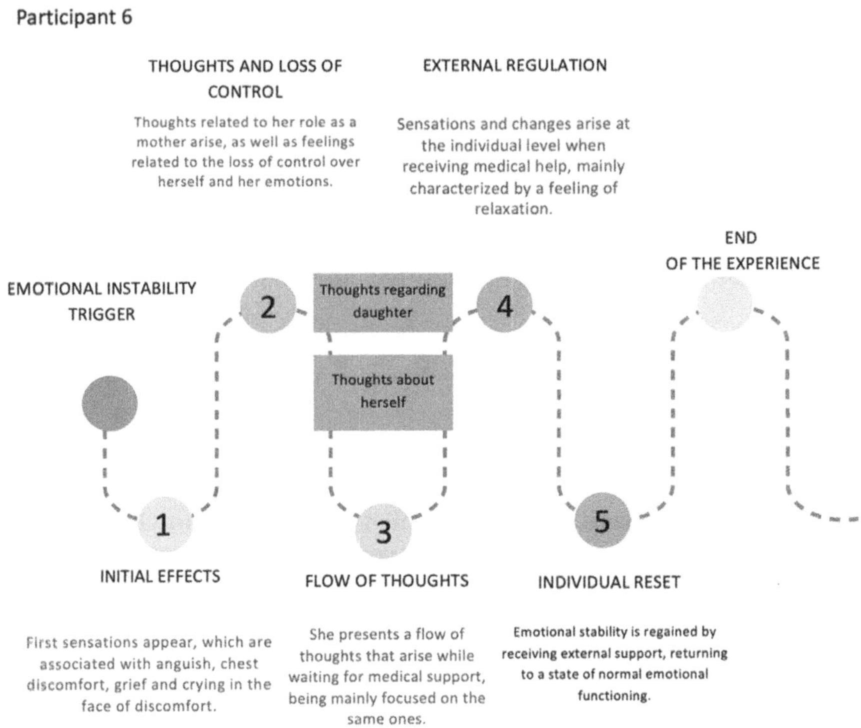

Figure 7.6 Specific diachronic analysis—participant N°6.

anything out of holding it in because I couldn't do it anymore. I exploded and I cried, I cried, I cried, that's it."

"It felt kind of tight, it was like a pressure in the chest, kind of distressing the thing."

Once the episode of emotional instability and effects described above has begun, a **second phase** arises, characterized by the emergence of thoughts and loss of control. These thoughts are associated with guilt regarding her role as a mother, which generates an emotional feeling of discomfort, then there is a loss of control over her emotional state at an individual level, which gives rise to the need for external support. The most representative statements of this phase are the following:

"Then I think I felt like a bad mom, for not being present during her school year I felt like a bad mom, you know?"

"I tell my partner that I feel bad and that I feel very bad, so, to take me to the hospital. I went to the hospital, I told him that I was in a rare crisis and that I would prefer him to inject me with a sedative so that I could be calmer."

While waiting for support in the assistance service, a **third phase** arises, which is characterized by the emergence of a flow of thoughts, characterized by the development of thoughts linked to her daughter, thoughts about herself, thoughts about having lost her daughter's graduation and thoughts associated with what led her to the present state of emotional instability. The most representative statements of this phase are the following:

"I was kind of sitting in the gutter and as I was thinking, I was thinking the same thing, Emy stuff."

"I was thinking, I was thinking about Emy, and about me, you know? [sic], but I was looking, I don't know, I was like lost, like I was only thinking and I was sitting and I didn't react."

"What led me to this, to feel so bad if one didn't…I went to a graduation, there wasn't, I didn't have anything for me to feel bad about, I was thinking about that what leads me to, like, decompensate?"

Subsequently, a **fourth phase** arises, which is associated with external regulation, constituting this moment the main effects experienced at the moment of receiving pharmacological support from the physician. These effects are associated with a feeling of tranquility, which is part of a typical sensation at the moment of receiving external support, achieving emotional stability. The most representative statements of this phase are described below:

"It's like routine, I've been there, well, I'd been there like several times, so it was like the same thing again."

"Because I knew it was, it was like my last step, I mean, I would go to the hospital, they would inject me and I would go home relaxed, you know, it was like I knew I was going to go there and they were going to inject me."

Finally, in the **fifth phase**, the presence of a state described as individual restart is observed. This state is characterized by a loss of memory at the individual level at the moment of receiving pharmacological support, which marks a return to emotional stability (Figure 7.7). The present verbalizations are the most representative of this phase:

"Because of medication, because, well, it was still for me it was more or less strong and I also had a medication treatment at night, so I took the whole thing at my time plus the other sedative, so I spent about two days where I don't remember well what I did."

"I felt normal, as if I had just come from the hospital, I don't know, it was like I recovered, you know, the emotions, the thoughts, what I felt in my body, it was like everything started again, I felt good."

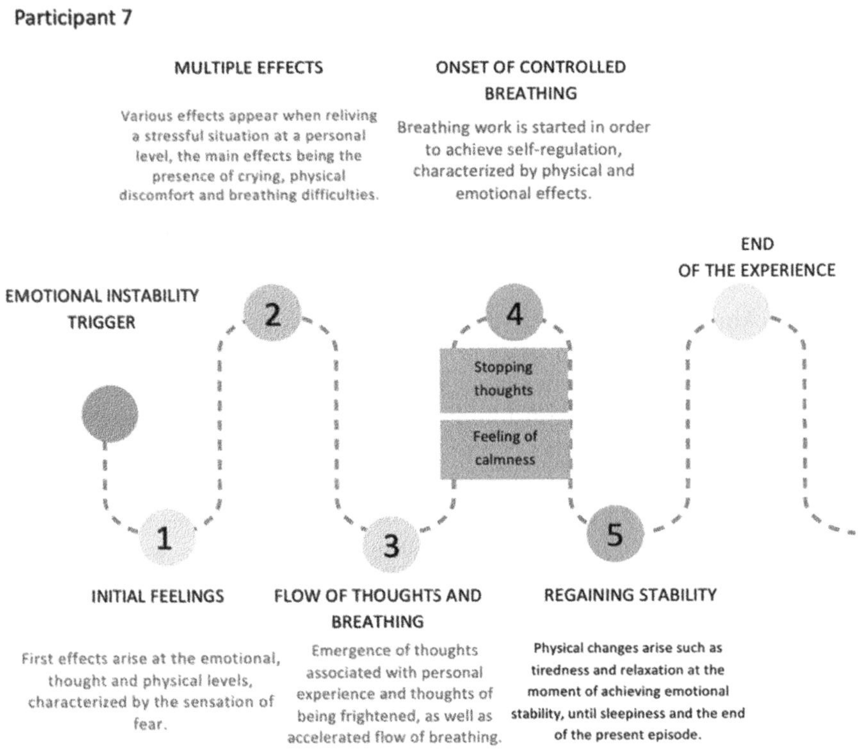

Figure 7.7 Specific diachronic analysis—participant N°7.

It is possible to distinguish in the present experience, five phases associated with the episode of emotional instability, which demarcate a clear differentiation in its presentation and course. The first phase is associated with the presence of initial sensations of emotional instability, which are characterized by the presence of effects at the emotional, physical and thought levels, mainly characterized by the emergence of a muscular contraction when recalling an event that produces fear. Some of the most characteristic statements of this phase are the following:

"I get scared and, in my mind, I feel like doing like this, but I don't, but..."

"The feeling I had like collapsing, I mean, I didn't do it in my mind, but of collapsing just like that, then I felt like contracted, it's like contracted the whole body."

Subsequently, a **second phase** arises, which is related to the multiple effects of reliving a stressful situation from the past. These effects are associated with the emergence of crying, physical discomfort and difficulties in regulating their own breathing, these sensations produce a general state of tension, presenting considerable difficulty in remaining in a state of calm. Some of the most representative statements of this phase are the following:

"From there it was getting harder and harder for me to try to calm down and it wasn't much of a thinking thing anymore, it was just that I was very agitated and breathing very fast."

"From then on I couldn't stop crying and I… what do you call it? What do you call this, but it was a lot, it was really like that, it's like a feeling that you're going to die, I don't know, I couldn't stop, I felt it was going to be infinite."

"Because it's hard for me to breathe like this, but my breathing is faster, my thoughts also go very fast, something I remember is like my hands were like this, contracted."

A **third phase** is associated with the emergence of a flow of thoughts, which are associated with personal experience, which is continuously relived during the present moment. The respiratory flow becomes more agitated and there remains a feeling of discomfort linked to the presence of fear. Characteristic statements of this phase are the following:

"Just the one I told you about the little girl who had a crisis, I remembered that."

"My breathing is still running fast, but my thoughts are not, I was just thinking I got scared, I got scared, I got scared, I got scared, I got scared, I got scared."

After receiving external support from the psychologist, a **fourth phase** begins, which is associated with the beginning of controlled breathing, presenting effects at the emotional and thought level, which are characterized by the arrest of thoughts and the emergence of a sense of calm. The present exercise favors the return to an initial state of emotional stability. The most characteristic statements of this phase are the following:

"My psychologist starts calming me down, he says, 'okay, breathe through your nose' and it takes me quite a while to kind of be able to stop breathing through my mouth, then I'm calming down, my thoughts, calming down, calming down, until I manage to calm down, that's basically it."

Finally, a **fifth phase** arises, which is associated with the resumption of emotional stability, at which time physical changes arise such as abdominal pain, a feeling of tiredness and relaxation, to conclude with sleep, a situation that marks the end of the episode of emotional instability

Participant 8

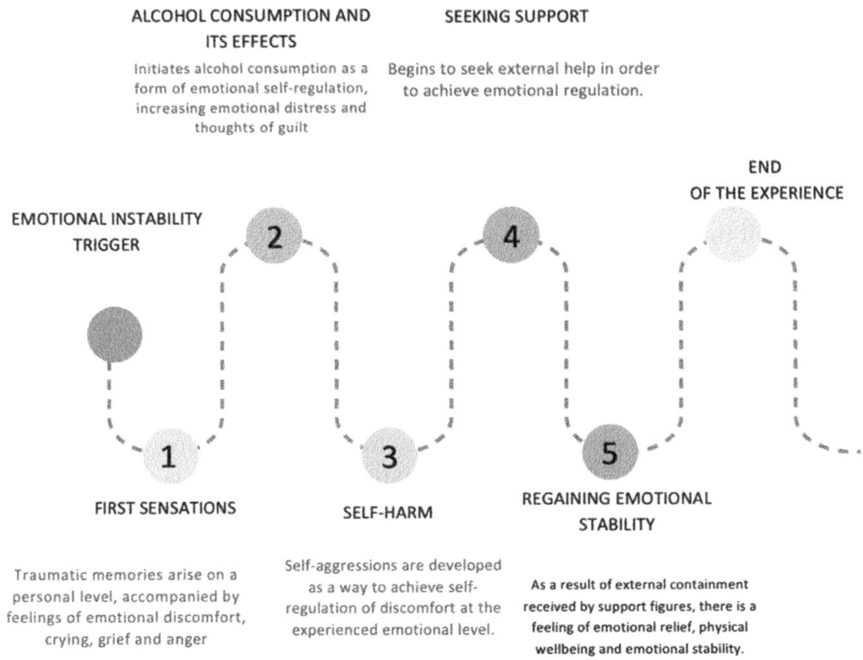

Figure 7.8 Specific diachronic analysis—participant N°8.

(Figure 7.8). The most characteristic statements of this phase are the following:

"I realize that my stomach starts to hurt, but as if when you laugh a lot, that feeling as if you had done sit-ups, because it's like… I don't know how to say it, the stomach, like… I don't know how to say it, it was already very contracted. I don't know how to say it, it was already very contracted."

"I almost totally calm down, I put aside thoughts that had to do with that, it made me very sleepy and I just think about getting home to sleep, that and nothing else."

In the present experience, it is possible to distinguish the presence of **five distinct phases**, which demarcate the presence of a variety of effects at the individual level during the episode of emotional instability. The **first phase** is associated with first feelings of emotional instability, which are associated with the emergence of traumatic memories at a personal level, accompanied by feelings of emotional discomfort characterized by the presence of crying, grief and anger. The most representative statements of this phase are the following:

"I started to remember a topic of an abuse, topics such as religious topics of my parents, of my family, and I felt that I was bad, very bad and I got out of control, I had started to cry, then I went to buy alcohol, I drank a lot, I was not aware of how much I had drunk."

"It was like between sorrow, anger, I didn't know how to distinguish, I felt sometimes that in reality my parents didn't love me or that they didn't love me, when it was the opposite, also a very internal conflict between what I was and God."

Subsequently, a **second phase** arises, which is associated with alcohol consumption as a way of managing the discomfort described in the first phase. Alcohol consumption presents effects at the emotional level, which are characterized by an increase in emotional distress and the emergence of an intense sense of guilt for their actions, as well as for their own existence. Representative statements of this moment are the following:

"I felt at that time that maybe I was not a good son, that I was not an example for my brothers and sisters, for my nephews and nieces, a mixture of things that my parents didn't want me to be as a son, maybe."

"I felt like dying, like disappearing, like not being a burden."

Given the permanence of emotional discomfort, a **third phase** arises, characterized by the emergence of verbal and physical self-aggressions, which are associated with a need to achieve self-regulation at the emotional level. Some representative statements of this moment are the following:

"I started to self-insult, I was saying I was useless and I shouldn't be and I was beating myself up, that."

"On my legs, on my arms or, all of a sudden, I would pull my hair a little bit as if to try to feel the external pain, rather than the internal pain."

When not visualizing an improvement in her emotional state, a **fourth phase** arises, which is based on the search for external support, in order to achieve a state of emotional regulation. This support comes from referents who provide physical and emotional support to the participant, managing to regulate the symptoms presented during emotional instability. Representative statements of this phase are the following:

"Seek help, call someone who will listen to me."

"I know I called several people, a friend, my older brother."

Finally, once external support has been received from close referents, a **fifth phase** arises, which is linked to regaining emotional stability, with characteristic physical and emotional effects as a result of this containment

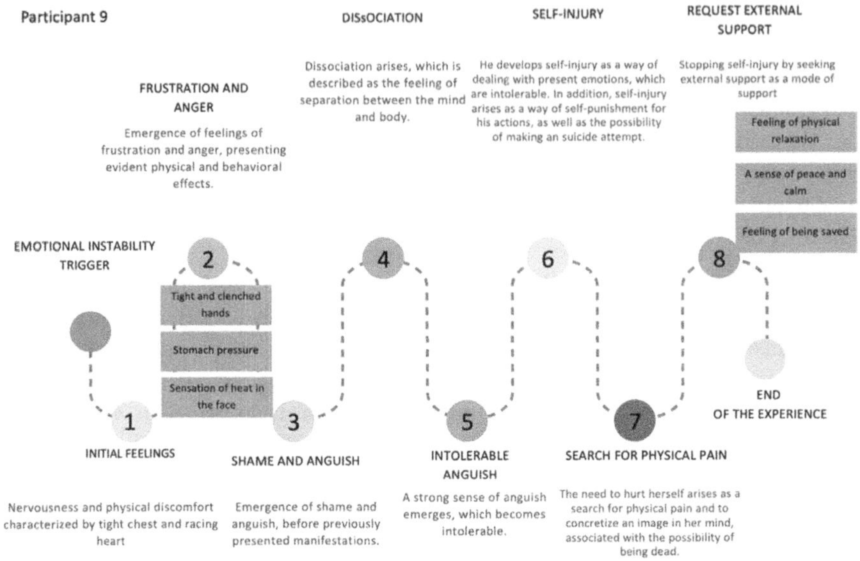

Figure 7.9 Specific diachronic analysis—participant N°9.

action (Figure 7.9). The most representative statements of this phase are the following:

> "They listened to me, they tried to tell me to calm down, to be calm. In fact, I think that time my brother came with my sister-in-law."
>
> "It was better, because I could get out what I had, everything that was happening to me, what I had choked here in my throat, I could get rid of the knot and it was like a relief to be able to verbalize it."
>
> "They go down like to a thousand, like that's where I was able to concentrate and I was able to kind of stay well or stay stable, I don't know if the word is well, I think broke, stable."

This experience is characterized by the presence of **nine distinct phases**, which group a set of symptoms at the physical, emotional, sensory and thought levels. The **first phase** associated with the experience of emotional instability responds to the set of initial sensations, which are associated with the presence of nervousness, physical discomfort characterized by a feeling of tightness in the chest and a racing heart. Some representative statements of this phase are the following:

> "Emotional instability begins, um, in a conversation I had with this person, where my dad went to support me, because I felt that I couldn't… I couldn't deal with that situation alone."

"As in physical discomfort, uh, I was very nervous, uh, I felt tense, mmm, chest kind of tight and my heart was racing."

As a **second phase**, emotions of frustration and anger arise, which are associated with the situation experienced with the ex-partner. These emotions present various physical and behavioral effects during this phase, including tense and clenched hands, stomach pressure, sensation of heat in the face and physical aggression toward the ex-partner. The most representative statements of this moment are the following:

"Like no, it didn't work out the way I really wanted it to, and that's why I got really frustrated and .... I was hostile just like him, it kind of infected me with that anger."

"It was like there that frustration kind of, ah, turns into anger, into rage, and I grab the phone and I throw it at him, or I throw it... I throw it like this, far away."

"It's like a heat, it's like it comes, sometimes from that.... discomfort in the stomach, like it's tight, like a heat starts to rise up to my face, like a fire is going to come out."

A **third phase** of the present episode of emotional instability is associated with the emergence of feelings of shame and anguish, which are related to actions of aggressions previously carried out, producing an individual maladjustment and instability. The main verbalizations of this phase are the following:

"Like an anguish in the chest, like all that stuff that comes out, it kind of decants."

"It's just, like, I kind of fall into guilt, like.... why did I allow it to get to that situation?"

Subsequently, the emergence of a **fourth phase** is appreciated, which is characterized by the emergence of an alteration called dissociation. This is described by the participant as a state of separation between the mind and the body, a situation that remains stable for the duration of the episode of emotional instability. The most representative verbalizations are the following:

"When this feeling comes back, which lodges in my chest, my mind kind of separates from my body, I become dissociated."

"I'm kind of absent, no.... I can no longer follow the conversation, or with the rational thoughts that I was having, but rather my emotions and my body are no longer attached."

The **fifth phase** is the emergence of a feeling of anguish, which is described as intolerable by the participant, a situation that produces an important discomfort at an individual level, linking to this emotion, sensations at a physical level such as tiredness at a bodily level. The most representative statements of this phase are the following:

"I feel intense distress."

"Em, like at.... also in the chest, like the weight stays on, em, and I also feel my body more tired, like my head is heavy, my shoulders."

"It comes to my mind that I kind of don't want to...I don't want to be there, I don't want to feel that. Em, I can't tolerate it."

As a way of dealing with emotions that are intolerable for the participant, in the **sixth phase** the emergence of physical self-harm is observed, which is characterized by the development of cuts on her wrists. The development of self-injury takes on a new meaning by presenting a dual utility characterized by the need to be punished for her actions and the possibility of attempting against her life as a way to stop her suffering. The most representative statements are the following:

"That's when I took a... like some kind of small knife, and I cut my wrists, I mean, I did cuts in my wrists."

"I thought it was going to hurt less this physical pain than the emotional pain I was feeling."

"I remember very much that it was very much tinged this as a "decision", in quotation marks, by the feeling of guilt, like I had to be punished."

After the sixth phase, a search for physical pain arises as a way of regulating emotional pain. This corresponds to a **seventh phase**, characterized by the need to achieve a certain amount of physical pain that allows an effective regulation of the emotional discomfort described, as well as the need to regain control of its own functioning, since it still remains in a state of dissociation. The most representative statements of this phase are the following:

"It had to do with... with feeling the pain, feeling my body, but I wasn't feeling it and I was looking for it."

"I was shocked to see the blood, it kind of a.... amazed me to see the blood and not feel the pain."

Faced with the situation experienced and the possibility of ending his life, an **eighth phase** arises, characterized by the need to seek external support as a rescue alternative to the behaviors presented. The participant turns to a support figure during the development of the farewell, a situation that favors the articulation of protective resources. The most representative statements of this phase are the following:

"There I kind of take a pause, I see that I'm going to kill myself, like I was determined to do it, and I talk to a friend to say goodbye."

"I kind of wanted him to know that it wasn't about him, that I valued him, um, because he was also an ex-partner that I had had before, that was a partner that didn't hurt me, it could be said."

"Uh, when I texted him, because I think it was like a message I sent him, an audio, I texted him on the phone. Um, he tells me he's coming immediately."

Finally, a **ninth phase** arises, which is associated with the arrest of emotional instability, with the support of an external referent, who provides physical and emotional support, allowing an effective regulation at the emotional level of the participant. The accompaniment by the external referent provides security to the participant and the possibility of openly expressing their emotions and discomfort associated with the episode of emotional instability (Figure 7.10). Some of the most representative verbalizations of this phase are the following:

"Em, peace, [laughs], like calm, and like this feeling of being saved."

"With a safe person, I feel safer, like nothing is going to happen to me, that they are going to stop me from continuing to hu…, to hurt myself."

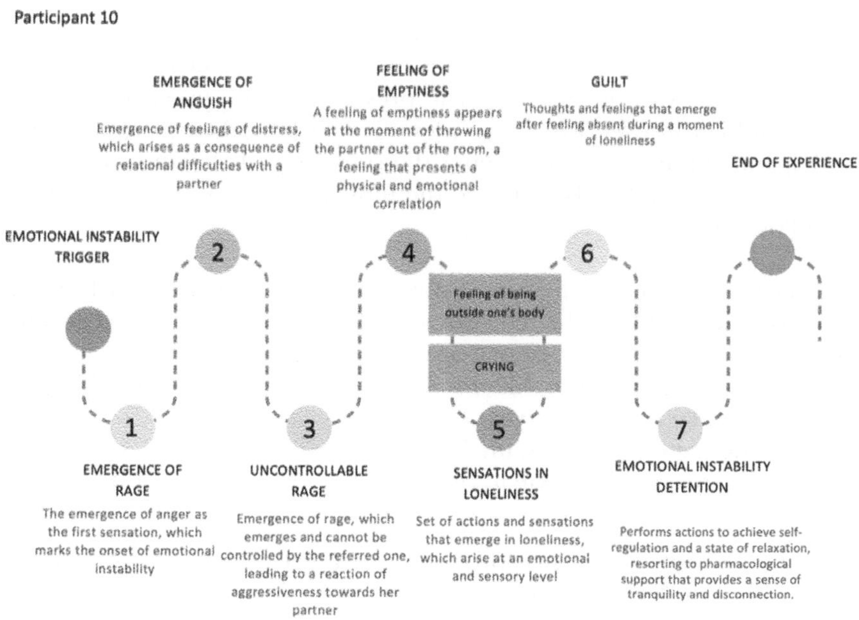

Figure 7.10 Specific diachronic analysis—participant N°10.

"I rested, like after this state came a very deep exhaustion, and already it kind of comes to my mind the next day at work."

In the present experience it is possible to distinguish **seven differentiated phases**, which demarcate a series of sensations that emerge during an episode of emotional instability. The **first phase** is associated with the emergence of rage presenting a correlation both at the emotional and physical level and at the level of thought, which is presented as a product of difficulties in interaction at the relational level, mainly associated with the perception of lack of attention from her partner. The most representative narratives of this phase are the following:

"It makes me angry. I mean, it makes me angry because I think that, if he's with me, I should be the most important. No, and I don't want to sound self-centered, but, but I should be the important thing at that minute."

"Estoy, eh, que, que, que estoy como emputecida en el fondo, que, que, que me está dando esta rabia y, y me empiezo a poner como entre nerviosa."

"I'm, uh, that, that, I'm enraged deep down, that, what's giving me this rage and, and I'm starting to get like a bit nervous."

"Like a knot, like a knot in my stomach, like... it's hard for me to identify it, I don't know, it's like I just feel it, eh, and, and, and, and, and, or I start to clench my hands, to bury my nails a little."

Subsequently, a **second phase** is presented, which is characterized by the emergence of anguish, a feeling that is related to relational difficulties during interaction with her partner. The present emotion presents effects at the physiological level, which are identified in a marked manner by the participant, the most striking being the sensation of shortness of breath and tingling in the hands. Some of the most representative narratives are the following:

"I start to get anxious because I don't want him to think that I'm like, like I don't know, like acting crazy or something, but, but I start to get anxious because I think that, that maybe we're going to break up."

"I feel a little bit like I'm, like I'm short of breath, uh, at times like, like nervous, but like I feel like crying."

"Like tingling in my hands, uh, like, like, like if..., it's just, it's weird, but it's like I'm, somewhere in me it's like I'm, I deserve all this for having bad choices."

As the present experience progresses, a **third phase** arises, characterized by the emergence of uncontrollable rage, a sensation that leads to the development of an aggressive action toward the partner, who is unable to regulate this manifestation effectively. Some of the most representative verbalizations of this phase are the following:

"That's when I got a little excited. I screamed, uh, I felt like I got really red with rage, I guess, I don't know."

"It's happening to me that I don't know how to control it. It's like... Ouch, how could I describe you, I don't know if you've ever seen the Katie Ka-Boom anime?"

"I kind of throw up anger, like I don't know how to regulate it well yet, so I say hurtful things [sighs], eh, and then I regret it later."

In relation to the third phase, there is a **fourth phase** which is described as the emergence of a feeling of emptiness, a feeling that is correlated at a physical and emotional level, mainly a feeling of sadness, loneliness and the need to punish her body in order to fill this emptiness. Some statements associated with this phase are the following:

"Loneliness. Loneliness, sadness. A lot of sadness."

"It's a feeling of... of fragility. Of weakness. And at the same time of, of wanting to like... some part of me like punishing myself too or, or, or, or seeing that I'm doing it wrong, like I can't get things right."

"Filling a void, I think, and, and, and, and, and I don't know, like from, also like from punishing myself, as well as punishing my body, from eating and eating and eating and eating and, and, and, and smoking a couple of cigars."

During the course of the feeling of emptiness, a **fifth phase** related to feelings of loneliness arises, which are associated with a set of sensations at the emotional and sensory level. The participant describes the experience of being outside her body, feeling strange and crying as the most representative elements of this moment. Some of the verbalizations associated with this phase are the following:

"I sat on the floor and lit a, a cigarette [sighs]. I cried and that was it. I mean, for a good while."

"Like, like everything I was feeling and, and what I was thinking, so I was like, I don't know, I felt like weird, like, like I wasn't even me."

"It was something like, I don't know, uh, like seeing me from the outside, like, like being there but not being there. I don't know if I'm explaining myself well."

Once the feelings of loneliness have passed, a **sixth phase** emerges, characterized by the appearance of thoughts of guilt, which are associated with their own behaviors, decisions and thoughts, a situation that is accompanied by a feeling of sadness linked to their personal situation. Some representative verbalizations of this phase are the following:

> "They are pure thoughts like guilt or, or, or, like thoughts that in the end I actually put together, a theme, a show, a little bit like I'm the one who always makes everything, that everything, that everything go a thousand percent."
>
> "Then the anger kind of subsided and, and this sadness came, this guilt, uh, I just wanted to lie down and have a cigarette."

Finally, the participant achieves a state of tranquility and relaxation through psychopharmacological support, this corresponds to the **seventh phase** of the experience, characterized by the arrest of emotional instability. In this phase there is a disconnection at an emotional level, as well as body relaxation once a medication is consumed as external support in the face of instability. Representative statements of this phase are the following:

> "I took half a Rize and threw myself on the bed, I didn't even put on pajamas, with what I had on and apparently fell asleep, I don't remember much."
>
> "Like stepping on clouds and like I'm there, like a plant or like a little leaf, like a leaf that I go wherever the wind takes me. Like I don't have much control of myself, emotionally disconnected and my body relaxed."

General Analysis

In the development of the diachronic description, it is possible to distinguish the presence of various effects at the symptomatological level, which representatively demarcate an episode of emotional instability. The main symptomatological effects observed are associated with the presence of discomfort at the physical, emotional, sensory and thought levels, being clearly perceptible emotions such as anguish and anger, as well as physical effects associated with the involuntary contraction of limbs, together with the permanence of physical tension at the general level.

As a representative part of alterations at the sensory level, the presence of dissociation episodes stands out in some of the observed experiences, which are described as manifestations similar to episodes of derealization and depersonalization, which generate alterations that lead to a subsequent feeling of strangeness on the part of those affected. From the level of thought it is possible to observe the development of thoughts of guilt, which in many moments are associated with the responsibility for their own behavior or verbal self-aggressions linked to the need to be punished for their mistakes.

In direct relation to elements associated with self-punishment, it has been distinguished that self-harm at the physical level occurs as a consequence of a triple need, which, in some cases, is linked to the need to achieve an effective self-regulation of their emotional discomfort, focusing on the physical pain that the wounds generate. On the other hand, self-harm at the physical level is associated with the need to be punished, a situation that is attributed in many experiences as an obligation or an action demanded as part of a ritual practice, linked to their wrongdoing. Finally, it is possible to distinguish that self-harm is associated with the possibility of making an attempt on one's life, actions that are carried out impulsively, but not in a calculated or organized manner, thus fulfilling the characteristics of parasuicides.

At a general level, the observed experiences involve multisymptomatic elements, characterized by effects at the physical, emotional, thought and sensory levels, a situation that exposes a clear complexity in the representation of the experience of emotional instability in the present population. In the following sections we will continue exploring episodes of emotional instability, from a synchronic perspective, orienting the exploration to a thematic dimension associated with the effects described above.

SPECIFIC SYNCHRONOUS ANALYSES

This section seeks to develop a detailed description of synchronic elements, which are associated with elements of the contents exposed in the explored phases. The approach proposed in the following section is linked to the detailed description of physical, emotional, behavioral, thinking and sensory effects, typical of the experiences of emotional instability, involving a description both at a graphic and qualitative level, thus allowing an organization that provides clarity and precision at an analytical level.

The results obtained in this dimension, based on the exploration of the 10 experiences of the participants considered in this research, are presented below at a graphic and descriptive level (Figure 7.11).

This graph shows the presence of effects at the physical, emotional, mental and sensory levels, which are associated with an episode of emotional instability, marking an experience that produces an imbalance at the level of general functioning. From the physical level, it is possible to distinguish the presence of body paralysis and pressure in the chest during the experience, sensations that generate discomfort in the participant.

"It's like everything comes to a standstill, everything comes to a standstill and I start to see chaos, from something so simple."

"I feel a kind of desperation in my chest, a pressure, like it's something I'm not going to be able to solve."

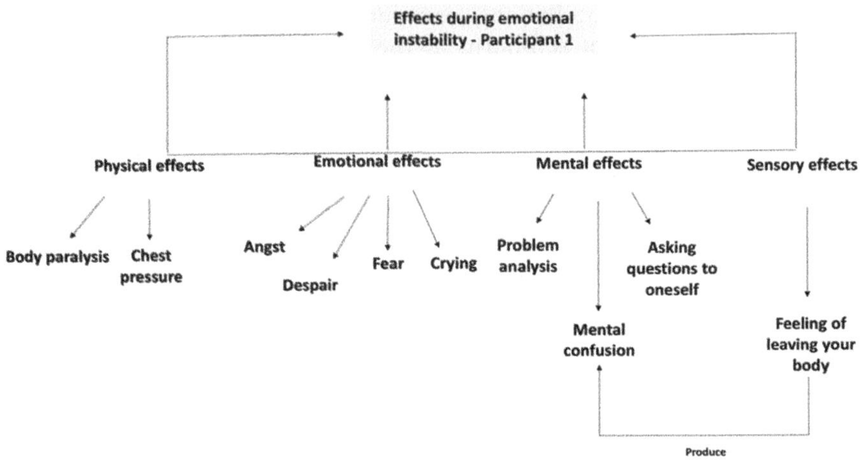

Figure 7.11 Specific synchronous analysis—Participant N°1.

From the emotional level, it is possible to distinguish the presence of emotions of anguish, hopelessness, fear and crying, which are associated with specific experiences, which are uncontrollable for the participant.

"And that's where the anguish enters and the fear comes in."
"A [feeling of] hopelessness, it's a super strange feeling and very, very strong, it's something uncontrollable."
"Then when I finish talking to this person, that's when the crying emerges."

At the mental level, there is the emergence of a flow of thought centered on the development of an analysis of her particular problem, a mental confusion when presenting a sensation of leaving her body during emotional instability, and, finally, the asking of questions to herself, which allow her to better understand her loss of control at the emotional level.

"I try to analyze the situation, which is when I start with that mental chaos and become paralyzed."
"I myself was asking myself 'why, why?' If it's a thing that I have to face, it's a normal thing, it's a simple thing, it's an everyday thing."
"I've tried to interpret that, this may sound crazy, right? That my own self is trying to take shelter, and is coming out of that chaotic body to observe what's going on or analyze what's going on."

Finally, it is possible to observe at the sensory level the presence of a sensation that emerges during an episode of emotional instability, which is described as the sensation of leaving her body, a situation that generates strangeness and confusion at the mental level, not being able to establish

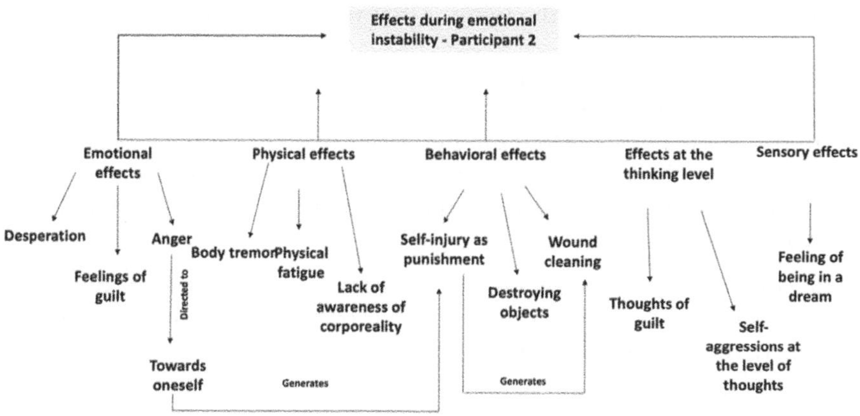

Figure 7.12 Specific synchronous analysis—Participant N°2.

a logical explanation or association regarding the occurrence of this phenomenon (Figure 7.12).

"When I go into the chaos, it's like I come out myself and see myself from the outside."

"It's a strange unfolding, because at the same time I observe myself from the outside, but very, very calmly, as if I were not myself."

In the present experience, it is possible to distinguish effects at the emotional, physical, behavioral, thought and sensory levels, which generate a set of manifestations that generate a high level of individual maladjustment in the participant. Regarding effects at the emotional level, the presence of feelings of despair, feelings of guilt and anger is observed, which is mainly directed toward herself as a product of her actions or mistakes at a personal level. This feeling of rage will lead to the development of physical self-injury as a form of self-punishment.

"Going into despair, into 'nobody cares about me,' blah, blah, blah, blah, blah, blah."

"All I could think, in a fit of tears, was 'sorry mom', that was the only thing that was going through my head, 'sorry mom, sorry mom', because I didn't want to go on."

"Hate, as well as self-hatred, anger, anger at the world, pity, self-pity, 'I'm alone', it's like poof... and on top of that guilt, too, a lot of guilt."

As for the physical effects of this experience, we observed the emergence of trembling in the body, a feeling of physical fatigue and a lack of awareness in the perception of one's own corporeality, a state that is associated with the moment of stopping the self-harm practices developed.

"Start shivering, start with crying... that you're not even [sic] crying, so like 'ah...'"

"Feeling the... But it's not like tired, it's not like you did sports or you're [having] [sic] a tired day."

"In the whole body, it's like I'm not aware that my hand is here, my arm is here, my leg is here, that I'm sitting like this, that it hurts here or that I'm uncomfortable, no, but it's like, it's really like the mind is completely blank, you don't feel anything."

Regarding the behavioral effects, it is possible to appreciate the emergence of self-harm as a punishment for her own actions or mistakes, which is directly related to the feeling of rage that she presents toward herself. There is also a tendency to destroy objects in her environment as a way of expressing her rage, as well as a ritualistic practice based on the cleaning of wounds resulting from self-harm.

"The self-injuries were getting deeper and deeper, go testing, it was like one is not enough, another one stronger, stronger, it's going to get stronger and stronger."

"Anger, anger, rage, it's a mixture, of course, anger at me, 'why is it happening to me again?'"

"There was no longer absolute control, I threw things; I'm not... I'm not... I'm not normally like that. Normally I'm not like that, I control my emotions a lot, but that time I completely overflowed, it was like... no, there was no way to contain it."

"After that, very automatically is like I get up, I start cleaning the wounds with soap, with water, the whole thing, it's almost a ritual, almost like a ritual, to clean, to see how the blood drains with the water, when it turns red, to clean the wounds well."

In relation to the effects at the level of thought, it is possible to distinguish the presence of thoughts of guilt associated with the actions of self-harm performed and the harm that this may cause to loved ones. On the other hand, it is possible to visualize the presence of self-harm at the level of thought, which arises persistently during the duration of the experience of emotional instability.

"I would cut myself [and] I would say 'I'm sorry, I'm sorry', because I was asking.... Why was it a sorry? Because it was... I already had the decision not to continue."

"Why [does this happen] to me, damn, 'I'm a failure, I'm a mistake, I'm never going to be fit to live in this world'."

Finally, it is possible to observe in the effects at sensory level, the emergence of a sensation that is experienced and described as being in a dream (Figure 7.13). This effect arises after the first signs of emotional

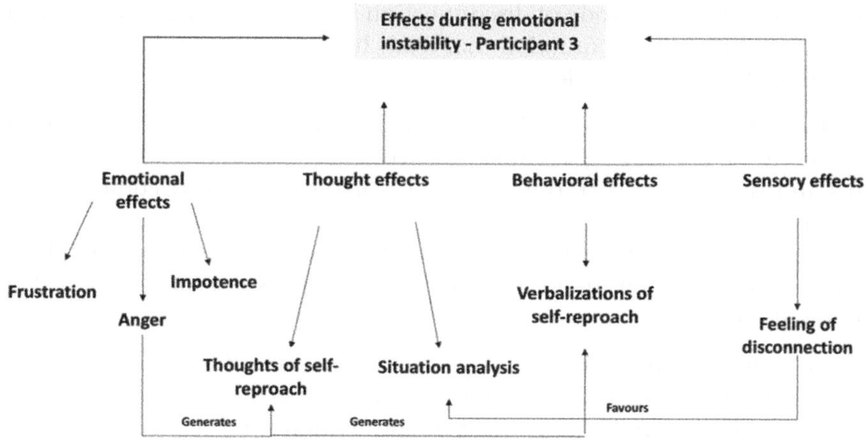

Figure 7.13 Specific synchronous analysis—Participant N°3.

instability are presented, showing a sensation of unreality, visualizing the world as a foreign space and there is an alteration in their perception at sensory level.

"It was like being in a dream, like a feeling of unreality, that what was happening was not happening, in fact, the view was different, the whole world seemed alien to me, everything seemed alien to me."

In this experience, it is possible to observe the development of effects at the emotional, thinking, behavioral and sensory levels, which are part of the experience of emotional instability. From the emotional level, emotions such as frustration at the moment of making a mistake, anger toward oneself, which is linked to thoughts of self-reproach and verbalizations of self-reproach, and finally, the feeling of helplessness at not being able to do anything about his personal situation are observed:

Frustration, anger, like:

> Oh, no, I'm not even good for that, I mean, for something as simple as remembering the keys, I'm a fool, how can I forget those things, things always go wrong for me, everything goes wrong, I shouldn't have existed, I'd better die, if in the end everything is already wrong.

"This time it was a form of helplessness, of anger, of, I don't have, I can't do anything."

Regarding the effects present at the level of thought, the development of thoughts of self-reproach for his mistakes at a personal level can be appreciated, as well as the development of an analysis of situations, an action that arises after an episode of disconnection sensation during an episode of emotional instability, a situation that leads him to reflect on his individual situation at an emotional level.

"I do everything wrong, it's like remembering another certain time I wanted to do something, it came out wrong, or the times I've tried to do this and they don't work out for me, it's like all that stuff comes in the moment."

"I start to analyze from the outside, that's like, it would be like what happens to me a little bit, that gives the feeling that it's not me that's in that moment there."

From the behavioral level, it is possible to observe the presence of self-reproach verbalizations, which are present during episodes of emotional instability. These are characterized by the tendency to take responsibility in an emphatic and drastic manner for their mistakes, developing a set of verbalizations with a clear focus on self-punishment.

"And the thoughts that I was having, I was also verbalizing them, and like, it's like I was reproaching myself for those things, like I was blaming myself that I have the fault for everything."

Finally, it is possible to observe at the sensory level, the development of a feeling of disconnection, which is described by the participant as a questioning as to whether what was experienced corresponds to reality, subsequently generating the development of a set of analyses at the level of thought regarding what happened at the emotional level (Figure 7.14).

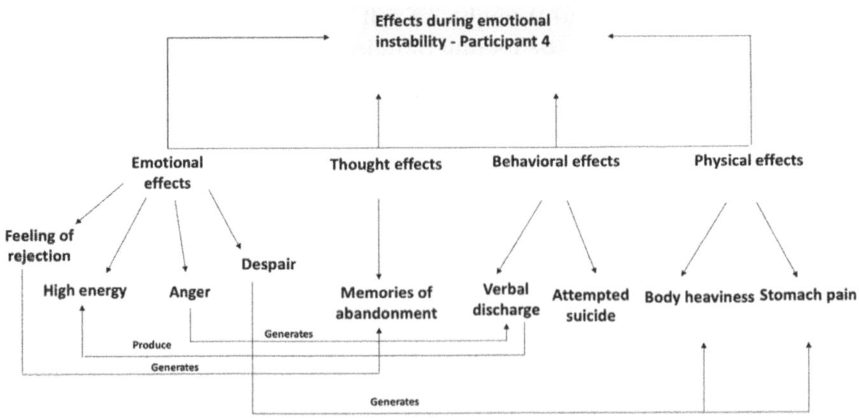

Figure 7.14 Specific synchronic analysis—Participant 4.

"At times it's like it doesn't seem to be happening, it seems like, like the situation isn't real."

"I'm like in a trance, like assimilating if it's true or not, if maybe I'm exaggerating, maybe it's not so much."

In the present experience, it is possible to distinguish the emergence of effects at the emotional, thought, behavioral and physical levels, which are mutually related during the course of the experience. From the emotional level, it is possible to refer to the presence of feelings of rejection, which are associated with the experience of abandonment by the ex-partner. This feeling gives way to the development of personal memories in which she has been abandoned before. It is also possible to observe the emergence of a great feeling of energy, which is associated with the development of verbal discharge actions, and it is also possible to observe feelings of anger and hopelessness, which will lead to specific behavioral and physical effects, respectively.

"I felt betrayed, I felt rejected and I felt like I was cheated, like I thought we were on the same page and in reality we weren't."

"I feel like a lot of energy, so it's like I have a lot of strength, so like I don't know, a feeling, it's weird, because in the moment, I feel like I have the power to be able to say whatever I want."

"Anger, I think mostly anger that he wasn't being honest with me."

"I'm not going to be able to live with so much grief, so if I can't live with so much grief and this grief is never going to go away better not to continue, it was like for me it was like the logical thing to do, it was like there was no other solution."

At the level of thought it is possible to observe an effect associated with the development of memories of situations in which he has been previously abandoned. The contact with these experiences on a personal level increases the sensation of emotional discomfort during the episode of instability experienced.

"You start to relive abandonment as a girl, so it's like that feeling all over again, it's like it's super difficult to describe the emotions and make them concrete."

From the behavioral level, two effects can be distinguished, which are associated with the development of a verbal discharge action toward the ex-partner, as a result of the feeling of rage associated with abandonment, generating a high feeling of energy at the emotional level. It is also observed the development of a suicide attempt through the consumption of medication, this decision is carried out due to the high emotional discomfort presented by the participant, as an alternative to stop her suffering due to the high level of hopelessness observed.

"I unloaded, like verbally everything I had to say, but it didn't relieve me, it wasn't a relief, it just kind of intensified everything" (Participant N°4, lines 166–167).

"I feel like a lot of energy, so it's like I have a lot of strength, so like I don't know, a feeling, it's weird, because in the moment, so like I feel like I have the power to be able to say whatever I want."

"I took some pills that I had saved, because at that point they hid the pills from me, that is, I had to take them in front of my mother every day."

Finally, it is possible to observe at the physical level the presence of two sensations which are the effects of a feeling of hopelessness, observed as part of the effects at the emotional level. The first physical effect observed is associated with a feeling of heaviness in the body, which detracts energy from the participant during the experience of emotional instability (Figure 7.15). On the other hand, there is pain at the stomach level, a sensation that has a direct correlation at the emotional level.

"With that feeling of weight in the body, as if it were a feeling of listlessness, of not wanting to continue."

"Pain in the stomach, but it's like gastric pain, as if there were, that is, it makes me want to go to the bathroom."

In the present experience it is possible to distinguish effects at the emotional, mental and physical levels, developing a set of symptoms that represent a loss of control during an episode of emotional instability. From the emotional level, it is possible to distinguish the emergence of feelings

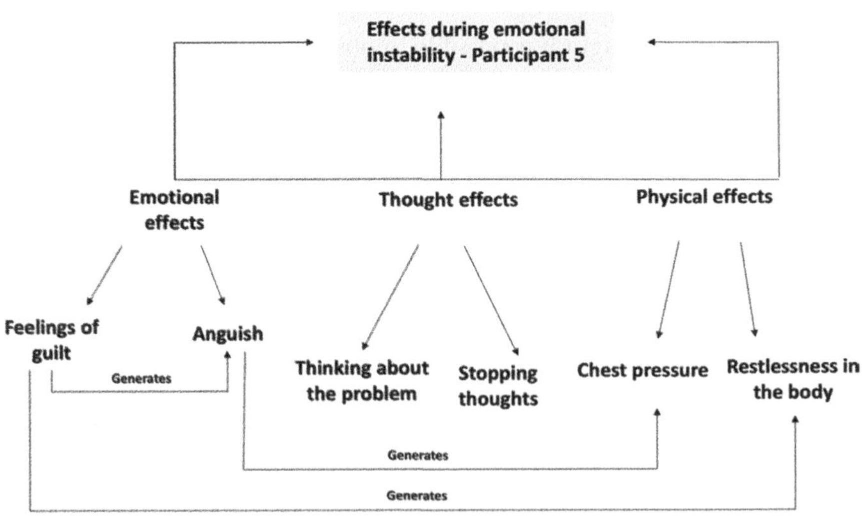

Figure 7.15 Specific synchronic analysis—Participant N°5.

of guilt, which influences the development of a feeling of restlessness at the body level, as well as in the generation of the second effect observed from the emotional level, which is related to the emergence of a feeling of anguish.

"First I feel guilty, I start thinking that he has a partner, that what we are doing is wrong."

"Then I feel my chest tighten and I feel a lot of anguish like in this whole area (points to chest)."

At the level of thinking it is possible to observe two effects which are linked to triggering emotional instability. The first one is associated with the development of thoughts regarding the problem that has generated the present episode, looking for alternative solutions to it and its discomfort. On the other hand, it is possible to distinguish the development of an autonomous action linked to thought stopping, which is used as a way to stop the flow of thoughts about the problem and to carry out concrete actions to solve it.

"My head is still thinking about what to do about this."

"Suddenly you say enough is enough and the thoughts stop, the emotions are paused and you say I have to have a conversation with him."

Finally, it is possible to observe at a physical level the presence of pressure in the chest, which is directly linked to the sensation of anguish presented at an emotional level (Figure 7.16). On the other hand, a feeling of restlessness is observed at the body level, which arises as a result of feelings of guilt previously referred to at the emotional level, a situation that generates discomfort in the participant.

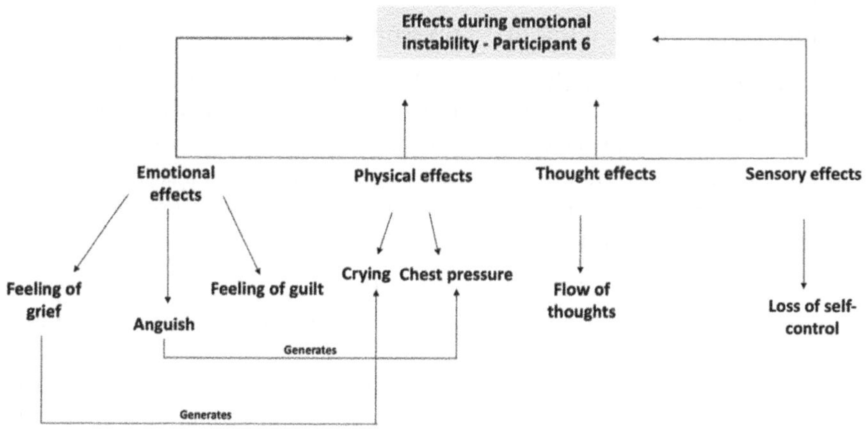

Figure 7.16 Specific synchronic analysis—Participant N°6.

"Then I feel like I'm kind of desperate in my body and I move like this (gestures with hands), then I stop."

"Then I feel my chest tighten and I feel a lot of anguish like in this whole area (points to chest)."

It is possible to observe in the present experience of emotional instability the development of effects at emotional, physical, mental and sensory levels, which show a loss of control in the patient, requiring external support for its regulation at a general level. From the emotional level, it is possible to distinguish the presence of feelings of grief at not having contact with her daughter, as well as anguish in this situation and feelings of guilt regarding her role as a mother. It can be observed that the feeling of anguish will lead to physical effects characterized by a feeling of pressure in the chest.

"As if I could no longer keep my sorrow, I affirm it, with sorrow, you know? [sic], as if I could not remain normal, I had to cry."

"It felt kind of tight, it was like a pressure in the chest, kind of distressing the thing."

"I felt like a bad mom because as a result of not being able to accompany the child to school [and] I felt like a bad mom for not being present in her school year, you know?"

At the physical level, the presence of crying can be observed, which arises as a result of the sensation of grief presented at the emotional level, also observing a feeling of pressure in the chest, which is directly related to the sensation of anguish described above at the emotional level.

"I feel like I kind of exploded, ¿cachai [sic], and I started crying, and cried, cried, cried."

"In the chest."

"It felt kind of tight, it was like a pressure in the chest."

From the level of thought, we can observe the development of a flow of thoughts which are associated with her daughter. On a personal level, they are states referring to how she came to be in such a problematic situation and how she has become emotionally unbalanced in such a significant way. This flow is maintained during a sustained period of time, generating a feeling of emotional discomfort in the participant.

"I was thinking, I was thinking about Emy, and about me, you know? [sic], but I was looking, I don't know, I was like lost, like I was only thinking and I was sitting and I didn't react."

"What led me to this, to feel so bad if one didn't…I went to a graduation, there wasn't, nothing happened to me to feel bad about, I was thinking about that what leads me to like decompensate?"

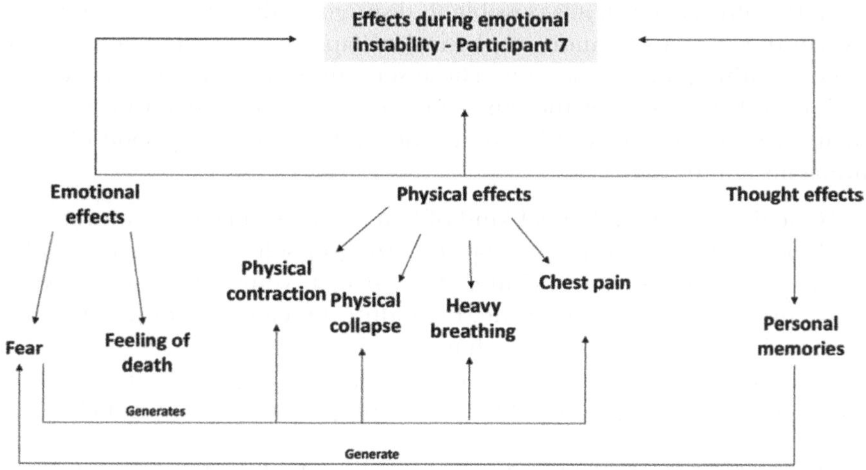

Figure 7.17 Specific synchronous analysis—Participant N°7.

Finally, it is possible to distinguish the presence of an effect at the sensory level characterized by the sensation of loss of control of herself (Figure 7.17). This sensation is described as a distancing from her own corporeality, which allowed her to observe herself externally, as if she were a person alien to herself, a situation that generates strangeness and difficulty in her understanding for the participant.

"As if I were a third person, I don't know if I explain myself, it was, it was the sensation. I didn't feel like I owned myself, you know? [sic] That."

In the present experience it is possible to distinguish the development of effects at the emotional, mental and physical levels, which compromise the general functioning of the participant, evidencing a loss of control during the duration of the experience of emotional instability. From the emotional level, it is possible to distinguish effects associated with the emergence of fear before the emergence of personal memories, associated with the situation experienced, which demarcates a strong fear at a personal level, a situation that is experienced again at that moment. On the other hand, the development of a sensation of death can be appreciated, mainly associated with the set of bodily manifestations that arise as a result of fear at an emotional level.

"I get scared and in my mind I feel like doing like this, but I don't."

"It's really like a feeling of like you're going to die, I don't know, I couldn't stop, I felt like it was going to be infinite."

At the physical level, it is possible to distinguish the emergence of physical contraction, a sensation of physical collapse, the development of agitated breathing and chest pain. These sensations are directly related to a feeling of fear arising at the emotional level, which is linked to personal memories that are revived by the participant during an episode of emotional instability.

"One thing I remember is I kind of had my hands like this, contracted."

"It was very hard for me to stop squeezing myself with my hands and it was hard for me as they told me, 'Now, stretch your hands, stretch your legs', and it was very hard for me, I couldn't, I mean, it's not that I didn't want to, but that I couldn't stretch my hands."

"I felt like I wanted to go to the floor, as I say a collapse, but not that feeling of bending down, but like contracting so much that you fall to the floor."

"Because it becomes difficult for me to breathe like this, but rather my breathing is faster."

"My chest started hurting from breathing really fast, so like… and I felt like my chest hurt, so like I told my psychologist, "my chest hurts, my chest hurts."

Finally, it is possible to identify from the level of thought the development of memories at a personal level, which are associated with the situation experienced by the participant, which generates a feeling of discomfort at an emotional level, representing a moment of tension and fear for the participant (Figure 7.18). These memories motivate the emergence of a feeling of fear, which leads to the development of the physical symptoms described above.

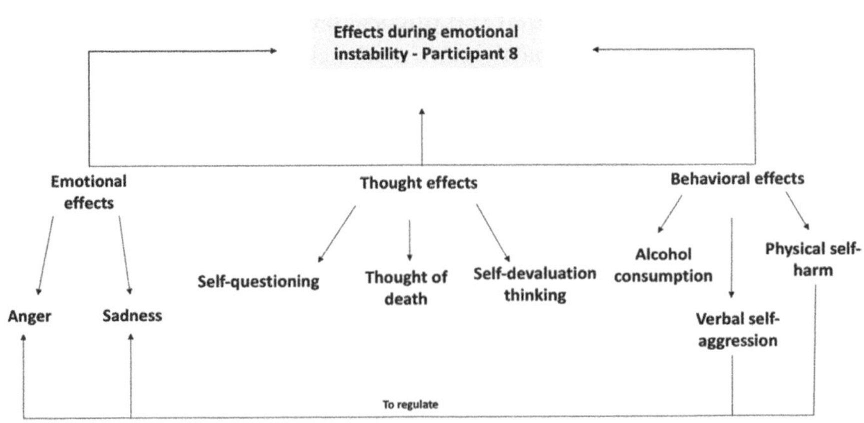

Figure 7.18 Specific synchronous analysis—Participant N°8.

"It came to my mind when I was in the psychiatric clinic [that] there was a girl who once had a crisis and screamed a lot, and hit things and broke things, hit people [so she] had to be injected very harshly with a painkiller."
"Just the one I told you about the little girl who had a crisis."

In the present experience, it is possible to distinguish the development of effects at the emotional, thinking and behavioral levels, elements that lead to a loss of control in the participant. From the emotional level, effects associated with the emergence of anger associated with a dissatisfaction with his own person, as well as with different episodes of his life, can be observed. On the other hand, the emergence of feelings of sadness can be appreciated, which are mainly associated with experiences lived at a family level, as well as episodes of vulneration experienced at an early age.

"At that time, obviously, it was like between grief, anger, I did not know how to distinguish, I felt sometimes that in reality my parents did not care about me or that they did not love me, when it was quite the opposite, also a very internal conflict between what I was and God."
"It was like several emotions, because it was between rage, sadness, anger, dissatisfaction with myself as a person."

From the level of thought, the development of self-questioning regarding his own person and his characteristics is observed, in addition to the emergence of thoughts of death linked to his emotional discomfort. On the other hand, and associated with the observed self-questioning, the development of self-devaluation thoughts is observed, centered on the manifestation of self-harming thoughts linked to his own person.

"I felt like dying, like disappearing, like not being a burden."
"I felt at that time that maybe I was not a good son, that I was not an example either for my siblings, for my nephews, a mixture of things was not what my parents wanted either as a son maybe."

Finally, it is possible to observe at the behavioral level the development of alcohol consumption by the participant, in addition to the presence of manifestations associated with verbal self-aggression, together with self-aggression behaviors at the physical level (Figure 7.19). These manifestations are linked to the regulation of emotional feelings of sadness and anger, focusing on physical pain over emotional pain.

"Then I went to buy alcohol, I drank a lot, I was not aware of how much I had drunk, until later when all this overflow was over, they told me how many bottles it had been."
"Because I started insulting myself, saying I was useless and I shouldn't be there and hitting myself, that."
"On my legs, on my arms or, all of a sudden, I would pull my hair a little bit as if to try to feel the external pain, rather than the internal pain."

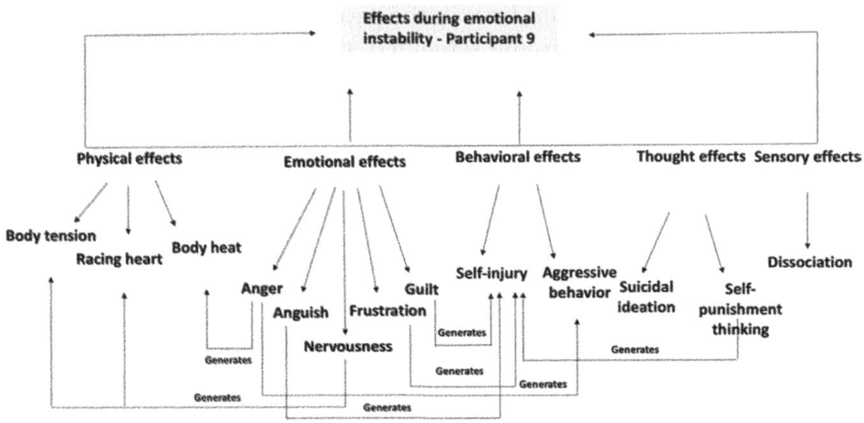

Figure 7.19 Specific synchronous analysis—Participant N°9.

In the present experience of emotional instability, it is possible to distinguish the development of effects at the physical, emotional, behavioral, thought and sensory levels, which are mainly linked to an experience characterized by a loss of control that threatens her emotional, psychological and physical well-being. From the physical level, it is possible to observe the presence of tension at body level and acceleration of their cardiac functioning, both sensations arise as a result of nervousness evidenced at emotional level during an episode of instability. In addition, it is possible to identify the presence of a sensation of heat at the body level, which is associated with a feeling of anger that emerges at the emotional level, which is also related to the personal situation that generated instability.

"As in physical discomfort, uh, I was very nervous, uh, I felt tense, mmm, with the chest kind of tight and my heart was racing."

"It's like a heat, like it's coming, sometimes from that… discomfort in the stomach, like it's tight, like a heat starts to rise up to my face, like a fire is going to come out."

It is possible to observe the emergence of effects at the emotional level, which are linked to the emergence of anger associated with a personal situation, also presenting a feeling of anguish, which produces significant discomfort in the participant. On the other hand, it is also possible to identify the emergence of a feeling of nervousness when exposed to interpersonal situations, as well as the development of a feeling of frustration linked to interpersonal bonding effects, and the emergence of a feeling of guilt linked to actions performed by the participant.

"It was like there that frustration kind of, ah, turns into anger, into rage, and I grab the phone and I throw it at him, or I throw it... I throw it like this, far away."

"Like an anguish in the chest, like all that stuff that comes out, it kind of decants."

"As in physical discomfort, uh, I was very nervous, uh, I felt tense, mmm, chest kind of tight."

"It's just, like, I kind of fall into guilt, like.... why did I allow it to get to that situation?"

The behavioral effects are associated with the development of self-harm in the form of cuts on the wrists as a way to deal with emotional feelings of anguish, frustration and guilt, focusing on physical pain over emotional pain. Also, it can be seen that these behaviors are associated with thoughts of self-punishment present during the development of the experience, demanding the need to articulate this type of actions. On the other hand, it is possible to distinguish the presence of aggressive behavioral manifestations, which arise from feelings of rage at an emotional level, as a result of difficulties experienced at an interpersonal level by the participant.

"And when I got home, uh, I self-injured myself to...like...evade those emotions."

"That's when I took a... like some kind of small knife, and I cut my wrists, I mean, I did cuts on my wrists."

"It turns into anger, into rage, and I grab the phone and throw it at him, or I throw it...I throw it like this, away."

From the level of the effects at the level of thought, the development of suicidal ideation can be appreciated, which is associated with the possibility of ending her life due to the suffering experienced at the emotional level. In addition, the development of thoughts linked to self-punishment emerge, which are associated with the feeling of guilt for actions performed and loss of control, which is experienced as a personal responsibility on the part of the person being evaluated.

"It comes to my mind that I kind of don't want to...I don't want to be there, I don't want to feel that, um, I can't tolerate it."

"I remember very much that it was very much tinged this as a 'decision', in quotation marks, by the feeling of guilt, like I had to be punished."

Finally, it is possible to identify as an effect at the sensory level the presence of a sensation of dissociation on the part of the person being evaluated, which is described as an instant of separation between the mind and the body, generating a differentiated perception at the sensory level (Figure 7.20).

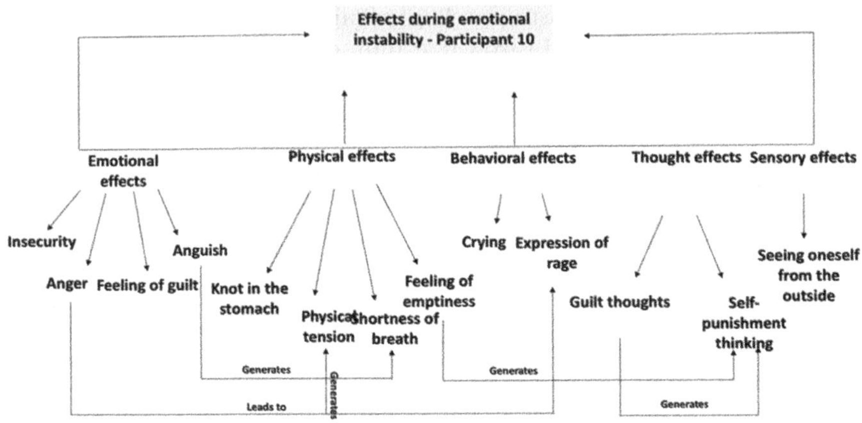

Figure 7.20 Specific synchronous analysis—Participant N°10.

"My mind kind of separates from my body, it dissociates from my body."

"I'm kind of absent, no.... I can no longer follow the conversation, or with the rational thoughts that I was having, but my emotions and my body are no longer attached."

In the present experience of emotional instability, the emergence of effects at the emotional, physical, behavioral, thought and sensory levels can be observed, showing a set of manifestations that generate a loss of control in the participant, requiring external support for her emotional self-regulation. At the emotional level, it is possible to distinguish the emergence of a feeling of insecurity associated with her current relationship with her partner, which arises when she has difficulty with this figure. In addition, it is possible to observe the development of a feeling of anger toward her partner, an emotion that leads to the presence of physical tension and expressions of anger that lead to difficulties at the interpersonal level. Finally, it is also possible to distinguish the emergence of a feeling of guilt, which is associated with actions performed by her, as well as with her emotional instability, observing the emergence of anguish, which leads to shortness of breath in the participant.

"I was watching the movie, so I immediately thought that he might be writing to some girl, because he, I don't know, he is, he is, he is attractive" (Participant N°10, lines 45 to 50).

"It makes me angry. I mean, it makes me angry because I think that, if he's with me, I should be the most important. No, and I don't want to sound self-centered, but, but I should be the important thing at that minute."

"Afterward I regret it, and I also feel that afterward I, like me, I'm to blame for a large part of the matter."

"I start to get anxious because I don't want him to think that I'm like, like I don't know, like acting crazy or something, but, but I start to get anxious because I think that, that maybe we're going to break up, that I'm not good enough for him."

From the physical level, a feeling of a knot in the stomach can be observed, which is linked to a feeling of anger that has arisen at the emotional level. In addition, it is possible to observe a sensation of physical tension, which is associated with feelings of anger, together with a sensation of shortness of breath, which emerges as a result of feelings of anguish experienced at the emotional level. Lastly, it is possible to observe the emergence of a feeling of emptiness during episodes of emotional instability, a situation that leads her to present thoughts of self-punishment, as a way to regulate this feeling that produces discomfort.

"Like a knot, like a knot in my stomach, like... it's hard for me to identify it, like I don't know, it's like what I feel."

"And like feeling tense, like really tense, like, like stiff, like really stiff jaw. Uh, I would say it's that, like tense."

"I feel a little bit like I'm, like I'm short of breath, uh, at times like, like nervous."

"Like a hole in the stomach."

Regarding the behavioral level, the development of crying as a result of discomfort experienced at an emotional level by the participant can be observed, as well as the expression of anger, which arises from a high sensation presented at an emotional level, emerging as a need for expression.

"I sat on the floor and lit a, a cigarette [sighs]. I cried and that was it. I mean, for a good time."

"That's when I got a little excited. I screamed, uh, I felt like I got really red with rage, I imagine, I don't know, uh, I cried, uh."

Regarding the effects at the level of thought, it is possible to observe the emergence of thoughts of guilt, which are associated with a sense of responsibility based on their own actions and functioning at the emotional level. Linked to these thoughts, the development of self-punishment thoughts is associated, which are also linked to the feeling of emptiness described above, and the possibility of self-punishment arises as an option to regulate this feeling.

"It's pure thoughts like guilt or, or, or, like thoughts that I actually put together a whole, a theme, a show, a bit like I'm the one who always does everything."

"Some part of me like punishing myself too or, or, or, or seeing that I'm doing it wrong, like I'm not getting things right."

Finally, from the sensory level, it is possible to observe an effect associated with the possibility of seeing oneself from the outside, a situation that is described with surprise by the person evaluated, indicating that this phenomenon generates a certain sensation at a physical level, characterized by tingling in the body, not being able to give a clear explanation regarding this sensation at a sensory level.

"I don't know how to explain it well in words, but it's like, like, as if I could see myself from the outside, no, I don't know how to explain it well, but, but it's like a very strange physical sensation, like a tingling."

"It was something like, I don't know, uh, like seeing me from the outside, like, like being there but not being there. I don't know if I'm explaining myself well."

General Analysis

Based on specific synchronic analyses, it is possible to refer to the general development of effects during an episode of emotional instability, which emerge at the emotional, physical, behavioral, thinking and sensory levels, producing a significant alteration at the level of functioning in the participants of this research. It is possible to distinguish that the effects observed from the emotional level are linked to the development of feelings such as anguish, anger, feelings of guilt and hopelessness, which show a correlation at the physical level, perceptible and reportable by each participant.

Effects such as body tension, increased heartbeat, physical sensation of emptiness, pain in the chest and stomach can be distinguished from the physical level, being these effects regularly associated to sensations developed at an emotional level, which allows participants to clearly identify changes in their general functioning. This symptomatology produces significant alterations in their individual functioning, requiring in many experiences support to achieve effective self-regulation.

From the behavioral level, the development of expressions of rage that entail aggression, behaviors linked to physical and verbal self-aggression, as well as the presence of crying during the development of emotional instability are observed. These effects present a direct relationship with sensations at the emotional level observed, as well as with effects at the level of thought, presenting a usefulness in the regulation of emotions and thoughts, being these practices instrumentalized from a perspective of self-regulation strategies.

It is possible to distinguish as effects at the level of thought the emergence of thoughts of guilt, thoughts of self-punishment, personal memories that are re-experienced during the development of an episode of emotional instability, as well as mental strategies that allow self-regulation at the emotional and thinking level. In general terms, the maintained thoughts compromise the development of specific actions at behavioral level, which may represent risk behaviors such as self-injury at physical level, being also related to observed emotional effects.

Finally, from the sensory level it is possible to identify the development of an episode that is described as dissociation, separation of mind and body, or externalized perception of one's own body. This sensation produces strangeness in the persons evaluated and occurs regularly during episodes of emotional instability, with similar characteristics in its development, marking a sensory change at the physical level and in the stimuli perceived by the participants.

GENERIC DIACHRONIC STRUCTURE

The results obtained show a detailed description of the characteristic moments of the episode of emotional instability, which is linked to micro-moments that represent a loss of control with the presence of various effects at the emotional, physical, thought, behavioral and sensory levels. The following is a graphic linked to a generic diachronic structure and its respective description (Figure 7.21).

It is possible to distinguish at a general level the development of **six differentiated phases** in the observed experiences of emotional instability, highlighting the beginning of a trigger of emotional instability, which is regularly linked to interpersonal relational difficulties or a set of actions performed by the participants, which produces a high level of frustration.

In **phase 1**, the first sensations of emotional instability appear, which are mainly associated with physical and emotional sensations, which describe an alteration in the particular functioning of the persons evaluated.

Phase 2 shows the emergence of physical, emotional, behavioral, thought and sensory effects, distinguishing sensations such as anguish, anger, guilt, thoughts and behaviors of self-harm, as well as a separation between mind and body, described as a state of unreality.

As a result of the sensations described above, there is a loss of emotional control on the part of the participants, resulting in the emergence of **phase 3**, a moment in which a need arises centered on the search for and development of actions that favor emotional regulation, in view of the significant discomfort experienced.

In **phase 4** it is possible to observe the development of actions to achieve emotional regulation, being mainly actions such as requesting external support, taking medications that favor emotional regulation or the use of

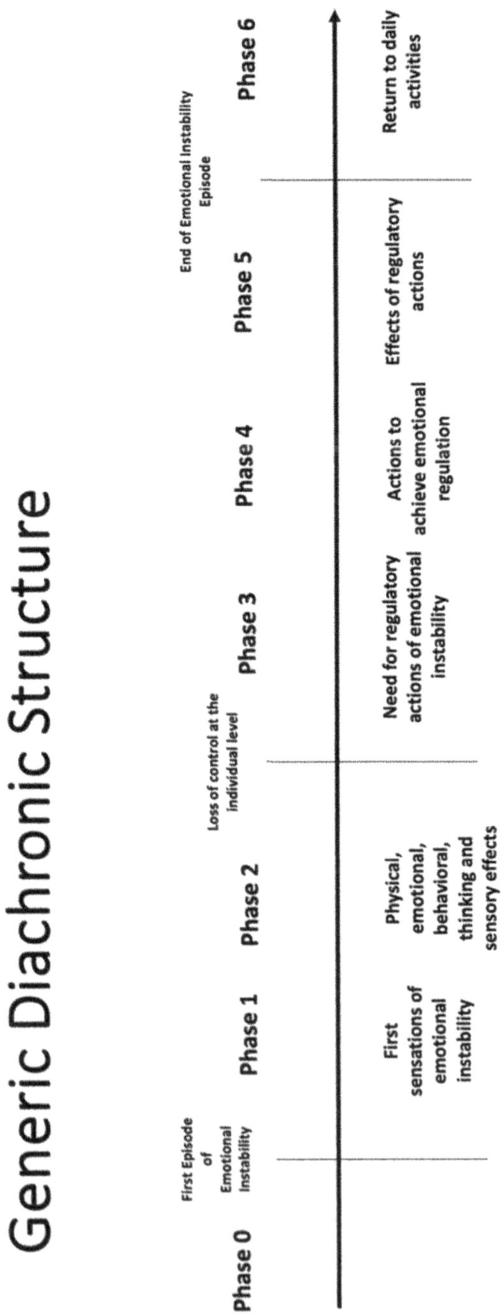

Figure 7.21 Generic diachronic structure.

thinking strategies that allow self-regulation at an emotional level by the participants.

It can be observed in **phase 5** the effects that arise in participants, as a result of regulation actions developed. These effects are linked to a feeling of physical relaxation and flow of thought, tranquility and calm at an emotional level, achieving later in **phase 6** to resume daily activities from an experience of emotional stability, product of actions performed at an individual level.

GENERIC DYNAMIC LINES

This section describes the development of effects observed at the emotional, physical, behavioral, thinking and sensory levels in different phases organized in a diachronic structure, involving the development of dynamic lines that describe in detail the temporal presence of specific effects in each participant.

The general organization of this section compromises the development of these generic dynamic lines:

- Generic dynamic line—Emotional effects on experiences
- Generic dynamic line—Physical effects on experiences
- Generic dynamic line—Thinking effects on experiences
- Generic dynamic line—Behavioral effects on experiences
- Generic dynamic line—Sensory effects on experiences

The following are the results obtained in the generic dynamic lines as part of the exploration of experiences of emotional instability (Figure 7.22).

In the present graph, it is possible to observe the presence of varied effects at the emotional level, during experiences of emotional instability explored. In general terms, a distribution in **phases 1, 2** and **5** of experiences at a general level can be seen, appreciating in **phase 1** the emergence of sensations such as despair, frustration, fright, insecurity, sadness and nervousness, which are directly related to triggers of emotional instability, constituting the first emotional sensations at an experiential level.

As for what was observed in **phase 2**, the emotional effects characterized constitute an evolution of the first effects of emotional instability observed, marking an instant in which a loss of control occurs in participants, in view of the significant symptomatology evidenced during the experiences explored.

With respect to the emotional effects observed in **phase 5**, these respond to the development of actions that favor the regulation of emotional instability, giving rise to sensations such as tranquility, emotional relief, calm,

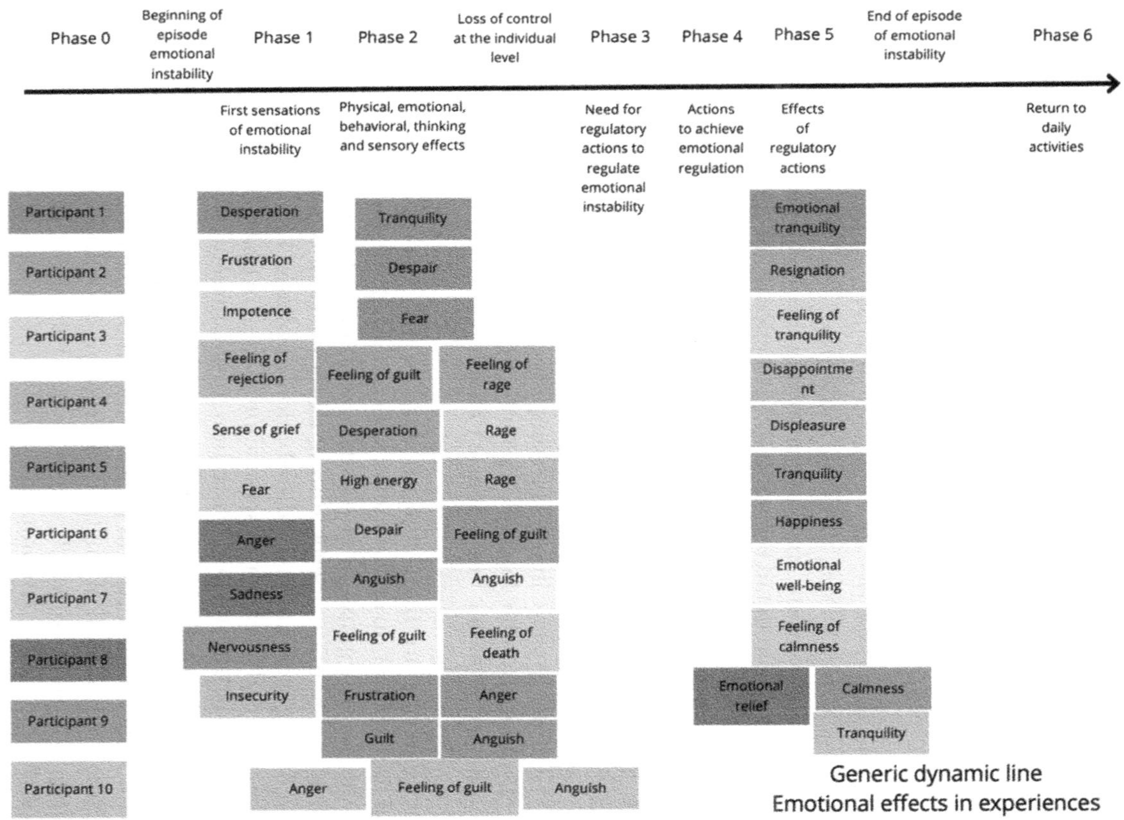

Figure 7.22 Generic dynamic line—Effects at the emotional level.

happiness and in one of the experiences a feeling of disappointment and displeasure, which is related to the failure in the suicide attempt presented.

Regarding to the emotional effects observed, it is possible to identify that in **phase 2** the set of emotions most representative of experiences of emotional instability fully emerges, constituting a critical moment at an experiential level, which significantly marks a loss of control at an individual level (Figure 7.23).

It is possible to observe in this graph a distribution of physical effects observed in the different experiences of emotional instability, which are mainly appreciated during the development of **phases 1, 2** and **5**, distinguishing an evolution in the experiential flow of physical manifestations. In **phase 1** it is possible to identify as first physical sensations the development of manifestations such as pressure in the chest, physical collapse, body tension and a feeling of a knot in the stomach. Although the present experiences are only observable in five participants, it is identified that first sensations are also directly related to physical correlates distinguishable by participants.

Regarding to what was observed in **phase 2**, it is possible to identify a more representative presence of physical effects in the observed experiences, distinguishing effects such as paralysis at body level, physical fatigue, stomach pain, pressure in the chest, agitated breathing, physical tension at general level and sensation of emptiness at physical level. In the present phase it is possible to observe that the flow of physical effects develops in an extensive and significant way for all the participants, constituting a moment in which the present physical experiences develop in a more significant way.

Finally, it is possible to observe in **phase 5** the development of effects at the physical level, which arise as a result of emotional regulation actions developed by participants. In eight of the visualized experiences, it is possible to distinguish the emergence of physical effects such as tranquility at the physical level, body relaxation, physical exhaustion, decrease of physical tension and sensation of well-being at the physical level. The present moment marks a set of physical signs that allow participants to distinguish the return to a state of emotional stability (Figure 7.24).

In the graph above, it is possible to observe a distribution of effects at the level of thought, which emerge from the triggering situation of the episode of emotional instability. The present distribution is associated with the development of thought effects in **phases 1, 2, 3, 3, 4 and 5**, being constitutive as a general part of the experience at a synchronic and diachronic level. In **phase 1**, it can be observed the emergence of effects at the level of thought in two cases, such as memories of abandonment experienced and memories of personal character, which favor the development of emotional instability characteristic of the observed experiences.

With regard to what was observed in **phase 2**, the presence of effects at the level of thoughts such as thoughts of guilt, suicidal ideation, thoughts

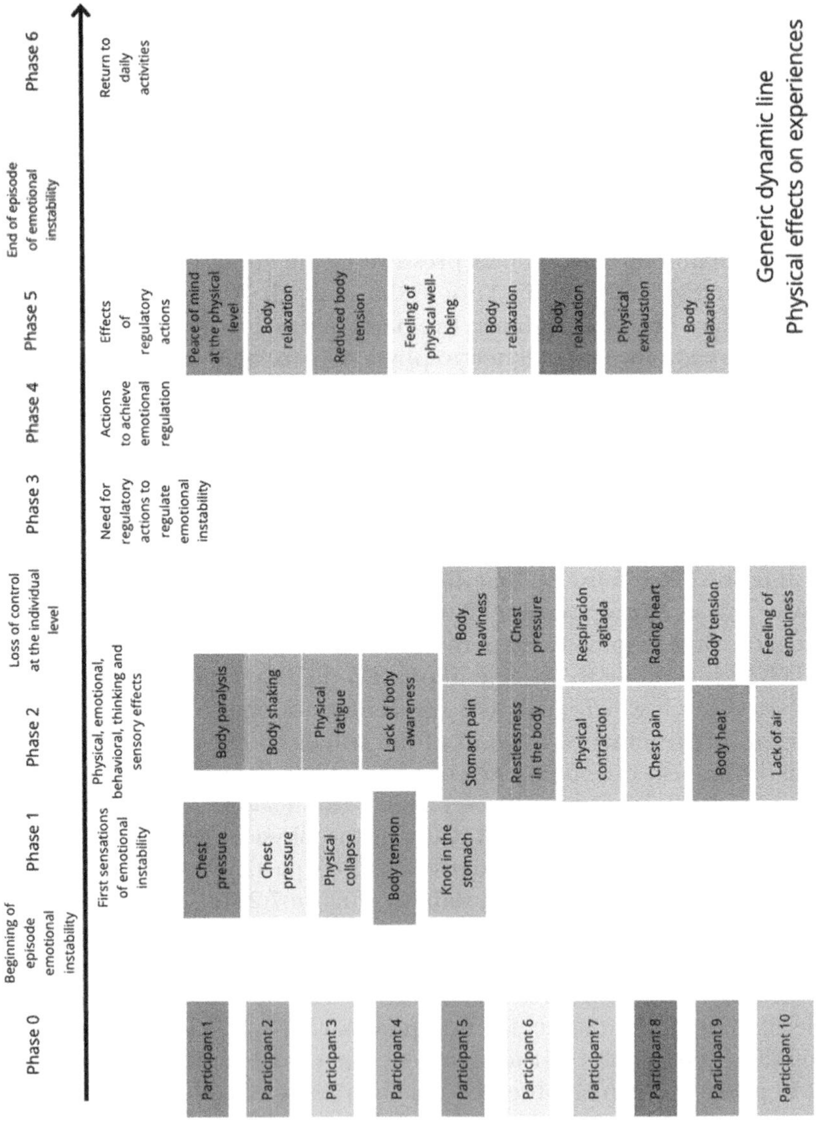

Figure 7.23 Generic dynamic line—Effects at the physical level.

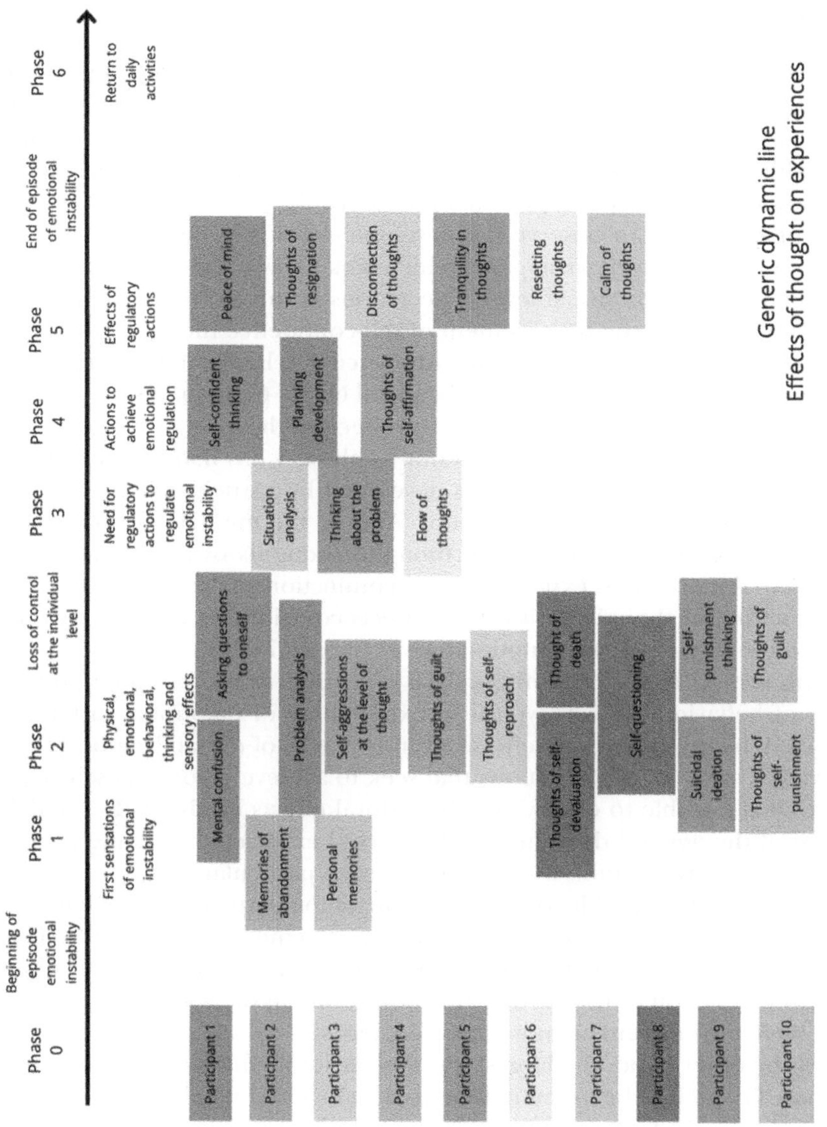

Figure 7.24 Generic dynamic line—Effects at the level of thought.

of self-punishment, self-harm at the level of thought, mental confusion and analysis of the problems presented can be indicated. These effects constitute the central moment in which a loss of control at the individual level is constituted, presenting together with effects at the emotional, behavioral, sensory and physical levels.

In **phase 3**, it is possible to observe the development of thoughts by three participants, which are linked to the possibility of developing actions or reflecting on the problems experienced, in order to reach a possible solution that favors greater emotional stability. The observed effects are associated with the development of situation analysis, thinking about problems and flow of thoughts about personal problems.

In **phase 4**, we can observe the development of specific actions at the level of thought by two participants, which seek to favor the return to a state of stability at the emotional level. The actions at the level of thought executed are linked to the development of self-confidence thoughts, development of individual planning and maintenance of self-affirmation thoughts, which seek to favor a new emotional control by the participants.

Finally, in **phase 5** we can observe the effects at the level of thought that the development of actions carried out in phase 4 has had, which can be mental practices or specific actions developed by participants in order to return to a state of emotional stability. Among the mental effects are the return to calmness at the level of thought, thoughts of resignation with respect to the problems experienced, disconnection at the level of thought and resetting of thoughts, with these effects contributing to the return to normal functioning at the emotional level (Figure 7.25).

With respect to the present graph, it is possible to refer to the development of behavioral effects typical of experiences of emotional instability observed, being the present effects a direct action of destabilization at the individual level, as well as actions that seek to achieve emotional self-regulation. It is possible to observe the behavioral effects in **phases 1, 2 and 4**, as part of the general distribution of observed experiences, distinguishing differentiated associations associated with each particular phase.

In **phase 1**, it is possible to observe in one of the participants a behavioral manifestation that represents the beginning of emotional instability. This is characterized by the development of destruction of objects, as part of an aggressive reaction by the participant at the moment of having experienced a problematic moment at an interpersonal level.

On the other hand, the largest set of behavioral effects can be observed in **phase 2**, which is the moment that marks a loss of control by participants. Some of the effects observed in the present phase are associated with the development of crying as a manifestation of anguish, self-injury as physical punishment, verbalizations of self-reproach, verbal discharge, alcohol consumption, verbal self-aggression and expression of rage through the

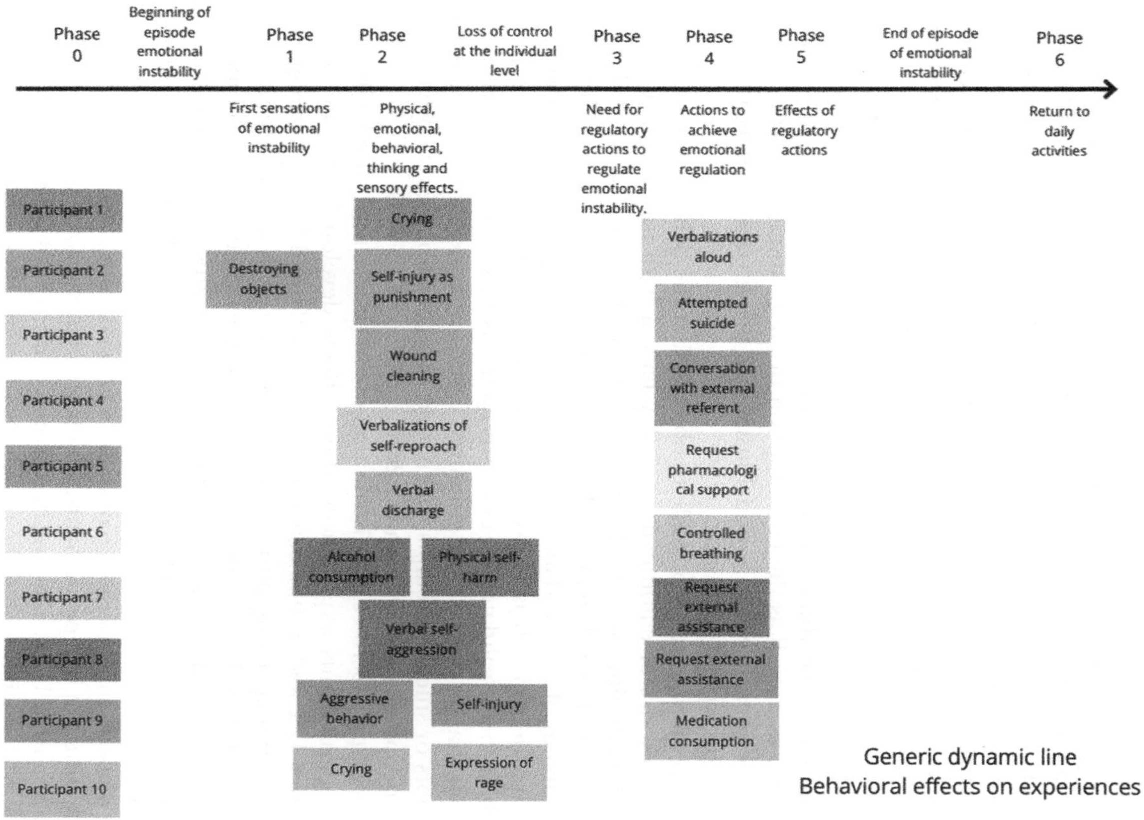

Figure 7.25 Generic dynamic line—Effects at the level of Behavior.

development of aggressive behaviors. These manifestations have a high impact on participants, leading to a subsequent loss of control in their emotional self-regulation, as well as in their interpersonal relationships, resulting in risk behaviors that may lead to the development of significant damage.

Finally, in **phase 4** it is possible to observe the development of actions that favor self-regulation at the emotional level. It is possible to distinguish in eight participants the development of individual practices, as well as the request for external support, presenting a regulating effect from the emotional level, being at the same time identified as practices that generate a state of well-being at the individual level. Among the actions developed are the development of verbalizations aloud, a suicide attempt—which seeks to stop emotional discomfort—, conversation or request for support to external referents—which develop practices of emotional support—, performing controlled breathing exercises—which favor emotional and physical regulation—, as well as the consumption of medications that arise as support in the presence of emotional instability, being consumed as an emergency in this type of situations.

In general terms, it is possible to observe that the behaviors maintained during episodes of emotional instability have a high impact on the individual functioning of the affected persons, leading to a social and daily maladjustment, which may result in risk behaviors that make possible the development of serious damage to the physical and psychological integrity of the participants. It is important to point out that many of these practices have been validated as effective methods of emotional self-control, methods that, in some of the visualized cases, are associated with self-harm behaviors or suicide attempts, a situation that compromises the well-being of the people evaluated (Figure 7.26).

This graph describes the distribution of effects at sensory level, observed in the participants experiences, these effects develop in a general way in **phases 1, 2 and 5**, not being able to be explained by the participants, emerging unexpectedly and generating a feeling of strangeness in them. In **phase 1**, it is possible to observe in one of the participants the development of the sensation of being in a dream, which generates the referred strangeness, not being able to attribute the emergence of this in any particular situation.

In **phase 2**, the emergence of sensory effects of emotional instability can be identified in five participants, which are characterized by the sensation of leaving their body, a feeling of disconnection, loss of control of their corporeality, dissociation and the possibility of seeing themselves from the outside. These effects will generate strangeness in the participants, in addition to providing an attribution to the high emotional impact of the emotional episode experienced.

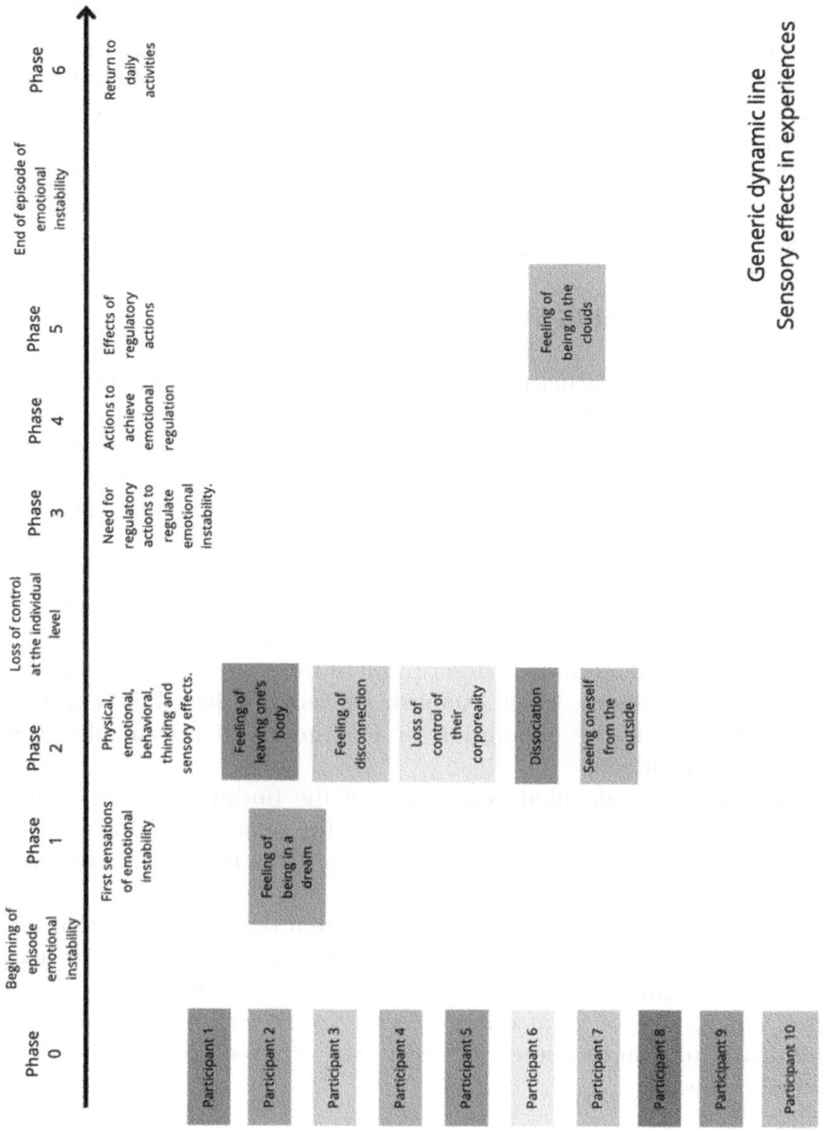

Figure 7.26 Generic dynamic line—Effects at sensory level.

Finally, in **phase 5** it is possible to observe in one of the experiences of emotional instability the presence of a situation that arises once a medication that serves as support and emotional regulator has been consumed, arising a the sensation of being in the clouds as a state of reverie and physical and emotional tranquility in the participant, a situation that marks the achievement of emotional stability.

It is important to mention that the present manifestations do not have a detailed understanding that allows identifying their respective emergence, which is why there is a need for a more in-depth exploration of this phenomenon in this population, being able to distinguish in greater detail its presentation and association with episodes of emotional instability described in this research.

GENERIC SYNCHRONIC STRUCTURE

This section develops a structure that synthesizes in general lines the results obtained from the analytical process linked to synchronic elements associated with experiences of emotional instability. The results to be delivered involve the articulation of a graphic representation and a description of the elements found in the totality of the experiences, demarcating a general analysis of elements of experiential content (Figure 7.27).

The present graph exposes the effects that emerge in experiences of emotional instability in the different cases explored, leading to a detailed description of the effects at the emotional, physical, thought, behavioral and sensory levels. In addition, a description of the respective relationships that these effects present, which establish a direct link based on a certain influence that favors the generation or emergence of certain observed effects, is also included.

The following is a detailed description of the findings that characterize the generic synchronic structure, defining the relational characteristics observed between different effects that emerge from the episode of emotional instability.

In the experiences it is possible to observe that the effects found at the emotional level are associated with the development of feelings of fear, hopelessness, anguish, anger, feelings of guilt, despair, frustration, helplessness, emergence of great energy, feelings of rejection, sadness, feelings of death, nervousness and insecurity. The observed relationships are described below:

- A direct relationship is observed between the experience of fear and physical tension present in participants, a situation that allows the identification of a clear correlation between emotional and physical effects.

Figure 7.27 Generic Synchronous Structure—Effects of emotional instability.

- The feeling of hopelessness generates in some of the participants a sensation of bodily heaviness, which translates as a feeling of weight in the extremities or trunk.
- It is possible to distinguish that the feeling of distress compromises the development of a physical sensation associated with a feeling of pressure in the chest, again showing a close link between emotional manifestations and physical correlates of participants. As a complement, it is observed that the feeling of distress generates a physical sensation of shortness of breath, which has a direct impact on the physical functioning of participants.
- The sensation of rage generates diverse manifestations at the behavioral level, distinguishing the development of physical self-injury as personal punishment, verbalizations of self-reproach, verbal discharge and aggressive reactions. A physical sensation of heat is also observed, which is directly associated with the emergence of rage at the emotional level.
- The presence of guilt feelings is directly associated with the emergence of emotional distress, as well as with the emergence of behaviors related to physical self-harm, characterized by the development of self-injury as a way to achieve effective emotional self-regulation.
- As for the sensation of despair, it can be seen that the present one is directly related to the physical sensation of restlessness at a bodily level.
- Regarding the feeling of frustration, it can be seen that the present one is directly linked to the development of physical self-injurious behaviors, which arise as a way to obtain an effective emotional regulation.
- It is not possible to observe a direct relationship between the emotional effect of impotence and manifestations or effects observed in other areas.
- The feeling of great energy emerges as an effect of the development of verbal discharge action, which is performed as an action of aggression that emerges from the feeling of rage evidenced by participants.
- As for the feeling of rejection, there are no direct relationships with other dimensions or effects observed in the different areas.
- Regarding the emotional sensation of sadness, this is linked to three behavioral effects observed. These are associated with the presence of crying as a representation of the sadness experienced. On the other hand, it is possible to distinguish that those evaluated consider the development of physical and verbal self-aggression behaviors as strategies to regulate the feeling of

sadness, constituting a set of practices that emerge autonomously in participants.

- In relation to the emotional effect of the sensation of death, it is not possible to distinguish any type of relationship with other effects observed in experiences.
- The feeling of nervousness at the emotional level directly influences the shaping of the feeling of physical tension, observed in the physical effects of participants.
- Finally, the feeling of insecurity is not associated with any observable effect on other associated categories.

In relation to the effects at the physical level, it is possible to distinguish the presence of sensations or manifestations associated with body paralysis, pressure in the chest, body trembling, physical tiredness, lack of awareness of corporeality, stomach pain, heaviness at the body level, restlessness in the body, feeling of a knot in the stomach, physical tension, feeling short of breath, feeling of emptiness, agitated breathing and chest pain. The following is a description of the relationships observable from the analysis carried out:

- As for the sensation of bodily paralysis, although the present one emerges as a representative element in some experiences, a direct relationship with other effects of explored experiences is not observed.
- The feeling of pressure in the chest emerges directly from the emotional sensation of distress, which generates significant discomfort in participants.
- The body tremor evidenced is not linked to any manifestation observed in any of the distinguished effects.
- The sensation of physical fatigue emerges directly once emotional self-regulation strategies have been articulated; however, it does not have a direct relationship with other effects observed in experiences.
- The effect of lack of awareness of corporeality responds to a loss of contact with one's own body, a sensation that mainly characterizes one of the observed experiences. No effects associated with this sensation are distinguished.
- Regarding the presence of stomach pain, it is possible to associate the present sensation to the emotional effect of hopelessness, which in turn generates a feeling of heaviness in the body.
- The effect of restlessness at the corporal level is directly associated with the sensation of desperation experienced at the emotional level, and a clear physical-emotional correlation can be distinguished in experiences.

- The physical sensation of a knot in the stomach is not directly related to any type of effect observed in participants.
- The effect of physical tension emerges directly from the sensation of fear, as well as from the nervousness evidenced in the participants during experiences of emotional instability.
- The sensation of shortness of breath emerges directly from the sensation of distress observed at the emotional level. This physical sensation increases the feeling of discomfort and loss of control in participants.
- The physical sensation of emptiness is not associated with any type of effect observed in the experiences explored; however, it is described in some of the experiences as a physical sensation that generates permanent discomfort.
- The agitated breathing arises as a result of an emotional sensation of fear experienced. This sensation marks the influence of previous memories or experiences associated with emotional instability, which may directly influence the physical functioning of participants.
- Finally, the sensation of chest pain is directly related to the sensation of fear present at the emotional level. This shows the strong influence of past experiences on the physical and emotional stability of participants.

From the behavioral level, the effects observed in participants of the present research are linked to the presence of self-injury such as punishment, destroying objects, cleaning wounds, verbalizations of self-reproach, verbal discharge, suicide attempts, alcohol consumption, physical self-injury, crying, physical and verbal expression of rage and verbal self-injury. The relationships between the present effects and manifestations observed in other categories are described below:

- As for the development of self-injury as a punishment practice, these emerge directly from self-punishment thoughts present in participants, as well as from the influence of the emotional sensation of rage. This allows us to distinguish that self-harm behaviors are strongly influenced by elements at the level of thought and emotion.
- Destroying objects is related to feelings of rage, representing a manifestation characterized by a low capacity for emotional and behavioral self-regulation, observed in participants.
- The cleaning of wounds is a ritualistic practice, which arises after self-injuries performed as a punishment. This practice is related to the development of self-injury, visualizing the emergence of blood as a regulating effect at a physical and emotional level.

- The verbalizations of self-reproach are directly related to the emotional effect of self-directed anger. The present practice aims to achieve a regulation of emotional discomfort that arises from the sensation described above.
- Verbal discharge is a behavior linked to the development of verbal hetero-aggressions, which have a liberating effect on participants. It is observed that the present ones emerge directly from feelings of rage, being verbal discharge behaviors useful forms for the regulation of such emotional feeling.
- Suicide attempts are directly linked to suicidal thoughts present in thought-level effects. These practices arise as a regulating effect at the emotional level, being destined to two purposes: To constitute conspicuous practices by way of requesting external support, or to stop the emotional suffering, attempting against their own life.
- Alcohol consumption emerges as an emotional regulation practice, which emerges as an emotional self-regulation strategy that provides a relaxation effect on participants. This practice is associated with emotional effects of anguish, sadness and feelings of guilt.
- Physical self-injury is associated with the set of self-injurious practices that arise as self-regulatory practices at the emotional level. It can be seen that these practices arise from feelings of distress evidenced in participants, feelings of rage, feelings of guilt and feelings of frustration observed.
- The emergence of crying as a behavioral manifestation is directly linked to the feeling of sadness observed in participants.
- The expression of rage is a set of behavioral and verbal manifestations characterized by the development of heteroaggressions, which emerge as a trigger of the emotional sensation of rage, which cannot be effectively regulated.
- Finally, verbal self-harm emerges as a practice aimed at achieving regulation of emotional feelings of anger and sadness. The present relationship allows us to identify again the direct relationship of self-aggressive behaviors as recurrent emotional self-regulation strategies in participants.

From the level of the effects observed at the level of thought, it is possible to distinguish a varied set of manifestations, which are associated with the presence of mental confusion, the development of an analysis of personal problems, asking oneself questions about personal problems, thoughts of self-reproach, analysis of personal situations, memories of experienced abandonment, thought arrest, thoughts about problems, thoughts of guilt, flow of thoughts that emerge from emotional instability, personal memories that generate emotional discomfort, self-questioning, thoughts of death, thoughts of self-devaluation, suicidal ideation and thoughts of self-punishment. It is possible to distinguish in general terms that the effects at the level of thought are associated with three elements specific to the observed experiences:

1. They constitute a set of strategies that favor emotional self-regulation (analysis of personal problems, asking questions to oneself, analysis of personal situations).
2. They contribute to the development of specific behavioral practices linked to physical or verbal self-harm (thoughts of self-reproach, self-questioning, thoughts of self-devaluation, thoughts of guilt, thoughts of death, suicidal ideation and thoughts of self-punishment).
3. They are directly associated with the reminiscence of an experience that produces emotional discomfort (memories of experienced abandonment, flows of thoughts that emerge from emotional instability and personal memories that generate emotional discomfort).

Based on the evidence, it is possible to distinguish that the effects at the level of thinking directly influence the emotional and behavioral development of observed participants.

Finally, regarding the emergence of effects at the sensory level, it is possible to distinguish the emergence of the sensation of leaving one's body, the sensation of being in a dream, the sensation of disconnection, loss of control of oneself, dissociation and the possibility of seeing oneself from outside of one's body. The present effects produce confusion in participants and demarcate a key moment of the experiences, which is marked by the presence of an important emotional instability, constituting the present sensations an instant of loss of control and important confusion at a mental level.

Summary of the Results of the Microphenomenological Interview

In the development of the micro-phenomenological interview, it is possible to distinguish in a precise way elements characteristic of the course and content of an experience of emotional instability in participants of the present study, a situation that groups a set of effects and phases as constitutive elements of the observed experiences. It is possible to realize that the experience of emotional instability in people with BPD is characterized by the presence of intense sensations and alterations at the emotional, physical, sensory, thinking and behavioral levels, effects that contribute to a loss of control in the course of the particular experience, demarcating a key moment in the experiential development of emotional instability.

In the development of the present experiences of emotional instability, the need arises on the part of participants to achieve emotional self-regulation, in order to regain stability and control, a situation that implies the use of various strategies, among which are the consideration of thinking strategies, pharmacological support, self-injurious practices or requesting support from external referents. The use of certain self-regulation strategies will depend on the set of skills or resources developed by each participant at a particular level, being appreciated as distinctive elements the development of this type of practices, which sometimes have a ritualistic value, based on their continuous repetition and automatic sequence of actions before every event of emotional instability experienced.

With respect to the effects observed at the emotional level, it can be highlighted that during the experience of emotional instability, manifestations arise that produce intense discomfort and represent a set of sensations that are intolerable for participants, in response to which they resort to practices that favor their respective regulation. Some of the practices observed are associated with the development of hetero- and self-aggressive behaviors, representing an important risk factor for their physical, psychological and emotional well-being.

In relation to the physical area, the effects show intense experiences at the corporal level, characterized by sensations of pain, discomfort or alterations that have direct repercussions on the individual functioning or stability of the persons evaluated. It is possible to identify a direct relationship between manifestations at the emotional level and physical effects observed, responding to clear manifestations at the psychophysiological level, which consistently accompany the experiences of emotional instability, observing an important capacity to identify and connect with physical sensations on the part of the participants.

From the behavioral level, a set of behaviors maintained by the participants can be appreciated, which arise as a direct response to sensations of physical and emotional discomfort, as well as to specific thoughts maintained during the development of the experience of instability. The present behavioral manifestations imply the execution of self- and hetero-aggressive behaviors, which arise as regulating behaviors at the emotional level, constituting their practice a form of effective self-regulation in the reduction of suffering at the emotional, physical and thought levels. On the other hand, the observed behaviors are associated with persistent thinking, linked to the need to be punished for their actions, a situation that leads to self-harming practices in order to respond to the set of ideas that arise obsessively.

At the level of thought, it is possible to distinguish the development of thoughts that arise automatically, which are linked to self-punishment or feelings of guilt, which in most cases leads to the development of verbalizations of self-reproach or self-injurious behaviors as a way to correspond directly to the present ideas of self-harm. A useful resolution is associated with the possibilities that the use of thinking strategies observed in the participants favor emotional self-regulation, appreciating that practices such as the search and analysis of situations and the suspension of thoughts have a direct impact on the articulation of emotional stability. However, the present strategies emerge in participants who already have significant psychotherapeutic support, integrating this type of thinking as part of their self-care resources.

From the sensory level, striking effects can be distinguished, which generate a feeling of strangeness in participants, distinguishing their emergence in moments of high emotional instability. Experiences related to dissociation, depersonalization or derealization emerge as characteristic elements of an important part of the lived experiences, a situation that implies the need to develop a greater exploration, in order to identify in a practical sense, the functionality of the present alterations, favoring a greater understanding of the emergence of sensory alterations in people with BPD, in view of their distinctive character during episodes of emotional instability.

It is central to make a synthesis that allows to clearly identify the main findings, establishing a synchronic-diachronic organization of the experiential elements. For this purpose, an integrative graph is developed that groups elements of organization in phases typical of generic diachronic structure and elements of experiential content typical of generic synchronic structure. The following is a graph that allows an integrative visualization of the main findings (Figure 7.28).

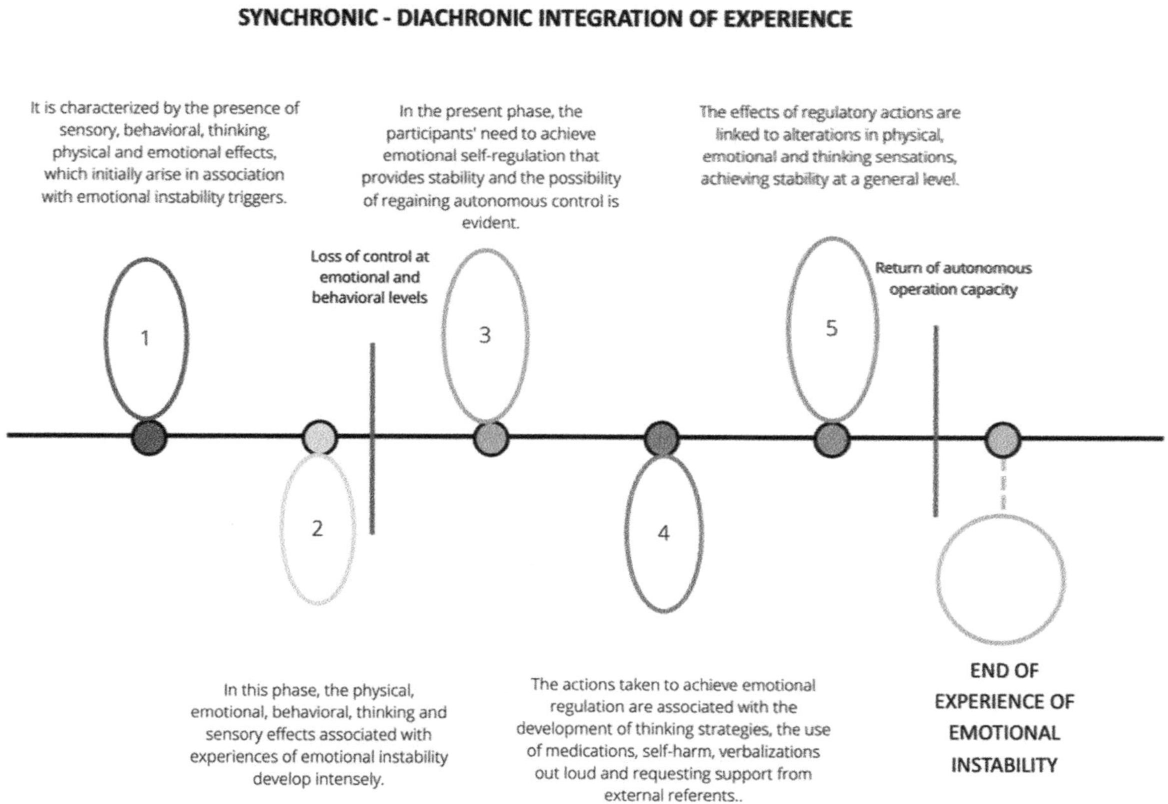

Figure 7.28 Integration of synchronic and diachronic structure of experiences of emotional instability.

CHAPTER 8

A STEP FURTHER IN THE UNDERSTANDING OF SUBJECTIVITY. THE INTEGRATION BETWEEN INTERPRETATIVE PHENOMENOLOGICAL ANALYSIS AND MICROPHENOMENOLOGICAL ANALYSIS

The present chapter represents a significant methodological challenge, since it contemplates an integrative exercise based on the results found in two types of phenomenological and hermeneutic explorations, which to date have not been combined in the state of the art associated with the understanding of particular experience. The development of the present integration seeks to respect the theoretical approaches of authors such as Martin Heidegger, Edmund Husserl, Maurice Merleau-Ponty, Paul Ricoeur, Hans-Georg Gadamer and Francisco Varela, synthesized in the experiential exploration proposals developed by Jonathan Smith and Mike Osborn (IPA [Interpretative Phenomenological Analysis]) and Claire Petitmengin

Phenomenological-Hermeneutical Approach to Borderline Personality Disorder, pages 151–160

doi:10.1108/978-1-80592-281-020251008

(microphenomenological interview). The present approaches have distinctive approaches based on phenomenology and hermeneutics (IPA) and the prereflexive exploration of experience from phenomenology (microphenomenological interview), favoring the development of an integrative perspective of experience from prereflexive, reflexive and linguistic dimensions.

In order to achieve an integrative exercise that provides clarity regarding the experiential flow that characterizes the experience of borderline personality disorder (BPD), it is necessary to initially plot the findings obtained in each exploratory phase, since both consider a differentiated perspective based on a general understanding of the experience associated with BPD (IPA) and a detailed understanding at a synchronic and diachronic level of a characteristic element at the experiential level (microphenomenological interview).

The exposition of two graphs that synthesize the findings obtained from the application of IPA and microphenomenological interview is shown, developing a brief descriptive exercise of the present results. Subsequently, an integrative exercise will be carried out in a visual and descriptive way of the results obtained, in order to have an integral perspective of the particular experience of people with BPD (Figure 8.1).

IPA RESULTS

The results of IPA are associated with the development of 5 superordinate themes, which are associated with the life experiences of 10 people with BPD, showing the development of these elements, which constitute an experiential representation that influences at the identity, social, emotional, cognitive and behavioral levels.

Superordinate theme 1: Types of particular thoughts.

Subtopics: Catastrophic thoughts, different perception of reality, perception of reality in limits.

The present experiences are associated with the development of beliefs or cognitive constructions that accompany the particular experience of the participants, which are associated with the maintenance of a thought characterized by the interpretation of a catastrophic future where events may occur that affect their own physical or emotional integrity. A differentiated perception of reality is also distinguished, characterized by the development of interpretations of a highly intimate and particular character, a situation that significantly influences their own self-definition as well as the adequacy of activities or interpersonal relationships at a daily level. On the other hand, the reality perceived in limits exposes participants to a dichotomous perception of their significant figures and daily events, establishing a classification of their experiences in negative or positive polarities.

Figure 8.1 Summary of IPA results.

Superordinate theme 2: Unstable personal relationships and experiences of vulneration.

Subthemes: Instability in couple relationships, feeling strange and different from others, dependence in couple relationships, early vulnerations.

It is possible to observe the maintenance of unstable relationships at the interpersonal level, which are characterized by a strong dependence on significant figures, which implies a continuous demand for attention toward them, a situation that makes it difficult to maintain stability at the romantic relationship level. This is linked to the continuous perception of incomprehension and lack of support that they perceive at the social level, a situation that is directly associated with BPD, in view of the fact that they do not regularly lack spaces of understanding or effective support for their particular suffering. Finally, in aspects related to their vital development, the participants have experienced instances of physical and emotional vulnerability from an early age, a situation that has contributed to the formation of unstable relational patterns, as well as in the development of severe psychopathological manifestations at the individual level, such as emotional and behavioral alterations, identifying that such violations may have a direct relationship with the subsequent development of this personality disorder.

Superordinate theme 3: Unstable emotions at the individual and relational level.

Subtopics: Anger, feelings of guilt and frustration, feelings of emptiness, emotional instability.

The presence of unstable emotions at the individual and relational level is a continuum at the experiential level and a significant element of their daily experience, an aspect that is described as a cornerstone and representative of the experience with BPD. The emergence of anger is appreciated as a characteristic emotion in the present emotional instability, which is mainly directed toward his own person, as well as in manifestations of heteroaggressive character, identifying that the present emotion arises as a representation of a high level of frustration before the nonsatisfaction of bonding needs, as well as a form of self-reproach for his own identity and behaviors, continuously presenting associated feelings of guilt. Feelings of emptiness emerge as a manifestation at emotional, cognitive and physical levels, characterized by the emergence of an important feeling of anguish associated with this experience, which leads to the need to establish strategies that favor self-regulation of this feeling at individual level. Emotional instability was explored in detail in the development of the microphenomenological interview.

Superordinate theme 4: Intense emotion-seeking and self-punishment.

Subthemes: Self-harm, self-sabotage, risk behaviors, need for self-punishment, continuous need for stimuli, impulsive decisions.

It can be seen that participants present an inclination to the continuous search for instances that generate adrenaline and intense stimuli as a way to achieve a sense of well-being, as well as a strategy to regulate the discomfort experienced at an emotional level, considering that these experiences provide a sense of temporary well-being. As significant elements in the present superordinate theme, it is important to refer to the presence of a continuous perception of the need to be punished, which emerges as a set of automatic thoughts that condition actions related to self-harm and self-sabotage. These behaviors present an intentionality based on the need to achieve emotional self-regulation, as well as to satisfy the persistent ideas of being punished.

Superordinate theme 5: Knowing your diagnosis and receiving mental health care.

Subtopics: Experience of being diagnosed, experiences in mental health care.

Regarding personal experiences associated with receiving the diagnosis of BPD, the participants indicate an experience characterized by a sense of tranquility, in view of the fact that through this diagnosis they have been able to explain characteristics of their own functioning, identifying elements of BPD that give meaning to their individual characteristics. On the other hand, some participants have considered that the diagnosis of BPD represents a tragic situation, since the present disorder constitutes a condemnation based on the impossibility of personal development, as well as the difficulty of achieving a sense of fullness and well-being at the emotional level or in their interpersonal relationships.

Regarding the mental health care received, favorable experiences can be appreciated, which have favored a better understanding of their own symptomatology and individual characteristics, as well as the development of emotional self-regulation strategies. On the other hand, experiences categorized as negative by the participants can be appreciated, indicating having received care from professionals with little professional preparation, as well as with a low empathic capacity or abilities to establish a human bond at a therapeutic level, highlighting the need to have therapists who present an adequate update in knowledge associated with this disorder, as well as empathic qualities that favor the therapeutic relationship (Figure 8.2).

RESULTS OF THE MICROPHENOMENOLOGICAL INTERVIEW

In the development of experiences of emotional instability explored from the development of microphenomenological interviews, it is possible to identify the appearance of **five distinct phases**, which synthesize elements at the diachronic and synchronic level of the experiences. **Phase 1** is associated with the emergence of the first feelings of instability in participants, which are directly related to triggers that generate a break in their emotional functioning, appreciating the emergence of experiential effects at sensory, behavioral, thinking, physical and emotional levels, marking the beginning of the episode of emotional instability.

In **phase 2**, it is possible to observe the development of emotional instability effects, showing that effects observed in the behavioral, emotional, physical, thinking and sensory areas develop with greater intensity and

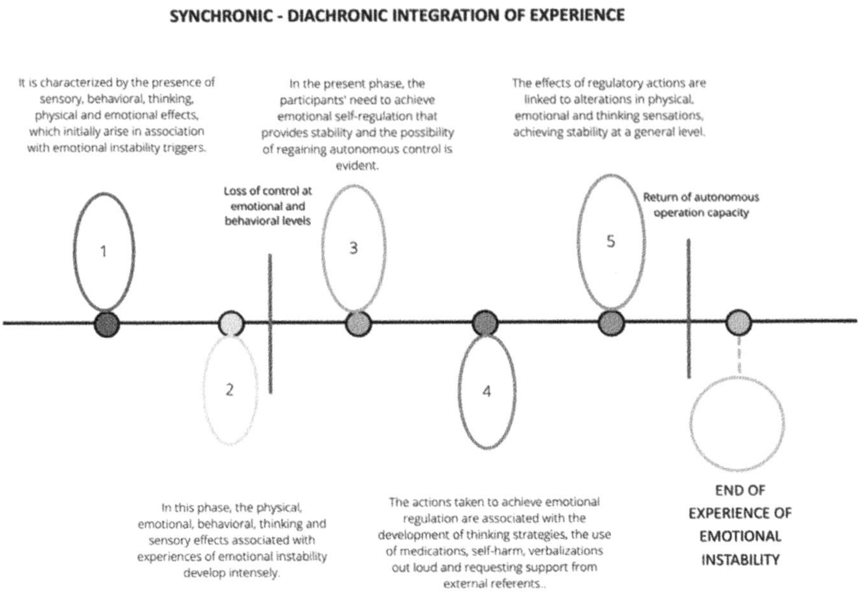

Figure 8.2 Integration of synchronic and diachronic structure of experiences of emotional instability.

show a loss of control at the emotional and behavioral level in the participants, with this phase being identified as a key moment in which it is possible to distinguish the impact that the effects described above have on the individual development of those being evaluated.

Regarding **phase 3**, it is possible to distinguish the emergence of the need to achieve emotional regulation in view of the loss of control experienced in the face of emotional instability. In the present phase, possibilities of emotional self-regulation begin to be distinguished, which favor the resolution of the trigger experienced, as well as the resumption of daily activities in an autonomous manner.

In **phase 4**, it is possible to observe the development of actions that favor emotional regulation, which are associated with the execution of thinking strategies, consumption of drugs, development of self-harm at a physical level, verbalizations aloud based on the course of actions to be executed and the request for support from external referents, who develop actions of physical and emotional containment. The present phase is striking, in order to clearly identify the strategies used by the participants in the development of emotional self-regulation, identifying elements that can be very useful in the strengthening or support at a psychotherapeutic level.

Finally, in **phase 5** it is possible to distinguish the effects of the regulatory actions performed, identifying the emergence of alterations at the physical, emotional and thinking levels, which favors the return to emotional stability, autonomous control of emotions and behaviors, as well as the return to daily activities, marking the end of the episode of emotional instability. The identification of effects present in participants allows identifying the effectiveness of the self-regulation practices implemented, which favors the visualization of the resources of the people evaluated to adapt to experiences that show instability and loss of emotional and behavioral control.

Integration of Results

For the development of this section, we propose the design of an integrative graph that synthesizes the results obtained in IPA and microphenomenological interview. Afterward, we will develop a description of the main findings that compose the representative elements of experiences with BPD from a phenomenological and hermeneutic dimension (Figure 8.3).

This graph integrates results obtained from a general perspective based on the experiences of people with BPD. By conducting an experiential exploration, central elements of the observed experiences are perceived, obtaining relevant information in different areas related to the present psychopathology. The main findings point to the emergence of **five central themes** associated with the presence of a particular type of thinking, characterized by the presence of a differentiated perception of reality, which leads to frequent difficulties at the individual and interpersonal level. The above is also observable within the central themes at the experiential level, being characteristic the tendency to present a catastrophic vision of the future or of possible new events, in addition to a very differentiated perception of reality based on very particular interpretations of events experienced from a particularity that often cannot be understood externally. That is, the perception of a reality in limits based on the continuous tendency to idealize or devalue its most significant links.

It is also important to highlight the presence of **unstable personal relationships** and **experiences of vulneration**, elements that demarcate a significant part of the observed experiences, which have been constituted by continuous difficulties at the interpersonal level, as well as the experience of early vulnerations, which have influenced according to the experiences of the participants in the subsequent conformation of the present disorder. It is also important to highlight the general perception of feeling strange and different from others, a situation that shows that the experience with BPD is marked by a sense of social isolation, characterized by the feeling of incomprehension and social prejudice.

Another relevant theme is associated with the **search for intense emotions** and the **tendency for self-punishment**, aspects that are directly related

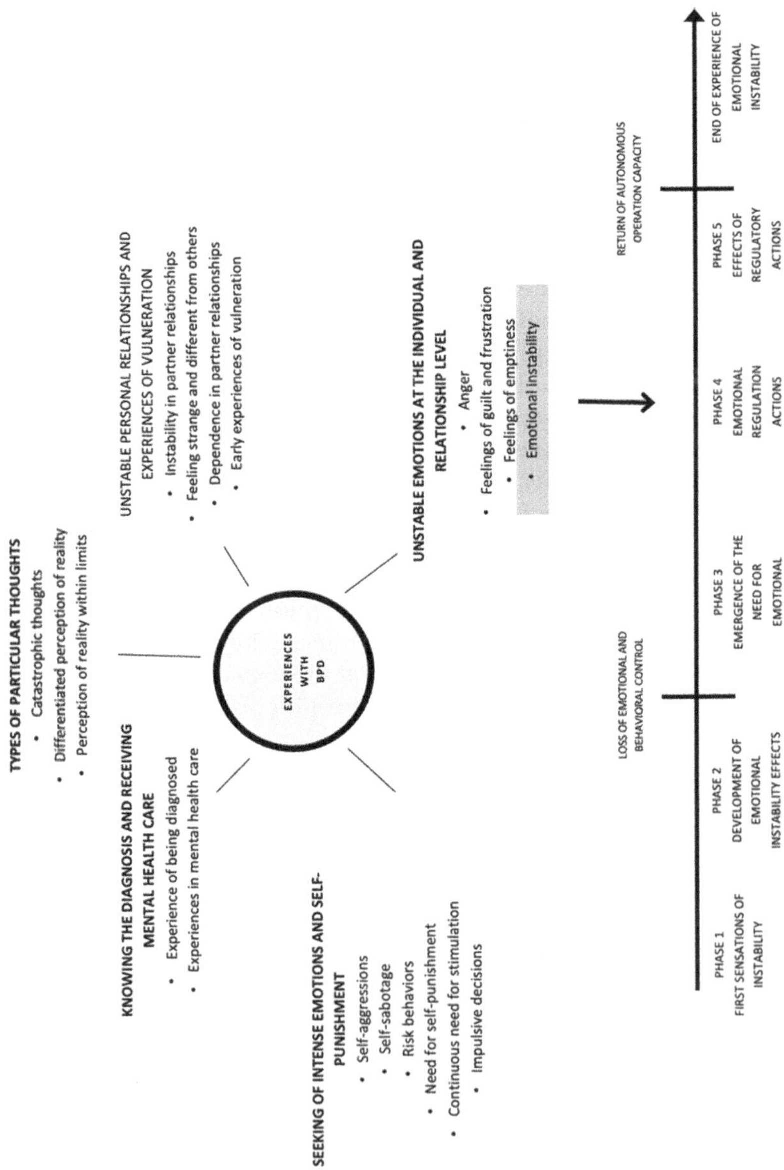

Figure 8.3 Integration of IPA results and microphenomenological interviews.

to the daily experience of BPD, establishing a relationship characterized by the presence of obsessive thinking, associated with the need to self-punish themselves for their actions and the development of ritualistic practices, associated with the development of practices of both physical and psychological self-harm, being able to appreciate that self-harm arises based on three central elements: As a need for self-punishment; as an emotional regulator; as a way of ending one's own life.

The search for intense emotions is associated with the presence of a continuous need to present stimuli that generate adrenaline, which translates into a feeling of emotional well-being, managing to forget daily problems and emotional suffering experienced, noting that in most cases, when this period of search for stimuli and experience of adrenaline ends, thoughts and feelings of guilt arise, commonly associated with self-punishment practices mentioned above.

It is also important to highlight the set of experiences associated with **knowing the diagnosis and having mental health care**, elements that refer to the fact that the experience of being diagnosed has had in some cases a positive attribution, since it provides greater clarity regarding personal characteristics and the possibility of receiving therapeutic support.

On the other hand, a catastrophic experience can also be appreciated, since the present diagnosis is experienced by a certain group of participants as a sentence or an experience that will mark a significant suffering at the individual and family level. At the moment of receiving psychotherapeutic support, the observed experiences are varied, since a certain group of participants highly value the support perceived at the psychotherapeutic and psychiatric level, referring to the important contribution that this represents in the acquisition of greater stability at the personal level.

However, another group of participants report negative experiences at the time of receiving mental health care, which have been characterized by a lack of knowledge at the professional level regarding BPD, as well as the lack of personal resources to achieve a favorable therapeutic link.

Finally, it is important to highlight the **presence of unstable emotions at the individual and relational level**, which is characterized by the regular presence of feelings of anger, guilt, frustration and a sense of emptiness that emerges both physically, cognitively and emotionally. These are emotions that fluctuate continuously, marking an experience of emotional instability, an element that marks a central part of the experience with BPD, implying a significant alteration that influences functioning at the individual level. It is from the identification of emotional instability, as a central element in the development of the present experiences, that a microphenomenological analysis of one episode of emotional instability in participants is developed, obtaining results that structure contents at a synchronic and diachronic level.

The microphenomenological analysis of episodes of emotional instability is demarcated in general terms by the development of five phases, which are linked to the emergence of emotional instability with effects at the physical, emotional, thinking, behavioral and sensory levels, a situation that involves a loss of control and autonomous functioning. In addition, it is possible to visualize the development of strategies that favor self-regulation at the emotional level and the subsequent possibility of regaining autonomy and control, constituting new ways of thinking, verbalizations, substance use, request for external support or self-harming behaviors.

As central phases of the present analysis, **phase 2** stands out, characterized by being the precise moment in which the physical, emotional, thought, behavioral and sensory effects that characterize emotional instability emerge significantly, represented by a loss of control and autonomy in functioning, constituting an instant that implies a high risk in the development of behaviors, thoughts or emotions that can generate serious damage to the integrity of the participants.

Another central phase to highlight is associated with **phase 4**, moment in which strategies that favor emotional self-regulation and management of its specific effects at an experiential level are articulated, appreciating that the articulation of this set of strategies favors a return to emotional stability and autonomous functioning, a situation that constitutes the end of the episode of emotional instability.

From the development of an integrative work it is possible to distinguish the elements that constitute the main experiences of people with BPD, which are characterized by elements that allow to achieve an understanding of their individual, relational and social bonding experiences, subsequently achieving an exploratory immersion at episodic level, appreciating the main characteristics that accompany the experience of emotional instability in the participants.

CHAPTER 9

TOWARD A HORIZON OF MEANINGS AND COMPREHENSIVE POSSIBILITIES. CONTRIBUTIONS AND CHALLENGES IN THE PHENOMENOLOGICAL HERMENEUTIC APPROACH

In the present study, it has been possible to identify from a hermeneutic phenomenological methodology, the experience of people who present borderline personality disorder (BPD), being an exploration that has favored the obtaining of diverse findings, which establish interesting lines of exploration both at a research and interventional level from the clinical-psychotherapeutic plane. The central findings of the present research can be divided into what has been observed from the general experience with BPD (IPA [Interpretative Phenomenological Analysis] analysis) and the episodic observation of a representative characteristic of the disorder (microphenomenological analysis). Once this differentiation has been made, we will proceed to report the findings of this research.

Phenomenological-Hermeneutical Approach to Borderline Personality Disorder, pages 161–170

doi:10.1108/978-1-80592-281-020251009

From the level of the general experience with BPD, a set of relevant findings point out that the experience with the present disorder, although it offers tranquility and the possibility of achieving greater knowledge, at the moment of being diagnosed it is also experienced as a condition that generates suffering. This means that the experience of BPD is lived intimately in loneliness, contributing to the person perceiving him/herself as someone strange, different from others, who will not be understood by others in his/her particular suffering. This intimate experience is characterized by a very particular system of thoughts, emotions and behaviors, observing from the level of thought, a particular interpretation of reality, which is experienced intensely in extremes of idealization and devaluation of significant figures, this perception of reality leads people with BPD to have a differentiated way of perceiving stimuli and everyday situations, failing to be understood in their particular interpretations.

They are continuously in search of intense emotions and experiences, which generate adrenaline and a sense of well-being, developing a dynamic in which they are regularly exposed to risky behaviors at a physical and emotional level, giving rise to thoughts and feelings of guilt, which have repercussions on the development of self-aggression practices at a physical, verbal and thought level. The behaviors they present are automatically associated with a way of thinking, which emerges continuously in the persons evaluated, associated with the need to be persistently punished, a situation that leads to the articulation of self-injurious practices mentioned above, which they regularly perceive a utilitarian attribution as: strategies of emotional regulation; strategies of self-punishment; possibility of making an attempt against their own life.

At the relational level, they usually present difficulties in interpersonal relationships, especially with significant figures, with whom they present relationships based on a high dependence on care and emotional support. These demands lead to the maintenance of interactions that result in significant damage to their relationship figures, subsequently leading to associated relational breakdowns. At a historical level, they have lived experiences of physical and emotional violation by parental or third-party referents, who have generated serious emotional affections, contributing to the development of early behavioral disorders, which later influence the present personality configuration, based on what has been reported by people with BPD. It is visualized that the present vulnerations are experienced with a high perception of betrayal and generate a high ambiguity in the perception of significant figures, who are seen as not very stable or reliable, a situation that contributes to the development of a generalized perception by external referents as figures with a dichotomous functioning, influencing this in the establishment of polarized relationships.

From the emotional level, it is possible to identify that a continuous emotional instability is maintained, characterized by episodes marked by the experience of effects at the physical, emotional, behavioral, thinking and sensory levels, these effects constituting an instant that marks a loss of control and autonomy in persons with BPD, who are intensely affected by the set of effects indicated. As a central part of an episodic analysis of emotional instability, it has been possible to identify that the described effects constitute a set of manifestations that expose people with BPD to an important instability, emerging strategies that favor emotional self-regulation. These strategies constitute practices at the level of thought, verbalizations, self-injurious practices, intake of medication and request for external support, appreciating the existence of effects at the level of thought, physical and emotional as signs of emotional regulation, before the development of the aforementioned practices.

As significant findings of episodes of emotional instability, we can indicate the existence of self-punishment thoughts that emerge automatically at a cognitive level, which sometimes lead to thoughts of self-harm or self-aggressive behaviors, being characteristic the presence of rage at an emotional level, which is regularly externalized or internalized as self-harm behaviors. From the physical level, physiological alterations emerge that show a loss of body autonomic control, characterized by involuntary physical contraction, physical tension and gastrointestinal problems. The findings associated with effects at the sensory level during episodes of emotional instability are striking, with the emergence of sensations of depersonalization and derealization, experiences that generate a high level of confusion and discomfort in the persons evaluated, being characteristic of their emergence during moments in which a high level of emotional instability is present.

The results obtained have been possible thanks to the articulation of a hermeneutic phenomenological research methodology, which has entailed the challenge of carrying out an integration between two modalities of analysis, which did not have previous integrations, observable from the state of the art. From this perspective, an integrative exercise has been developed, which considers as central the respect for phenomenological traditions of authors such as Martin Heidegger, Edmund Husserl and Maurice Merleau-Ponty, the contributions of hermeneutics of authors such as Hans-Georg Gadamer, Paul Ricoeur and Martin Heidegger, synthesized in the models of analysis proposed by Jonathan Smith, Mike Osborn and Claire Petitmengin.

The methodology considered has been carried out on the basis of a systematic and rigorous structure, which entails a work of theoretical suspension based on the assumptions of phenomenology and an interpretative—not explanatory—exercise based on the contributions of hermeneutics, as traditions that develop a joint contribution to the understanding of the particular experience. The unprejudiced approach proposed in Edmund Husserl's "epoché" articulates a continuous need for the researcher's work, for which the development of a field notebook was very useful for the experiential emptying, in addition to the continuous interaction with other researchers belonging to the phenomenological tradition, facilitating the maintenance of a continuous objectivity and focus on the experience over the a priori theory of the phenomenon.

The structures from which the results of this research have been presented are understandable from a visual and descriptive perspective, developing inputs that allow a clear and detailed reading of the findings and their respective steps in the interpretative process. It is central the articulation of clear strategies at the research level that allow an immersion in the particular experience from the traditions of phenomenology and hermeneutics, which arise from a philosophical universe as a promise of approach and interpretation of phenomena that occur in nature, but that have not exposed in this universe clear or replicable forms of methodological approach at the research level. That is why the present research also sought to clearly expose the main models of hermeneutic phenomenological analysis and how they can be articulated step by step, in order to subsequently make a selection and integration of two modalities of analysis.

The usefulness of implementing this type of methodology in the capture of the particular experience of people with BPD is clear from the perspective that it represents a methodological consideration that exposes the researcher as a relevant figure in the observational process, in that its usefulness lies in the possibility of having a suspension of their prior knowledge, work that involves an important task prior to and during the development of the research process, as a possibility of achieving an approach to the experience as it is lived by the figure of the participant. This situation extends to the fact that phenomenology and hermeneutics are traditions that allow deep levels of analysis, which encompass not only the reflective experience, but also experiences that reside in a prereflective dimension at an existential level. It is from this perspective that the consideration of the present methodology not only resorts to the value of remembering a set of experiences, but also seeks to immerse oneself in the reminiscence of a certain experience at a certain moment, from the possibilities that prereflection offers.

New reflections that arise from the results obtained are associated with the perception of BPD, not only as a psychiatric pathology that generates high emotional and behavioral instability, but also as a profound sense of social isolation and a perception at the experiential level, characterized by the continuous sensation of individual differentiation, an element that complicates the identity definition of people who present this pathology. It is possible to affirm that people with BPD perceive themselves as individuals with significant difficulties, a situation that compromises their self-definition from a perspective of impossibilities and challenges at the individual level, which contributes to the development of an identity perception based on self-reproach and self-sanctification, as governing elements of the personality, leading to the need to provide significant therapeutic support in elements of the constitution of their own identity characteristics.

From the findings it is also possible to establish as a new reflection the identification of emotional self-regulation strategies in people with BPD, which arises as a need based on the existence of resources that allow an effective achievement of stabilization in people with this pathology. However, the present regulatory resources can be beneficial from a perspective based on self-care, as well as representing an important risk factor, since their respective articulation considers a possible transgression of self-injurious character. The need arises for interveners to identify and differentiate the self-regulation strategies present in people with BPD, as a care strategy and perception of emotional regulation alternatives, evident in each participant.

It is also central to establish new reflections regarding elements of emotional instability present in people with BPD, which is regularly considered as a general dimension of manifestation of this disorder, and which has been observed in the present research to represent a deep dimension at the experiential level, which involves the experience of multiple effects at the physical, emotional, thought, behavioral and sensory levels, in addition to specific moments at the experiential level. As an element of the experience with the present disorder, it is central to consider that the criterion of emotional instability entails the need for a deep immersion in the particular experience of each person, in view of the possible effects and manifestations that may arise as representative in their particular experience at a daily level, being a function of the evaluator and clinical intervenor to achieve an approach that favors an approach to the experiential depth of the present manifestation.

Finally, as a new reflection it is possible to establish that the thought system of people with this disorder has particularities that involve not only a particular interpretation of everyday experiences, but also the articulation of cognitive structures based on the negative perception of their own person, associated with an automatic thought regarding the need to be punished on a recurrent basis. From this perspective, it is important to establish the consideration that people with BPD present a link to self-punishment from a cognitive level, as a belief system rooted in their own identity and personality functioning, arising the need to establish interventions that allow to deepen both elements based on cognitive and identity constructs at a psychotherapeutic level, as central elements of the interventions to be carried out.

It is possible to establish a dialog between the results of the present research and the state of the art associated with BPD and its respective diagnostic course. As a significant element found in the present study is the continuous feeling of stigmatization linked to living with BPD, which is consistently experienced in social contexts, as well as in clinical intervention spaces. These elements have also been observed by authors such as Ring and Lawn (2018), Ahmed et al. (2021), Klein et al. (2022), Masland and Null (2022) and among others, who have managed to identify the stigma experienced in people who have been diagnosed with BPD, both socially and in contexts of psychotherapeutic support, counting on several occasions with the support of mental health professionals who show little preparation for addressing this pathology. The present results are consistent with what was observed in this research, in view of the fact that the feeling of being perceived as strange or misunderstood subjects constitutes a form of stigmatization, which can lead to clear difficulties in the approach to care and support systems in mental health, thus hindering integration at the social level in this population.

The changes at the sensory level observed in people with BPD in this research have allowed a clear distinction of the emergence of episodes of derealization and depersonalization, episodes that are experienced with strangeness by those affected, constituting significant moments in the course of this disorder. Authors such as Löffler et al. (2019), Shah et al. (2020), Krause-Utz (2022), Yang et al. (2022) and among others, have reported the relevance of episodes of depersonalization, dissociation and derealization in the present population and how the understanding of these episodes can represent a significant imprint for the treatment models considered in BPD.

The present research has managed to identify how the sensory alterations presented by this population not only produce an alteration that generates strangeness or confusion, but also emerge as systems of protection and self-care in situations that represent a high impact at an emotional level, arising the need to achieve new levels of understanding regarding the experiential complexity associated with the emergence of these episodes in people with BPD.

An element that is always of interest to the researcher is related to the development of self-injury in the present population, achieving in the following research to distinguish three types of motivation associated with them, a finding that provides relevant knowledge that self-injurious behaviors should be understood from their intentionality, not only as a generalizable sign, since they can be instrumentalized in an ideographic way, pursuing a particular logic.

In the literature it is possible to distinguish from authors such as Martino et al. (2020), Colle et al. (2020), Reichl and Kaess (2021) and among others, a relationship between the presence of self-harm practices in people with BPD as manifestations of emotional instability, as well as their respective articulation as strategies of connection with aspects of their own corporeality, which contributes to achieve self-control again. From the understanding appreciated in the state of the art and the results of the present research, it is possible to affirm the complexity of the emergence of self-injurious behaviors in people with BPD, in that their emergence should be explored in a differentiated way in each case, allowing to go beyond a mere behavioral manifestation, being able to distinguish deep attributions to these practices from a particular dimension of meanings.

In direct relation to the above, it has been possible to clearly distinguish in this research the strong link between BPD and actions or thoughts associated with punishment or self-punishment, developing a permanent attribution regarding the need to develop practices that threaten their physical and emotional well-being. Authors such as Berenson et al. (2021) have managed to identify the high sensitivity that people with BPD present in comparison to the population without mental health pathologies, in relation to reward and punishment stimuli, identifying that this high sensitivity predisposes the development of reactions or behaviors of emotional and behavioral hyperactivity to this type of stimuli. These findings are consistent with what was observed in the participants of the present study, who maintain a continuous perception of self-punishment as a representative element at the level of thought, which leads to self-injurious behaviors that generate a sense of tranquility in the participants.

Based on the work of authors such as Kaufman et al. (2020), Choukas-Bradley et al. (2020), Marques-Feixa et al. (2021) and among others, it has been possible to distinguish the presence of various risk behaviors in people with BPD, among which are the development of sexual promiscuity, problematic alcohol and substance use, as well as the development of behaviors that expose this population to risk situations at the physical and emotional level. These results are similar to what was observed in the present research, regarding the relationship between emotional instability observed in people with BPD and risk behaviors, among which are problematic alcohol consumption, sexual promiscuity and impulsive behaviors, showing that these manifestations emerge as an alternative to achieve an effective regulation of their emotional instability and states of discomfort at the individual level, serving as self-regulation strategies that have a counterproductive character in the welfare of the affected persons. A psychotherapeutic challenge will be the recognition of self-regulation strategies present in this population, in order to identify what kind of strategies maintained by patients may involve emotional, psychological and physical damage.

It is possible to observe in the work of various researchers such as Fertuck et al. (2018), Lo Monte and Englebert (2018), Cavicchioli and Maffei

(2021), Dell'Osso et al. (2021) and among others, the presence of differentiated thinking systems in people who present BPD, a situation that leads to various findings among which are: The presence of autistic traits; low social cognition; the form of thinking based on hyporeflexivity and the prevalence of continuous ruminations based on suicidal and uncontrolled thinking.

Furthermore, it is possible to establish a link between the observed research and the results obtained in the present investigation based on the consideration that an important part of the findings of this research are linked to the presence of a particular way of thinking in people with BPD, which imply a very differentiated understanding of social situations, as well as of their own experiences and experiences. The particular type of thinking may be directly associated with the findings described above, constituting a comprehensive complement, which provides clarity as to the elements that make the type of thinking observed in the present population unique.

Authors such as Daros et al. (2018), Daros and Williams (2019) and among others, have explored the emotional self-regulation strategies used by people with BPD, appreciating the use of coping strategies based on the avoidance of situations, such as self-injurious behaviors and a tendency to rumination, appreciating a low level of analysis and reflective capacity in problems of a personal nature.

The present research has complemented the set of self-regulation strategies considered by people with BPD, observing a set of strategies which may constitute a set of beneficial behaviors (thinking about problems, self-verbalization, requesting external support, regulated breathing and consumption of regulating medication). It has also been possible to observe risk behaviors that may affect emotional and physical stability (substance use, self-injurious behaviors). It has been observed that patients who are actively involved in psychotherapeutic processes have greater resources that favor self-regulation in moments characterized by emotional instability and loss of control at the individual level.

As findings of the present research, it is possible to make a differentiating distinction from what has usually been appreciated in the literature, establishing an originality from the plane of experiential exploration and methodological character. At the experiential level, a dialog has been established with research that has provided clarity regarding the characteristic elements of BPD. However, the findings of this research have provided greater depth in aspects such as sense of isolation, particular type of thinking, self-regulation strategies used and their respective usefulness, which is a clear visualization of the sequential effects of emotional instability, being core elements of people with BPD, such as early experiences of physical, emotional and psychological vulnerability. These findings provide clarity as to what marks the experience of BPD in people who have lived the present pathology, as an alternative to achieve favorable psychotherapeutic approaches to individual suffering, carrying out interventions that fully consider the characteristics of the experiences of the present pathology.

From the methodological point of view, an exploration proposal has been established that differs considerably from what is regularly observed in the state of the art, integrating two models of interview and narrative analysis, which consider elements of phenomenological and hermeneutic traditions. A review has been carried out that has sought to develop an access to experience at a prereflexive and reflexive level, following the approaches of authors such as Schleirmacher, Husserl, Heidegger, Gadamer and Merleau-Ponty, and their respective influence on qualitative research methodology.

The present research has been nourished by two forms of approach that had not been integrated before in the state of the art: the joint use of IPA and the micro-phenomenological interview. Both have been very useful in order to respond to the following needs: to achieve an understanding of the experience from a general and micro-experiential perspective; to provide an approach, analysis and reflection articulated on the basis of an organized methodology; and finally, to unite two proposals of approach to the particular experience that have specific traditions from phenomenology and hermeneutics.

The relevance of the present study is given in the lines described above, at the experiential and methodological level, being useful for figures such as researchers and interveners, who will have information regarding lines of intervention in the present pathology, identifying characteristic experiences of BPD that allow the development of intervention proposals tailored to the needs of the present population. From the methodological point of view, the present research provides light on how to conduct research based on the hermeneutic phenomenological methodology, establishing a useful guide for the researcher, as it represents the possibility of replicating future studies based on the exploration of the particular experience, using the present methodology and associated theoretical considerations.

The methodological approach of the present study is novel, considering two approaches that seek to capture the subjective experience from differentiated theoretical and practical approaches, appreciating an articulated integration in phases, which allows a clear replication in future studies on this subject. The benefits of achieving a methodological integration in phenomenology and hermeneutics are associated with the development of approaches that respect both the prereflexive value of the experience and its interpretative possibilities at a linguistic level, favoring from their integration to achieve new approaches to different moments of the subjective experience.

The aim is not only to transmit ways of approaching the particular experience, but also to develop reflections to researchers and therapists regarding the value of alternative approaches that respect the phenomenological and hermeneutic tradition, being a possibility of linking to a new field of study, in which psychiatric pathologies can have a new line of understanding and approach to the experience and constitutive characteristics of their experience, over an explanatory denomination based on the use of a generalist classification.

The results expose a clear challenge for the figure of the intervenor and researcher in the thematic, in terms of the need to achieve a deep immersion in the elements of experiencing, which shows that the establishment of generalizations during the research process may lead to a possible annulment of significant elements in the development of an experiential understanding. The establishment of a process based on the consideration of the subjective experience, as the intervening and investigative axis, allows a differentiated distinction of particular needs, which adjusts the intervening frameworks to the challenge of subjective exploration.

From a psychiatric and psychological perspective, the results of the present study complicate the understanding of the functioning of BPD, in view of the dynamic value presented by the development of the subjective experiences observed in the findings, which expose a general perspective that demarcates a set of central themes from the experiential section, which are developed beyond a definition of an objective nature. On the other hand, it is possible to distinguish that the flow from which a loss of control develops in the present disorder exposes the need to visualize in a differentiated way how the experience of emotional instability, which significantly affects the present population, is produced in detail.

By having detailed results regarding the experience of BPD, it is possible to identify specific moments of the experiential flow that require greater support from interventionists, favoring the identification of personal resources that allow effective self-regulation in affected individuals. This work provides clarity regarding the continuous comprehensive and interventional challenges with the present population, complexifying diagnostic criteria and experienced moments that require important psychotherapeutic and psychopharmacological support.

CHAPTER 10

CONCLUSION

The present hermeneutic phenomenological research has allowed a deep and nuanced understanding of the subjective experience of people with borderline personality disorder (BPD). Through a detailed analysis of individual experiences, several central themes that characterize the daily existence of these individuals have been identified. These findings not only provide a rich and complex insight into the inner experiences of people with BPD, but also highlight the importance of integrating multiple methodological approaches to gain a more complete and humanized understanding.

In conclusion, this research has proposed to develop a hermeneutic phenomenological research methodology to understand the particular experiences of people with BPD. This work has been associated with the development of a new methodological approach, which considers elements of phenomenological and hermeneutic traditions, constituting a combination of two interview modalities that maintain these philosophical perspectives as a base.

The first objective of the present work was to establish an approach to the phenomenon of the particular experience, using a structured methodology that considers a hermeneutic phenomenological perspective in people with BPD. In relation to this objective, the following conclusions were reached:

1. **Feeling of Emptiness and Existential Angst:** A recurring theme among participants was a sense of emptiness and a persistent existential angst. This feeling seems to be intrinsically linked to a fragmented identity and difficulty finding meaning and purpose in life.

Phenomenological-Hermeneutical Approach to Borderline Personality Disorder, pages 171–175

doi:10.1108/978-1-80592-281-020251010

2. **Intense and Unstable Interpersonal Relationships:** Participants' interpersonal relationships were described as intense but unstable, often marked by cycles of idealization and devaluation.
3. **Self-injury and Impulsive Behaviors:** Self-injury and other impulsive behaviors were frequently mentioned as coping mechanisms to manage intense emotional pain.
4. **Fear of Abandonment and Loneliness:** Fear of abandonment was a pervasive theme, manifesting itself in a deep fear of loneliness and desperate behaviors to avoid rejection or separation.
5. **Emotional Instability:** Participants described significant emotional ambivalence, experiencing contradictory emotions simultaneously or in rapid succession.
6. **Search for Identity:** The search for a coherent identity was another central theme. Participants expressed a sense of confusion and lack of a stable identity, which exacerbates their emotional discomfort and difficulty in setting long-term goals.

The integration of phenomenological and hermeneutic methodologies in this research has been especially significant. Phenomenology has allowed us to explore participants' lived experiences in a direct and detailed manner, while hermeneutics has provided an interpretive lens for understanding the broader meanings and contexts of these experiences. This methodological combination has enriched the research, allowing for a deeper and more nuanced understanding of the complexity of BPD.

As a second objective, the present research aimed to obtain a set of representative narratives in people with BPD, allowing to obtain from an unprejudiced approach a better understanding of the particular experience associated with this disorder. The results obtained in this objective can be described as follows:

1. From an unprejudiced approach to the phenomenon under study, it has been possible to clearly distinguish narratives that give an account of the subjective experience linked to the particular experience with BPD.
2. The narratives obtained had to be part of an interpretative process that exposed the consideration of principles of phenomenological and hermeneutic analysis of the information, maintaining at all times a posture of unprejudiced observation of the study phenomenon.
3. The third objective focused on describing the particular experiences related to BPD in an organized and comprehensible manner.

The results obtained in this sense confirmed that:

Five key dimensions were identified that shape the approach to reality of people with BPD, including particular types of thinking, the experience of knowing the diagnosis and receiving mental health care, unstable personal relationships and experiences of violation, intense emotion seeking and self-punishment, and unstable emotions at the individual and relational level.

Through a microphenomenological analysis, it was possible to visualize the development of five phases that characterize the experience of emotional instability in individuals with BPD, which include: First sensations of emotional instability; Development of emotional instability effects; Emergence of need for regulation at the emotional level; Emotional regulation actions; and Effects of regulatory actions.

Taken together, these findings provide a deeper understanding of the lived experiences of individuals with BPD, which may contribute significantly to a better understanding of the pathology and to the identification of areas for future intervention to improve the management and treatment of this disorder.

The present approach exposes benefits and challenges for the figure of the researcher, being able to point out within its main benefits to have a link to the prereflective and reflective experience at an experiential level, from an immersive possibility in the linguistic analysis as a set of particular meanings. Another benefit observed is associated to the fact that the methodology considered exposes holistic meeting points, under a consideration that the particular experience can be constituted from multiple experiential dimensions, encompassing meanings of a psychological, physical, emotional, sensory, relational nature, among others, thus managing to visualize the particular experience as a significant source of information that facilitates a broad understanding of a study phenomenon.

As challenges associated with the consideration of this research methodology, there is the need to have an important preparation in philosophical traditions arising from the approaches of phenomenology and hermeneutics, which have sought since the late 19th century an approach to experience beyond any label or added explanation. This considers an additional factor: the need for the researcher to ascribe to a continuous exercise, linked to the need to regulate his or her aprioristic explanatory desires with respect to all types of phenomena. Another important challenge arises in the practical application of the concept of "epoché" proposed by Edmund Husserl, as an alternative of aprioristic suspension, which beyond constituting a theoretical consideration of approach, responds to a type of attitude of encounter with a given phenomenon, an attitude that will favor the observation and distinction of elements proper to the experience from its natural context, beyond any explanatory interest.

RECOMMENDATIONS

The present study represents a significant first step in the exploration of the experiences associated with BPD. Further research in this area is recommended to broaden the understanding of the complexities of this disorder and its impact on the daily lives of those who experience it. In addition, it is crucial to continue providing empirical evidence that supports and enriches our understanding of the particular experiences associated with BPD, designing new proposals for approaching the subjective experience, arising the need for researchers in the area to have a rigorous concern of theoretical postulates that respect comprehensive traditions from the epistemological level.

To approach this study, it was necessary to adopt a posture of aprioristic suspension, which implies the regulation of all personal judgment during the research process. In this sense, practices that facilitated this approach were implemented, such as the use of a researcher's notebook or diary to record individual perceptions and the triangulation of information through interaction with experts in hermeneutic phenomenological research. These strategies allowed a more objective and rigorous approach to the analysis of the experiences collected.

The methodology developed in this study reveals considerable complexity and offers a detailed view of the experiences of individuals with BPD at the macro- and micro-phenomenological level. This holistic approach has made it possible to identify the main daily experiences of individuals with this disorder, as well as to discriminate constituent and representative elements of these experiences at the micro-phenomenological level. The results obtained have validated the established theoretical assumptions, highlighting the usefulness of the hermeneutic phenomenological methodology to explore the particular experiences of BPD in various dimensions, including cognitive, emotional, physical, sensory and behavioral. Taken together, these findings underscore the holistic value of understanding the BPD experience from multiple perspectives.

LIMITATIONS

Among the limitations of the present study, it is possible to distinguish that there is still a low state of the art regarding the joint consideration of two modalities of hermeneutic phenomenological interviews, so that the present work was also constituted as a set of considerations, opinions and approaches based on the experience of experts in hermeneutic phenomenological research, developing together with the researcher a form of experiential exploration rarely observed in the existing literature. Another limitation of the present research was associated with the researcher's handling of bias. Although strategies that favored self-regulation of individual opinions or perceptions regarding the data obtained were continuously used, the emotional aspects that arose during the capture of the experiences may have influenced the direction of the research developed.

As future lines of research associated with the present topic, it has been observed the need to continue with further exploration regarding the usefulness of the integration of experiential exploration methodologies from the hermeneutic phenomenological tradition, which represents a new field of approach to the understanding of both physical and mental health pathologies, from the perspective of the affected person. This will entail studies to distinguish the benefits and disadvantages of different models of experiential approach, proposing improvements or integrations that allow a structured and replicable methodological approach based on the respect of basic philosophical traditions.

Another future line of research is associated with elements of BPD, and there is a need for further exploration of the characteristics of the thinking of people with this pathology, since both this research and several international studies show that the thinking of people affected by this pathology has differentiating characteristics, which exposes an interesting field of exploration at the research level.

There is a need to explore in greater depth elements associated with sensory alterations present in people with BPD, which are linked to the emergence of episodes of derealization and depersonalization, in order to achieve a better understanding of their genesis and their respective usefulness as a defense mechanism during the development of experiences of emotional suffering. Another future line of research is associated to continue establishing new proposals of approach for BPD, in order to favor new approaches that allow the affected persons and their families to have resources that contribute to the remission of risk factors, as well as the constitution of identity elements in the affected persons, which are regularly altered and oriented to self-sanction, and this may contribute to the articulation of self-injurious behaviors in the present population.

REFERENCES

Abettan, C. (2015). Phénoménologie et état limite. Séminaires de l'Ecole Française de Daseinsanalyse (Conferencia del 12 de diciembre de 2015).

Ahmed, S., Newman, D., & Yalch, M. (2021). The stigma of borderline personality disorder. In A. M. Columbus (Ed.), *Advances in psychology research* (Vol. 146, pp. 163–183). Nova Science Publishers.

Álvarez, E. (2001). Terapia cognitivo-conductual del trastorno borderline de la personalidad. *Anales de Psiquiatría, 17*(9), 53–60.

American Psychiatric Association. (2013). *Diagnostic and statistical manual of mental disorders* (5th ed., text revision). American Psychiatric Association.

Anosike, P., Ehrich, L., & Ahmed, P. (2012). Phenomenology as a method for exploring management practice. *International Journal of Management Practice, 5*(3), 205–224.

Arndt, A. (2013). *Friedrich Schleiermacher als philosoph.* De Gruyter.

Balzani, C., Micoulaud-Franchi, J. A., Yunez, N., Fagot, A., Mariaud, A. S., Chen, C., & Vion-Dury, J. (2013). L'accès aux vécus pré-réflexifs. Quelles perspectives pour la médecine en général et la psychiatrie en particulier? *Annales Médico-psychologiques, 171*(2), 118–127.

Barbera, N., & Inciarte, A. (2012). Fenomenología y hermenéutica: dos perspectivas para estudiar las ciencias sociales y humanas. *Multiciencias, 12*(2), 199–205.

Bateman, A., & Fonagy, P. (2006). *Mentalization-based treatment for borderline personality disorder: A practical guide.* Oxford University Press.

Bateman, A., & Fonagy, P. (2009). Randomized controlled trial of outpatient mentalization-based treatment versus structured clinical management for borderline personality disorder. *The American Journal of Psychiatry, 166*(12), 1355–1364.

Berdzenishvili, N. (2016). The question of truth in sciences of spirit (Geisteswissenschaften). *Bulletin of the Georgian National Academy of Sciences, 10*(2), 71–77.

Berenson, K. R., Van De Weert, S. M., Nicolaou, S., Campoverde, C., Rafaeli, E., & Downey, G. (2021). Reward and punishment sensitivity in borderline and avoidant personality disorders. *Journal of Personality Disorders, 35*(4), 573–588.

Bergson, H. (1963). *Obras escogidas.* Aguilar.

Bevan, M. (2014). A method of phenomenological interviewing. *Qualitative Health Research, 24*(1), 136–144.

Bitbol, M., & Petitmengin, C. (2013). A defense of introspection from within. *Constructivist Foundations, 8*(3), 269–279.

Bitbol, M., & Petitmengin, C. (2016). On the possibility and reality of introspection. *Mind and Matter, 14*(1), 51–75.

Bolio, A. (2012). Husserl y la fenomenología trascendental: Perspectivas del sujeto en las ciencias del siglo XX. *Reencuentro. Análisis de Problemas Universitarios,* (65), 20–29.

Bonnington, O., & Rose, D. (2014). Exploring stigmatisation among people diagnosed with either bipolar disorder or borderline personality disorder: A critical realist analysis. *Social Science & Medicine, 123*(2), 7–17.

Borschmann, R., Henderson, C., Hogg, J., Phillips, R., & Moran, P. (2012). Crisis interventions for people with borderline personality disorder. *The Cochrane Database of Systematic Reviews,* (6).

Brentano, F. (1874). *Psychologie vom Empirischen Standpunkte.* Duncker & Humblot.

Cammell, P. (2016). *Reinterpreting the borderline: Heidegger and the psychoanalytic understanding of borderline personality disorder.* Rowman & Littlefield Publishers.

Cavicchioli, M., & Maffei, C. (2021). Rumination as a widespread emotion-based cognitive vulnerability in borderline personality disorder: A meta-analytic review. *Journal of Clinical Psychology, 78*(6), 989–1008.

Charlick, S., Pincombe, J., McKellar, L., & Fielder, A. (2016). Making sense of participant experiences: Interpretative phenomenological analysis in midwifery research. *International Journal of Doctoral Studies, 11,* 205–216.

Chávez-León, E., Ng, B., & Ontiveros-Uribe, M. (2006). Tratamiento farmacológico del trastorno límite de la personalidad. *Salud Mental, 29*(5), 16–24.

Choi-Kain, L., Finch, E., Masland, S., Jenkins, J., & Unruh, B. (2017). What works in the treatment of borderline personality disorder. *Current Behavioral Neuroscience Reports, 4*(1), 21–30.

Choukas-Bradley, S., Hipwell, A. E., Roberts, S. R., Maheux, A. J., & Stepp, S. D. (2020). Developmental trajectories of adolescent girls' borderline personality symptoms and sexual risk behaviors. *Journal of Abnormal Child Psychology, 48*(12), 1649–1658.

Clarkin, J. F., Yeomans, F. E., & Kernberg, O. (2006). *Psychotherapy for borderline personality: Focusing on object relations.* American Psychiatric.

Colaizzi, P. F. (1978). Psychological research as the phenomenologist views it. In R. S. Valle & K. Mark (Eds.), *Existential phenomenological alternatives for psychology.* Oxford University Press.

Colle, L., Hilviu, D., Rossi, R., Garbarini, F., & Fossataro, C. (2020). Self-harming and sense of agency in patients with borderline personality disorder. *Frontiers in Psychiatry, 11*(449), 1–11.

Cremers, H., van Zutphen, L., Duken, S., Domes, G., Sprenger, A., Waldorp, L., & Arntz, A. (2021). Borderline personality disorder classification based on brain network measures during emotion regulation. *European Archives of Psychiatry and Clinical Neuroscience, 271*(6), 1169–1178.

Creswell, J. W. (2012). *Qualitative inquiry & research design: Choosing among five approaches* (4th ed.). Sage.

Cristea, I. A., Gentili, C., Cotet, C. D., Palomba, D., Barbui, C., & Cuijpers, P. (2017). Efficacy of psychotherapies for borderline personality disorder: A systematic review and meta-analysis. *JAMA Psychiatry, 74*(4), 319–328.

Daros, A. R., Guevara, M. A., Uliaszek, A. A., McMain, S. F., & Ruocco, A. C. (2018). Cognitive emotion regulation strategies in borderline personality disorder: Diagnostic comparisons and associations with potentially harmful behaviors. *Psychopathology, 51*(2), 83–95.

Daros, A. R., & Williams, G. E. (2019). A meta-analysis and systematic review of emotion-regulation strategies in borderline personality disorder. *Harvard Review of Psychiatry, 27*(4), 217–232.

Dell'Osso, L., Cremone, I. M., Amatori, G., Cappelli, A., Cuomo, A., Barlati, S., Massimetti, G., Vita, A., Fagiolini, A., & Carmassi, C. (2021). Investigating the relationship between autistic traits, ruminative thinking, and suicidality in a clinical sample of subjects with bipolar disorder and borderline personality disorder. *Brain Science, 11*, 621.

Denzin, N. K., & Lincoln, Y. S. (2013). *Strategies of qualitative inquiry.* Sage.

Depraz, N., Gyemant, M., & Desmidt, T. (2017). A first-person analysis using third-person data as a generative method: A case study of surprise in depression. *Constructivist Foundations, 12*(2), 191–203.

Dilthey, W. (1986). *Introducción a las ciencias del espíritu: Ensayo de una fundamentación del estudio de la sociedad y de la historia.* Alianza Universidad.

Dilthey, W. (2000). *Dos escritos sobre Hermenéutica: el surgimiento de la Hermenéutica y los esbozos para una crítica de la razón histórica.* Prólogo, traducción y notas de Antonio Gómez Ramos. Ediciones Itsmo.

Doerr-Zegers, O. (2011). Phenomenology of intersubjectivity in bipolar disorder and schizophrenia. *Crossing Dialogues Association, 12*(1), 1–9.

Dor, M. (2015). *A study of the lived world of the patient with borderline personality disorder in New Zealand.* Doctor of philosophy and literature. University of South Africa.

Duarte, J., Martinez, C., & Tomicic, A. (2020). Episodes of meeting in psychotherapy: An empirical exploration of patients' experiences of subjective change during their 326 psychotherapy process. *Research in Psychotherapy: Psychopathology, Process and Outcome, 23*(1), 56–66.

Fertuck, E. A., Fischer, S., & Beeney, J. (2018). Social cognition and borderline personality disorder: Splitting and trust impairment findings. *The Psychiatric clinics of North America, 41*(4), 613–632.

Figueroa, C. (2008). La psicología fenomenológica de Husserl y la psicopatología. *Revista Chilena de Neuro-Psiquiatría, 46*(3), 224–237.

Finlay, L. (2008). A dance between the reduction and reflexivity: Explicating the phenomenological psychological attitude. *Journal of Phenomenological Psychology, 39*, 1–32.

Gadamer, H. G. (1982). *Truth and method.* Crossroads.

Gadamer, H. G. (2010). *Verdad y método II.* Sígueme.

Giorgi, A. (1986). The meaning of psychology from a scientific phenomenological perspective. *Études phénoménologiques, 2*(4), 47–73.

Giorgi, A. (2009). *The descriptive phenomenological method in psychology: A modified Husserlian approach.* Duquesne University Press.

Giorgi, A. P., & Giorgi, B. M. (2003). The descriptive phenomenological psychological method. In P. M. Camic, J. E. Rhodes, & L. Yardley (Eds.), *Qualitative research in psychology: Expanding perspectives in methodology and design* (pp. 243–273). American Psychological Association.

Grant, B. F., Chou, P., Goldstein, R. B., Huang, B., Stinson, F. S., Saha, T. D., Smith, S. M., Dawson, D. A., Pulay, A. J., Pickering, R. P., & Ruan, W. J. (2008). Prevalence, correlates, disability, and comorbidity of DSM-IV borderline personality disorder: Results from the Wave 2 National Epidemiologic Survey on Alcohol and Related Conditions. *The Journal of Clinical Psychiatry, 69*(4), 533–545.

Gunderson, J., & Links, P. (2008). *Borderline personality disorder: A clinical guide* (2nd ed.). American Psychiatric Publishing, Inc.

Hatch, J. A. (2002). *Doing qualitative research in education settings.* State University of New York Press.

Heidegger, M. (1989). *Contribuciones a la filosofía (Del acontecimiento).* Introducción, traducción y notas de Pablo Oyarzun R. Santiago de Chile.

Heidegger, M. (2008). *Ontologia, hermenéutica de la facticidad.* Alianza Editorial.

Heidegger, M. (2020). *Ser y tiempo.* Trotta.

Holroyd, A. (2007). Interpretive hermeneutic phenomenology: Clarifying understanding. *Indo-Pacific Journal of Phenomenology, 7*(2), 1–12.

Houben, M., Vansteelandt, K., Claes, L., Sienaert, P., Berens, A., Sleuwaegen, E., & Kuppens, P. (2015). Emotional switching in borderline personality disorder: A daily life study. *Personality Disorders: Theory, Research, and Treatment, 7*(1), 50–60.

Howard, K., Katsos, N., & Gibson, J. (2017). Using interpretative phenomenological analysis in autism research. *Autism: The International Journal of Research and Practice, 23*(7), 1871–1876.

Husserl, E. (1982). *La idea de la fenomenología. Cinco lecciones.* FCE. Traducción de Miguel García-Baró.

Husserl, E. (2002). *Renovación del Hombre y de la cultura: cinco ensayos.* Coedición de Editorial Antropos y Universidad Autónoma Metropolitana.

Husserl, E. (2012). Investigaciones Lógicas. In *Investigaciones Lógicas.*

Iqbal, N., Radulescu, A., Bains, A., & Aleem, S. (2017). An interpretative phenomenological analysis of a religious conversion. *Journal of Religion and Health, 58*(3), 426–443.

Irarrázaval, L. (2015). The lived body in schizophrenia: Transition from basic self-disorders to full-blown psychosis. *Frontiers in Psychiatry, 6*(41), 1–9.

Isabirye, A., & Makoe, M. (2018). Phenomenological analysis of the lived experiences of academics who participated in the professional development programme at an open distance learning (ODL) university in South Africa. *Indo-Pacific Journal of Phenomenology, 18*(1), 1–11.

Jardine, J. A., & Szanto, T. (2017). Empathy in the phenomenological tradition. In H. L. Maibom (Ed.), *The Routledge handbook of philosophy of empathy* (pp. 86–97). Routledge.

Jaspers, K. (1959). *Allgemeine psychopathologie.* Springer-Verlag.

Jaspers, K. (1965). *Wahrheit und Leben. Ausgewählte Schriften.* Buchklub ex libris.

Jhagroo, J. R. (2012). *A hermeneutic phenomenological study of the lived experiences of immigrant students in their mathematics classrooms at a secondary school in Auckland, New Zealand.* Doctoral Thesis. Auckland University of Technology.

Kaufman, E. A., Perez, J., Lazarus, S., Stepp, S. D., & Pedersen, S. L. (2020). Understanding the association between borderline personality disorder and alcohol-related problems: An examination of drinking motives, impulsivity, and affective instability. *Personality Disorders: Theory, Research, and Treatment, 11*(3), 213–221.

Kim, Y., & Park, J. (2021). A phenomenological study on the experience of physical education classes of peer relations alienation students: Max van Manen's hermeneutic phenomenology. *Journal of the Korean Society of Sports Education, 28*(1), 103–134.

Klein, P., Fairweather, A. K., & Lawn, S. (2022). Structural stigma and its impact on healthcare for borderline personality disorder: A scoping review. *International Journal of Mental Health Systems, 16*(48), 1–46.

Krause-Utz, A. (2022). Dissociation, trauma, and borderline personality disorder. *Borderline Personality Disorder and Emotion Dysregulation, 9*(1), 9–14.

Lambert, C. (2006). Edmund Husserl: la idea de la fenomenología. *Teología y Vida, XLVII*(4), 517–529.

Larkin, M., Watts, S., & Clifton, E. (2006). Giving voice and making sense in interpretative phenomenological analysis. *Qualitative Research in Psychology, 3*(2), 102–120.

León, E. (2009). El giro hermenéutico de la fenomenológica en Martin Heidegger. *Revista de la Universidad Bolivariana, 8*(22), 267–283.

Lichtman, M. (2011). *Understanding and evaluating qualitative educational research.* Sage.

Linehan, M. (2018). *Cognitive-behavioral treatment of borderline personality disorder.* Guilford Publications.

Linehan, M. M. (1993). *Cognitive-behavioral treatment of borderline personality disorder.* Guilford Press.

Lo Monte, F., & Englebert, J. (2018). Borderline personality disorder and lived time. *L'évolution psychiatrique, 83*, 37–45.

Mancilla, M. (2020). El arte de comprender en la hermenéutica de Freidrich Schleiermacher. *Utopía y Praxis Latinoamericana, 25*(9), 98–106.

Marques-Feixa, L., Moya-Higueras, J., Romero, S., Santamarina-Perez, P., Rapado-Castro, M., Zorrilla, I., Martín, M., Anglada, E., Lobato, M. J., Ramírez, M., Moreno, N., Mayoral, M., Marín-Vila, M., Arias, B., Fañanás, L., & Group, E. S. (2021). Risk of suicidal behavior in children and adolescents exposed to maltreatment: The mediating role of borderline personality traits and recent stressful life events. *Journal of Clinical Medicine, 10*(22), 5293.

Martínez Ávila, B., & Alvarez Aguirre, A. (2021). Aplicación de la fenomenología de Amedeo Giorgi como sustento metodológico. *ACC CIETNA: Revista De La Escuela De Enfermería, 8*(1), 106–112.

Martino, F., Gammino, L., Sanza, M., Berardi, D., Pacetti, M., Sanniti, A., Tangerini, G., & Menchetti, M. (2020). Impulsiveness and emotional dysregulation as stable features in borderline personality disorder outpatients over time. *Journal of Nervous & Mental Disease, 208*(9), 715–720.

Masland, S. R., & Null, K. E. (2022). Effects of diagnostic label construction and gender on stigma about borderline personality disorder. *Stigma and Health, 7*(1), 89–99.

Merleau-Ponty, M. (1945). *Phénoménologie de la perception.* Gallimard.

Merriam, S. B. (2009). *Qualitative research: A guide to design and implementation.* Jossey-Bass.

Mook, B. (2010). Hermeneutic phenomenology and psychotherapy. In *Les Collectifs du Cirp* (édition spéciale, Vol. 1, pp. 209–222).

Moreira, V. (2004). O método fenomenológico de Merleau-Ponty como ferramenta crítica na pesquisa em psicopatologia. *Psicologia: Reflexão e Crítica, 17*(3), 447–456.

Mosquera, P. (2004). *Borderline personality disorder: A cinical guide.* Desclée De Brouwer.

Navarro González, A. (2001). ¿Es la filosofía de Dilthey Hermenéutica? *Themata,* (27), 269–276.

Pacheco, C. (2021). Estrés en el trastorno límite de la personalidad: Una revisión de la vivencia particular desde una perspectiva microfenomenológica. *Revista De Investigación En Psicología, 24*(1), 223–244.

Paris, J. (2019). Suicidality in borderline personality disorder. *Medicina, 55*(6), 223.

Parnas, J., Sass, L. A., & Zahavi, D. (2013). Rediscovering psychopathology: The epistemology and phenomenology of the psychiatric object. *Schizophrenia Bulletin, 39*(2), 270–277.

Parnas, J., & Urfer-Parnas, A. (2017). The ontology and epistemology of symptoms: The case of auditory verbal hallucinations in schizophrenia. In K. S. Kendler, & J. Parnas (Eds.) *Philosophical issues in psychiatry IV: Psychiatric nosology* (pp. 201–216). Oxford University Press.

Patton, M. Q. (2002). *Qualitative research & evaluation methods* (3rd ed.). Sage.

Petitmengin, C., Remillieux, A., Cahour, C., & Carter-Thomas, S. (2013). A gap in Nisbett and Wilson's findings? A firstperson access to our cognitive processes. *Consciousness and Cognition, 22,* 654–669.

Petitmengin, C. (2006). Describing one's subjective experience in the second person: An interview method for the science of consciousness. *Phenomenology and the Cognitive Sciences, 5*(3), 229–269.

Petitmengin, C. (2007). Towards the source of thoughts: The gestural and transmodal dimension of lived experience. *Journal of Consciousness Studies, 14*(3), 54–82.

Petitmengin, C. (2011). Describing the experience of describing? The blindspot of introspection. *Journal of Consciousness Studies, 18*(1), 44–62.

Petitmengin, C., Remillieux, A., & Valenzuela-Moguillansky, C. (2019). Discovering the structures of lived experience. *Phenomenology and the Cognitive Sciences, 18,* 691–730.

Petitmengin, C., van Beek, M., Bitbol, M., Nissou, J. M., & Roepstorff, A. (2017). What is it like to meditate? Methods and issues of a micro-phenomenological description of meditative experience. *Journal of Consciousness Studies, 24*(5–6), 170–198.

Petreca, B. (2016). *An understanding of embodied textile selection processes & a toolkit to support them.* Phd thesis. Royal College of Art.

Plagenz, V. (2015). *The lived experience of nurses working in a modified therapeutic community.* UNLV Theses, Dissertations, Professional Papers, and Capstones.

Przyrembel, M., & Singer, T. (2018). Experiencing meditation. Evidence for differential effects of three contemplative mental practices in micro-phenomenological interviews. *Consciousness and cognition, 62,* 82–101.

Quepons, I. (2012). Intencionalidad de horizonte y reducción trascendental en la fenomenología de Husserl. *Investigaciones Fenomenológicas, 9*, 269–289.

Ramsook, L. (2018). A methodological approach to hermeneutic phenomenology. *International journal of humanities and social sciences, 10*, 14–24.

Reichl, C., & Kaess, M. (2021). Self-harm in the context of borderline personality disorder. *Current Opinion in Psychology, 37*, 139–144.

Ricoeur, P. (1969). *Le conflit des interpretations*. Seuil.

Ricoeur, P. (1975). *La métaphore vive*. Seuil.

Ricoeur, P. (1981). *Hermeneutics and the human sciences*. Cambridge University Press.

Ricoeur, P. (1996). *Si mismo como otro*. Siglo Veintiuno Editores.

Rietdijk, W. (2018). A micro-phenomenological study of processes and mechanisms of insight meditation. International Symposium for Contemplative Research, Phoenix, AZ, Phoenix, United States. 08–11 Nov 2018.

Rubin, H. J., & Rubin, I. S. (2012). *Qualitative interviewing: The art of hearing data* (3rd ed.). Sage.

Ruocco, A., Amirthavasagam, S., & Zakzanis, K. (2012). Amygdala and hippocampal volume reductions as candidate endophenotypes for borderline personality disorder: A meta-analysis of magnetic resonance imaging studies. *Psychiatry Research, 201*(3), 245–252.

Ruocco, A. C., Daros, A. R., Chang, J., Rodrigo, A. H., Lam, J., Ledochowski, J., & McMain, S. F. (2019). Clinical, personality, and neurodevelopmental phenotypes in borderline personality disorder: A family study. *Psychological Medicine, 49*(12), 2069–2080.

Said, F., Ali, I., & Javed, T. (2020). An interpretative phenomenological analysis of challenges faced by the university teachers in Pakistan amid Covid-19. *IJERI: International Journal of Educational Research and Innovation*, (15), 260–272.

Sansone, R., & Sansone, L. (2012). Borderline personality and externalized aggression. *Innovations in Clinical Neuroscience, 9*(3), 23–26.

Sansone, R., & Sansone, L. (2015). Borderline personality disorder in the medical setting: Suggestive behaviors, syndromes, and diagnoses. *Innovations in Clinical Neuroscience, 12*(7–8), 39–44.

Schleiermacher, F. (2012). *Vorlesungen zur Hermeneutik und Kritik (Kritische Gesamtausgabe. Vorlesungen)*. De Gruyter.

Schütz, A. (1932). *La construcción significativa del mundo social. Introducción a la sociología comprensiva* (Ediciones Paidós). 1ª reimpresión en España, 1993.

Shah, R., Temes, C. M., Frankenburg, F. R., Fitzmaurice, G. M., & Zanarini, M. C. (2020). Levels of depersonalization and derealization reported by recovered and non-recovered borderline patients over 20 Years of prospective follow-up. *Journal of Trauma & Dissociation, 21*(3), 337–348.

Sheppard, H., Bizumic, B., & Calear, A. (2023). Prejudice toward people with borderline personality disorder: Application of the prejudice toward people with mental illness framework. *The International Journal of Social Psychiatry, 69*(5), 1213–1222.

Skodol, A. E., Gunderson, J. G., Pfohl, B., Widiger, T. A., Livesley, W. J., & Siever, L. J. (2002). The borderline diagnosis I: Psychopathology, comorbidity, and personality structure. *Biological Psychiatry, 51*(12), 963–950.

Slattery, P. (2006). *Curriculum development in the postmodern era* (2nd ed.). Taylor & Francis.

Slavin, R. E. (2007). *Educational research in an age of accountability*. Allyn & Bacon.

Smith, J. (2004). Reflecting on the development of interpretative phenomenological analysis and its contribution to qualitative research in psychology. *Qualitative Research in Psychology, 1*(1), 39–54.

Smith, J., Flowers, P., & Larkin, M. (2009). *Interpretative phenomenological analysis: Theory, method and research*. Sage.

Smith, J. A., & Osborn, M. (2003). Interpretative phenomenological analysis. In J. A. Smith (Ed.), *Qualitative psychology: A practical guide to methods* (pp. 51–80). Sage.

Stanghellini, G., & Lysaker, P. H. (2007). The psychotherapy of schizophrenia through the lens of phenomenology: Intersubjectivity and the search for the recovery of first- and second-person awareness. *American Journal of Psychotherapy, 61*, 163–179.

Stoffers, J. M., Völlm, B. A., Rücker, G., Timmer, A., Huband, N., & Lieb, K. (2012). Psychological therapies for people with borderline personality disorder. *Cochrane Database of Systematic Reviews, 8*, CD005652.

Valenzuela-Moguillansky, C., & Vásquez-Rosati, A. (2019). An analysis procedure for the micro-phenomenological interview. *Constructivist Foundations, 14*(2), 123–145.

Valenzuela-Moguillansky, C. (2013). Pain and body awareness. An exploration of the bodily experience of persons suffering from fibromyalgia. *Constructivist Foundations, 8*(3), 339–350.

Valverde, S. (2003). Hermenéutica y simbolismo. *Revista de Filosofía de la Universidad de Costa Rica, 41*(104), 51–59.

Van Manen, M. (1990). *Researching lived experience: Human science for an action sensitive pedagogy*. SUNY Press.

Van Manen, M. (2002). Care-as-worry, or "don't worry, be happy". *Qualitative Health Research, 12*(2), 262–278.

Van-Quynh, A. (2017). Intuition in mathematics: A perceptive experience. *Journal of Phenomenological Psychology, 48*, 1–38.

Varela, F. (1996). *Ética y acción*. Dolmen.

Vásquez-Rosati, A. (2017). Body awareness to recognize feelings: The exploration of a musical emotional experience. *Constructivist Foundations, 12*(2), 219–226.

Vermersch, P. (1994). *L'entretien d'explicitation*. ESF.

Vermersch, P. (2009). Describing the practice of introspection. *Journal of Conscisuness Studies, 16*(10–12), 20–57.

Vermersch, P. (2012). *Explicitation et phénoménologie*. PUF.

Yang, J., Millman, L. S. M., David, A. S., & Hunter, E. C. M. (2022). The prevalence of depersonalization-derealization disorder: A systematic review. *Journal of Trauma & Dissociation, 24*(1), 8–41.

Young, J. E., Klosko, J. S., & Weishaar, M. E. (2003). *Schema therapy: A practitioner's guide*. Guilford Press.

Young, J. E., Klosko, J. S., & Weishaar, M. E. (2006). *Schema therapy: A practitioner's guide*. Guilford Press.

Zahavi, D. (2003). How to investigate subjectivity: Natorp and Heidegger on reflection. *Continental Philosophy Review, 36*(1), 155–167.

Zanarini, M. C. (2009). Psychotherapy of borderline personality disorder. *Acta Psychiatrica Scandinavica, 120*(5), 373–377.

Zanarini, M. C., Yong, L., Frankenburg, F. R., Hennen, J., Reich, D. B., Marino, M. F., & Vujanovic, A. A. (2002). Severity of reported childhood sexual abuse and its relationship to severity of borderline psychopathology and psychosocial impairment among borderline inpatients. *The Journal of Nervous and Mental Disease, 190*(6), 381–387.

ADDITIONAL READINGS

Bozzatello, P., Garbarini, C., Rocca, P., & Bellino, S. (2021). Borderline personality disorder: Risk factors and early detection. *Diagnostics, 11*(11), 2142.

Chapman, A. L. (2019). Borderline personality disorder and emotion dysregulation. *Development and Psychopathology, 31*(3), 1143–1156.

Depraz, N., Varela, F. J., & Vermersch, P. (2003). *On becoming aware: A pragmatics of experiencing.* Benjamins Press.

Dolling, E. (1997). Kritik der Urteilslehre: Land versus Brentano, mit Blick auf Frege. *Brentano Studien, 7,* 123–146.

Dörr, O. (2008). Los trastornos de personalidad desde una perspectiva fenomenológica. *Actas Españolas de Psiquiatría, 36*(1), 10–19.

Føllesdal, D. (2007). Husserl's reductions and the role they play in his phenomenology. In *A companion to phenomenology and existentialism* (pp. 105–114). John Wiley and Sons.

Fonagy, P., & Bateman, A. W. (2006). Mechanisms of change in mentalization-based treatment of BPD. *Journal of Clinical Psychology, 62*(4), 411–430.

Hernández, R., Fernández, C., & Baptista, P. (2014). *Metodología de la investigación.* Mcgraw Hill.

Husserl, E. (1970). *The idea of phenomenology.* Nijhoff.

Husserl, E. (1990). *Artículo de la Enciclopedia Británica,* (cuarta y última versión). UNAM.

Jain, S., Kuppili, P. P., Pattanayak, R. D., & Sagar, R. (2017). Ethics in psychiatric research: Issues and recommendations. *Indian Journal of Psychological Medicine, 39*(5), 558–565.

Löffler, A., Kleindienst, N., Cackowski, S., Schmidinger, I., & Bekrater-Bodmann, R. (2020). Reductions in whole-body ownership in borderline personality disorder - A phenomenological manifestation of dissociation. *Journal of Trauma & Dissociation, 21*(2), 264–277.

Luyten, P., Campbell, C., & Fonagy, P. (2020). Borderline personality disorder, complex trauma, and problems with self and identity: A social-communicative approach. *Journal of Personality, 88*(1), 88–105.

Nehls, N. (1999). Borderline personality disorder: The voice of patients. *Research in Nursing & Health, 22*(4), 285–293.

Parnas, J. & Henriksen, M. (2018). Selfhood and its disorders. In G. Stanghellini, M. Broome, A. Raballo, A. V. Fernández, P. Fusar-Poli, & R. Rosfort (Eds.), *The Oxford handbook of phenomenological psychopatology.* Oxford Press.

Pereira, Z. (2011). Los diseños de método mixto en la investigación en educación: Una experiencia concreta. *Revista Electrónica Educare, 15*(1), 42–58.

Pögeller, O. (1986). *Spur des Worts: Zur Lyrik Paul Celans.* Alber.

Ring, D., & Lawn, S. (2019). Stigma perpetuation at the interface of mental health care: A review to compare patient and clinician perspectives of stigma and borderline personality disorder. *Journal of Mental Health, 12,* 1–21.

Rossi Monti, M. (2016). The window and the wound: Dysphoria and anger in borderline disorders. In G. Stanghellini & M. Aragona (Eds.), *An experimental approach to psychopatology. What is like to suffer a mental disorder* (pp. 61–77). Springer.

Stanghellini, G. & Mancini, M. (2018). The life-world of persons with borderline personality disorder. In G. Stanghellini, M. Broome, A. Raballo, A. V. Fernández, P. Fusar-Poli, & R. Rosfort (Eds.), *The Oxford Handbook of phenomenological psychopatology.* Oxford Press.

Stoffers, J., Völlm, B., Rücker, G., Timmer, A., Huband, N., & Lieb, K. (2010). Pharmacological interventions for borderline personality disorder. *Cochrane Database of Systematic Reviews, 6.*

Surmiak, A. (2020). Should we maintain or break confidentiality? The choices made by social researchers in the context of law violation and harm. *Journal of Academic Ethics, 18*(1), 229–247.

Taylor, S. J., & Bogdan, R. (2010). *Introducción a los métodos cualitativos de investigación.* Paidós.

Van Manen, M. (2003). *Investigación educativa y experiencia vivida. Ciencia humana para una pedagogía de la acción y de la sensibilidad.* Idea Books.

Printed and bound by CPI Group (UK) Ltd, Croydon, CR0 4YY

13/09/2026

14961029-0006